Teaching in Rural

This teacher education textbook invites preservice and beginning teachers to think critically about the impact of rurality on their work and provides an overview of what it means to live, teach, learn, and thrive in rural communities. This book underscores the importance of teaching in rural schools as an act of social justice—work that dismantles spatial barriers to economic, social, and political justice.

Teaching in Rural Places begins with a foundational section that addresses the importance of thinking about rural education in the U.S. as an educational environment with particular challenges and opportunities. The subsequent chapters address rural teaching within concentric circles of focus—from communities to schools to classrooms. Chapters provide concrete strategies for understanding rural communities, valuing rural ways of being, and teaching in diverse rural schools by addressing topics such as working with families, building professional networks, addressing trauma, teaching in multi-grade classrooms, and planning place-conscious instruction.

The first of its kind, this comprehensive textbook for rural teacher education is targeted toward preservice and beginning teachers in traditional and alternative teacher education programs as well as new rural teachers participating in induction and mentoring programs. *Teaching in Rural Places* will help ensure that rural students have the well-prepared teachers they deserve.

Amy Price Azano is a teacher educator in the School of Education at Virginia Tech. She grew up in Virginia's Shenandoah Valley and focuses her scholarship on issues of equity for rural learners.

Devon Brenner transplanted from Michigan to Mississippi over 20 years ago. A professor of literacy teacher education at Mississippi State University, she engages in research that focuses on rural education policy and practice.

Jayne Downey is a professor at Montana State University where she directs the Center for Research on Rural Education. Born and raised on a farm on the prairies, her research and service are dedicated to working with and for rural schools and communities around the world.

Karen Eppley is a former fifth grade teacher who has lived her entire life in one rural valley. Her research interest is at the intersection of literacy education and rural education. She is an associate professor of curriculum and instruction at Penn State University where she teaches in the reading specialist certification program.

Ann K. Schulte is a professor at California State University, Chico. She has been a teacher and teacher educator in primarily rural contexts for 30 years. Her scholarship interests focus on self-study, teacher identity, and university–community partnerships in rural contexts.

Teaching in Rural Places

Thriving in Classrooms, Schools, and Communities

Amy Price Azano, Devon Brenner,
Jayne Downey, Karen Eppley
and Ann K. Schulte

Routledge
Taylor & Francis Group

NEW YORK AND LONDON

First published 2021
by Routledge
52 Vanderbilt Avenue, New York, NY 10017

and by Routledge
2 Park Square, Milton Park, Abingdon, Oxon OX14 4RN

Routledge is an imprint of the Taylor & Francis Group, an informa business

Library of Congress Cataloging-in-Publication Data
A catalog record for this title has been requested

Names: Azano, Amy Price, author. | Brenner, Devon, author. | Downey, Jayne, author. | Eppley, Karen, author. | Schulte, Ann Katherine, author.
Title: Teaching in rural places : thriving in classrooms, schools, and communities / Amy Price Azano, Devon Brenner, Jayne Downey, Karen Eppley, Ann K. Schulte.
Description: New York, NY : Routledge, 2021. | Includes bibliographical references and index.
Identifiers: LCCN 2020024622 (print) | LCCN 2020024623 (ebook) | ISBN 9780367617486 (hardback) | ISBN 9780367376383 (paperback) | ISBN 9781003106357 (ebook)
Subjects: LCSH: Education, Rural–United States. | Rural schools–United States. | Community and school–United States.
Classification: LCC LC5146.5 .A93 2021 (print) | LCC LC5146.5 (ebook) | DDC 370.9173/4–dc23
LC record available at https://lccn.loc.gov/2020024622
LC ebook record available at https://lccn.loc.gov/2020024623

ISBN: 978-0-367-61748-6 (hbk)
ISBN: 978-0-367-37638-3 (pbk)
ISBN: 978-1-003-10635-7 (ebk)

Typeset in Palatino
by Taylor & Francis Books

Dedicated to our rural beginnings in Addison, the Bald Eagle Valley, Luray, Saskatchewan, and Yankton.

Contents

Introduction: Teaching in Rural Places

This book is intended to help you think about and prepare for the work of being a rural teacher. We, the authors of this book, grew up in rural communities, taught in rural schools, and we have been preparing educators for work in rural schools for many years. This book represents our love for rural communities and our very real concerns about inequality in education, economics, and resources—inequalities that exist both within rural communities and between rural and non-rural places. We wrote this book because we want to ensure that rural schools are staffed with teachers who are ready to take a caring and critical stance toward the places they teach— who are ready to find the assets in rural places and work with rural families. Rural students deserve well-prepared teachers who are ready to address the challenges and leverage the strengths of rural schools and communities.

As you will see throughout the chapters, we invite teachers to engage in the important work of *remembering* what is strong about rural communities, *restoring* that which benefits rural people and places, *conserving* qualities of rural communities that should be protected, *changing* that which oppresses or divides us, and *creating* new, innovative ways to help rural communities thrive (Greenwood, 2013).

We have written this book because we recognize a need for resources to support new and aspiring teachers for rural schools. We are especially aware that many rural places have trouble staffing their classrooms. There are a variety of reasons for this that we will explore in this book. Rural schools have unique challenges, but they also have many strengths— strengths that may not be obvious but are real nonetheless. Teacher education has not traditionally examined what it means to live and teach in a rural place. We believe that an explicit focus on rural school contexts and the strategies that rural teachers can use to feel connected to their communities and their profession can help new (and experienced) teachers *thrive*.

We have chosen the term "thrive" deliberately. In order for rural communities to do well economically, politically, and socially, so that all residents (including all children) have the resources and opportunities they deserve, schools need to be strong. Strong schools depend on teachers— teachers who care about children, who are knowledgeable about their practice and their communities, who build relationships and shared goals

[handwritten notes in margin:] Remembering Restoring Conserving Changing Creating

with families, who see their work as connected to the community. Thriving teachers find satisfaction and joy in their work as they draw upon strategies and resources to positively impact the challenges they encounter in their classrooms and communities. We want you to thrive as a rural teacher.

This book has four main sections. **Section One: Rural Contexts** focuses on understanding and framing rural places. The chapters in Section One explore definitions of rurality and unpack the ways in which rurality is a socially constructed concept. These chapters explore the unique challenges and opportunities found in rural places and explain why rural teaching is a project of social justice—that is, why rural teaching is inexorably tied to the work of dismantling barriers to equity that are present in the United States and the ways in which rural places have often been denigrated and deprived of resources, recognition, and representation. This section introduces a framework that is central to this book—a critical pedagogy of place—which is teaching that prioritizes learning connections between local, regional, national, and global contexts while also taking a critical and thoughtful lens to understanding and challenging power, privilege, and sources of inequities in rural places.

Section Two: Thriving in Rural Communities recognizes that schools are embedded in and engaged in work on behalf of the community and examines what it means to live, work, and thrive in rural places. The chapters in this section invite you to examine assumptions about rural places and ways of living. The chapters offer strategies for learning about and becoming a member of the community in which you'll teach, including the Rural Community Walk—a process that new teachers can use to develop a greater understanding of a place and identify the assets and strengths that challenge stereotypes and support place-conscious pedagogy. This section also explores the rural teacher's responsibilities related to building positive relationships with rural families and explores what it means to be from, or not from, the place where you teach.

Section Three: Thriving in Rural Schools discusses the various roles and responsibilities that are unique to rural contexts and examines what it means to be a member of the staff at a rural school. Chapters in this section provide concrete strategies for working in and thriving in rural schools. These include building a professional network both within and beyond the school building and teaching in the midst of and responding to trauma. In this section, we also address education policy, particularly state and federal policies that impact rural schools, and unique organizational structures that are more common in rural schools, including multi-grade and itinerant teaching.

Section Four: Thriving in Rural Classrooms provides an overview of what it means to teach in rural classrooms. The chapters in this section address specific instructional theories and practices related to rural teaching and provide concrete strategies for planning and implementing place-conscious instruction. The chapters examine the affordances and challenges of technology use in rural classrooms, consider diversity in the rural classroom, and provide support for educators who will teach exceptional learners. The chapters in this section also address the issue of planning effective instruction based on different kinds of evidence and provides an overview of teaching as inquiry, a mindset toward teaching that can help rural educators reflect on and generate evidence about effective instruction.

Thriving as a Rural Teacher: This closing chapter will revisit the central themes of the book as it sets you up to write your personal purpose statement about thriving in rural communities, schools, and classrooms. This chapter offers a vision in which rural teachers have opportunities to become active leaders in rural places and suggests that the ideas and strategies in this book can support teachers in becoming active leaders in their classrooms, schools, and communities.

The sections of this book are nested in a particular way to convey that the role of the rural teacher is contextualized by rural classrooms, schools, communities, and contexts. This book is filled with examples and stories of rural teachers who are thriving even as they work to address the daily challenges they face in their schools. We also tell stories about ourselves that exemplify the themes and that are grounded in rural education theories. Each of us, the five authors of this book, are from rural communities and help prepare educators for rural schools. We will tell our own stories, and the stories of our students (both K-12 and education students), throughout this volume. It might be helpful to introduce ourselves:

Amy grew up in Luray, Virginia, a small town in the Shenandoah Valley, and attended the same rural school where her parents attended and became first-generation high school graduates. Amy is a first-generation college graduate and taught high school English before pursing her doctoral degree from the University of Virginia. She lives in Southwest Virginia and works at Virginia Tech as a teacher educator and rural education scholar.

Devon lives and works in Starkville, Mississippi. She grew up in a small community in Michigan and graduated with 89 students in her class. After completing her teacher education degree at Michigan State University (where she learned a lot about teaching in urban places), she returned to her hometown to teach fourth grade. For the last 20 years, she has been preparing teachers and researching rural education at Mississippi State University in northeast Mississippi, where rural traditions are strong and where the legacy of the region's oppressive past are still being dismantled.

Jayne is a professor at Montana State University where she works with rural preservice and in-service teachers and directs the Center for Research on Rural Education. Born and raised on a farm on the prairies, her research and service are dedicated to working with and for rural schools and communities around the world.

Karen is a former fifth grade teacher, who after earning a master's degree with an emphasis on children's literature while teaching, left the classroom to pursue a PhD program full time. She now prepares reading specialists at Penn State University. She is a first-generation college graduate who has lived her entire life within a 20 mile radius of the rural Bald Eagle Valley where she grew up. Her children now attend the same rural school from which she graduated.

Ann grew up and went to college in her hometown of Yankton, South Dakota. She was a teacher and high school debate coach for several years in nearby small towns. After earning her Ph.D in Wisconsin, Ann moved to northern California where she prepares teachers and mentors first-generation college students like herself. California State University, Chico stands on lands that were originally occupied by the Mechoopda, and it serves a very large rural region in the northern part of the state.

We imagine that you will read this book as part of a teacher education course or as part of your rural district's induction and mentoring program for new teachers. We have written the book as a textbook, and we hope that you and your instructor and classmates spend time talking about the discussion questions or investigating the resources for further reading. If you are reading this book on your own, we hope that you will stop and think or write about the discussion questions or call a friend or colleague to talk about the issues that are being raised. We believe you will learn more if you actively engage with the ideas presented.

You may read the book in order, from start to finish. It also may be that you will jump around, reading related chapters together. Many of the ideas in this book are introduced in early chapters and revisited multiple times, with more concrete and explicit strategies for practice in later chapters. However you read the book, we hope that you will engage with the stories and examples, reflect on the ideas, find useful strategies that help you prepare for the work of rural teaching, and enjoy learning about what it means to be ready to thrive in rural communities, classrooms, and schools.

Rural Teachers for Changing and Uncertain Times

As we write the final sections of this book in April of 2020, the world is shut down. Each of us is staying home as much as possible due to the coronavirus pandemic (COVID-19). We have been moving our courses online, attending video meetings, spending extra time with our families, and finding out what our dogs and cats do all day long. We are concerned for our students who may be struggling with food insecurity or housing issues, and all of us are struggling to do our jobs from our homes in isolation. We are worrying about what comes next and, at the same time, calling our friends for virtual book clubs. All the time, we recognize that our privilege has defined our experience during the pandemic. We indeed know that we are not "in the same boat"—only in the same storm.

As we write, we have paid careful attention to media coverage about the impact of COVID-19 on rural communities. First, there was hope that rural places would be able to avoid the virus. It was hoped that smaller populations and lack of population density would help limit the spread of the virus. Unfortunately, that was not the case. Now, rates of the virus in rural places are growing exponentially. Native American communities in particular are struggling. Rural communities are dealing with the crisis with limited resources. The growing crisis highlights decades of inequity in rural places—as evidenced by communities with inadequate health care systems and other resources. Shortages of medical personnel in rural places are real, and in recent years, many rural hospitals have closed, in part due to underfunding or the shifting demographics and smaller populations in many rural places. The long term impact on families, workers, and businesses is yet to be determined.

At the same time, rural communities are dealing with the crisis as best as they can—with the strength and resilience they have always had, and with the challenges that are ever present. People in rural communities are still working if they can—growing food and driving trucks and delivering the mail. Other rural residents have come home from the parks and tourist destinations that are closed during the crisis, filing for unemployment, and figuring out how to scrape by. Neighbors are helping neighbors, bringing groceries and toilet paper. Many rural schools are taking extraordinary measures to deliver school lunches and finding new ways to provide educational resources for students. Hospitals and nursing homes are running out of personal protective equipment, and so quilting guilds, and anyone with a sewing machine, are stitching masks out of fabric leftover from projects from simpler times. Families are sitting around fire pits and walking their properties, watching spring come in spite of the crisis, and hoping that mortgage payments and rent can wait just a little longer. These months of social distancing and shelter-in-place are bringing out the best, and highlighting the challenges, of rural communities.

This crisis will end, and rural places will continue to be populated with strong, proud, resilient people and will continue to have great economic and social needs. As with all places impacted by the crisis, we expect that rural places will change in ways that we cannot yet imagine when we all get back to work. One thing is certain about rural places—our schools hold us together. We are no longer meeting in classrooms or gathering for athletic events and graduation. Social distancing has been a stark reminder of the importance of our schools in caring for children and as the social glue that holds communities together. When students and teachers come back to school, rural schools will need effective teachers who are committed to their places, who see the potential of all of their students, and who will work with families and students to help raise a new generation of citizens for our changing world. We hope this book helps you prepare to be one of those teachers.

Reference

Greenwood, D. A. (2013). A critical theory of place-conscious education. In R. B. Stevenson, M. Brody, J. Dillon, & A. E. J. Wals (Eds.), *International handbook of research on environmental education* (pp. 93–100). Routledge.

Part One
Rural Contexts

1

Becoming a Rural Teacher

Devon, one of the authors of this book, graduated from a small high school in rural Michigan—there were 89 people in her graduating class—a mix of farming families, families who commuted an hour to work in automotive plants, and families that operated tourist places for the summer people who came to boat and fish on the lakes in the area. After Devon graduated from college with a degree in elementary education, she got married and got a job teaching fourth grade in her hometown. The principal remembered her from middle school. Her teaching partner was her former sixth-grade reading teacher. Her high school health teacher now took her students for physical education (PE) twice a week.

There were so many wonderful things, and so many challenges, about teaching in this small rural community she loved so much. She already knew the families of most of her students. Based on their addresses, she had a good idea of how long each student spent on the bus to get to school and whether they were lake families or farm families. She ran into parents at Tuesday $2 Taco Night at the Highland Beach Inn (because everyone goes to $2 Taco Night) and hoped no one noticed when she ordered a second beer. She went to wrestling matches and the Homecoming parade because these are important in the Addison Schools community.

Devon taught fourth grade with a team of three other teachers—and together they shared the work of planning lessons. She mostly planned social studies. She also came in early to teach one section of eighth-grade Spanish for a little extra pay. The middle school wanted to start Spanish early, and she had a minor in Spanish—and pretty limited language skills. She was glad that a new class of eighth-graders rotated through every nine weeks. As a fourth-grade teacher, Devon got to teach Michigan history. Together, she and her students studied the Native Americans that first lived, and continue to live, in Michigan. She and her students learned about the French explorers and Polish miners, and the history of the logging industry that changed the landscape from forest to farmland. She taught about the role Michigan played in the Civil War, the northern migration of African Americans from the south in the middle of the twentieth century and the history of desegregation. Devon had limited resources for teaching these topics—the textbook she was given was out of date, for example, and she had limited technology. But she brought in local resources (the director of the community museum) and got ideas from the magazine of the state's social studies organization. As she taught, she tried to help her students understand the history and evolution of the place they all lived. She loved teaching in her small hometown district and hoped that reading and writing about the history of the state helped her students have a greater sense of their place in the world and their potential to make the world a better place.

This book is about teaching in a rural place. The chapters in this book are intended to help you prepare to be successful, and to thrive, in a rural community, in rural schools, and in your own rural classroom. In a lot of ways, teaching is teaching. No matter where you teach, much of the work of the profession is the same. Teachers everywhere build relationships with students and their families, set goals for learning, plan units and lessons, assess student learning, and celebrate growth. At the same time, your work as a teacher in a rural school can be very different from that of your colleagues in non-rural places—different contexts, different resources, unique challenges, and many powerful advantages that are the reasons that many teachers choose to work in a rural place.

Some people know from the start that they plan to spend their career teaching in a rural community. They already have reasons that spark their interest in being a rural teacher. You might be thinking about rural teaching because you want to be near family or you love the mountains or the prairie or because suburban life does not appeal to you. On the other hand, some people are hesitant about the idea of teaching in a rural place. Maybe you are considering rural teaching because you want to follow a partner or because your teacher preparation program is placing you somewhere rural or because someone assigned this text as reading, and you wonder whether teaching in a rural place will be a good fit for you. We, the authors of this book, care about, work in, and love rural places, but we recognize that not everyone sees the advantages we see. We believe that rural teaching is a great option for any new teacher, and we are not the only ones. Many rural teachers report that they really like their jobs. On average, rural teachers *why?*

report greater satisfaction about their work than their non-rural colleagues (Player, 2015). We hope you will, too.

> **For Discussion**
>
> Think about teaching in a rural school. What appeals to you about this kind of work? What are you looking forward to, and why? What makes you uncertain about teaching in a rural school? Why?

Rural schools, and the communities they serve, are diverse. Whatever makes the place you teach unique will also make the job of teaching in that place unique. Rural schools are found on the rolling hills of farmlands, in the winds of wide-open prairies, nestled in the valleys of mountains, deep in the woods, and on the slopes of desert landscapes. Rural schools may be located in places with great natural beauty with amazing opportunities for outdoor recreation. Other rural schools may be in more industrialized settings with oilfields and wind farms. Rural communities may have thriving economies or may be grappling with economic uncertainty and decline. Some rural areas thrive because of tourism or the arts, others are growing because of new technologies and the rise of telecommuting. The students in rural schools may have lived in the area for generations, or they may be relative newcomers, or both. Some rural schools are incredibly small, with just a handful of students in one room serving grades K–8. Other rural schools are quite large, with hundreds of students in each grade, often coming from many miles away after district consolidation. In some ways, this diversity makes it hard to generalize about rural teaching, but there are some commonalities that are worth noting. In this chapter, we are going to talk about some of the advantages, and the challenges, of teaching in a rural school. Not all the benefits or challenges apply to every school, but many rural schools share these characteristics.

Living in Rural Places

Many rural teachers come to a rural community to be close to family. If you grew up in a rural area, rural teaching may allow you to go back home after earning your college degree. This is not uncommon. Compared to other college graduates, teachers are more likely to live and work in or near the community where they graduated from high school (Reininger, 2011).

Some people choose to work in a rural place because of natural resources and outdoor recreation. If you have an interest in outdoor activities that your rural community provides—hiking or skiing or mountain climbing or hunting or canoeing or just watching the sun set and gazing at the stars—teaching in a rural school can place you in or near outdoor spaces and great natural beauty. Increasingly, some rural schools are offering a four-day school week, in part to aid in rural teacher recruitment and retention. Teachers who enjoy the outdoors may appreciate three-day weekends and the opportunities they provide for recreation (Turner et al., 2019). Likewise, some teachers choose to live in a rural place because they prefer a more peaceful lifestyle—places with less traffic, less congestion, and often much lower crime rates than metropolitan areas (National Center for Victims of Crime, 2014).

Some teachers also note the lack of amenities in many rural places can be a deterrent to a career as a rural teacher. Depending on the location and the community, there may be few (or no) restaurants or coffee shops near where you teach, or you may have to drive a long way to find a gym or a grocery store or live theater or concerts by the bands you love. There may be other resources that you appreciate more in your rural place, but the lack of dining, shopping, and entertainment options can be a source of concern.

Living in Smaller Places

Not all rural teachers choose to or have the ability to live in the community where they teach—but if you do get to live where you work, you may have a greater chance to become a member of the community and get to know your neighbors. Whether you are from there, or new to a place, if you teach in a smaller community you may have opportunities to build deep roots in a community. If you are a member of a religious or social organization, or as you go about your day-to-day activities outside of school, you will have many opportunities to interact with the community, to make friends, and to find ways to be a leader in the community. As you do, you will gain knowledge that will help you in your work as a teacher. You are more likely to know if there are changes or challenges or needs in the community that impact students or that you may want to address in your teaching (McGranahan et al., 2010).

Sense of Community

One of the biggest advantages of being a rural teacher is the opportunity to build relationships with students and their families (Ulferts, 2016). Teaching is primarily about building relationships. In a rural school district, you may be more likely to get to know your students and watch them grow and develop. You may have opportunities to teach the same student in more than one grade or class, or to teach multiple siblings from the same family. These lasting relationships can be rewarding, giving you the opportunity to watch children learn and grow over time. They can also be helpful in your work as a teacher. Relationships with students and their families can serve as the foundation for solving problems and supporting student learning. Ms. Cummins worked as the gifted and talented program director in the St. Francis Indian School in South Dakota after teaching there. She told us:

> When I talk about rural communities, I think about knowing entire famil-ies, them walking in the door and me being able to talk to Grandma about the fry bread she makes that's my favorite and talk about the kid's kinder-garten teacher whom I know. It's a whole lifestyle, a way of being that feels so different from what I know my friends in cities experience.

Smaller communities can help you build familiarity that leads to relationships and that can help you as a teacher (Ulferts, 2016). As a rural educator, you will have opportunities to meet students or their families in out-of-school set-tings. You may see your students' families at the local diner or cross paths with them hiking on a trail on Saturday afternoon. You may run into your students at a Scouting event or volunteering in a community clean up, riding their bike on the side of the road or at work at the convenience store. Encounters outside of school can give you a new perspective on your stu-dents. You come to see them as whole people and learn about their interests and their passions. You may see a student that you find challenging to work with during the school day in a new light outside the classroom. Knowledge about their interests or families can help you understand what makes your student unique or have more compassion for their challenges. Also, bumping into students and their families outside the classroom can give you a chance to reinforce what's happening in the classroom, to remind students to return permission slips or complete an upcoming project.

Knowing families also poses challenges. Teachers can develop pre-conceived notions about students based on interactions with their siblings or their parents. When you teach the fourth sibling in a family, your memories of the older siblings, and their behavior, may influence your expectations. Students and families might already have concerns about you if their older students did not do well in your classroom. Navigating this familiarity can be tricky. Devon taught in the same hometown where she grew up, and one year she taught the child of someone she thought of as a personal rival during high school. She had to work pretty hard to get beyond that feeling of rivalry.

It is also important to recognize that not all rural communities have the same feeling of community and stability that we describe here. Some communities are marked by economic and social division, and in many rural communities the student enrollment is in flux, for example, as migrant workers follow the growing season or new industries attract new residents. In these cases, your work as an educator can help create a welcoming environment that builds a feeling of community for you and for your students. Wille and colleagues (2019) described how school districts in Colorado welcomed displaced persons new to their community, saying, "Schools are an important institution in rural communities and as such, can serve as a leader in facilitating the integration of refugee families."

Overcoming Isolation

Of course, becoming a member of a tight-knit community is not automatic, and many rural teachers have reported that one of the greatest challenges they face is a sense of social isolation (Anttila & Väänänen, 2013). This particularly can be the case if you do not have friends or family members outside of school. A feeling of social isolation can arise if you do not feel as though you have a strong network of friends or opportunities for social engagement where you live and work. If you are not from the community where you end up teaching, you may have few social contacts outside of school when you first start teaching. For people who are single, teaching in a rural area may mean a relatively small dating pool. You may be able to make friends through work, religious institutions, or social clubs in the area, but a feeling of closeness may not be automatic. In the second section of this book, we provide some guidelines that can help you to learn about, and possibly put down roots in, your rural community.

Professional isolation can also be a challenge, particularly in smaller or more remote schools where you may be the only teacher of a particular subject or the only person teaching your grade. Even in larger schools, some rural teachers may not have a strong feeling of collegiality with the teachers down the hall. A feeling of being part of a community of colleagues can help teachers, especially new teachers, thrive in their profession. When that community is not present, your work can be more challenging. Chapter 9 will give you ideas for how to build a sense of professional community no matter how small your school.

The potential for feeling a sense of community or a sense of isolation varies greatly from school to school and region to region. Schools that are located in sparsely populated and remote areas—mountain top communities in the Rockies, remote prairie locations in the West, or island communities off the Atlantic coast—may feel more remote, and more isolated, from other communities. That feeling of isolation may not be as acute in small towns in rural New England or the Midwest that have larger school districts, nearby small towns, and easy access to more urban places. Of course, teachers can feel a sense of isolation and loneliness anywhere, even in big cities, where you might be surrounded by tens of thousands of people. Wherever you teach, if you work to understand and put down roots in the community and build a network of friends, you will be more likely to avoid that sense of social isolation.

Anonymity and Privacy

Another challenge of living in a smaller place is that it is difficult to be anonymous. You may have a feeling that you are never off-duty or do not have much privacy. When you live and teach in a small rural community, wherever you go you are likely to see or be seen by a student, a parent, or a colleague. While more urban and suburban locations may give you a feeling of relative anonymity, life in a small town means that word might get around about that joke on your t-shirt, that night you closed the bar down, or the time your car died on the side of the road. You may not care if one of the moms from your schools sees that you have decided to wear the same sweatshirt every day of spring break, but if you do care, someone will likely notice. Some rural teachers report that this feeling of living "in a fishbowl" can be a deterrent to rural teaching.

You may find that you are teaching alongside one of your students' parents, or dating one of your students' relatives, or you are friends with several of your students' family members. These situations can provide added richness and a feeling of community. However, they also present a greater need to attend to the confidentiality of your students. There is a federal law that protects the personal information of your students, no matter what your relationship is to them or their family. The Family Educational Rights and Privacy Act (20 U.S.C. § 1232g; 34 CFR Part 99), also known as FERPA, requires you to protect the privacy of children's educational records. Until a student is 18 years old, only the parents or guardians can give you permission to share any personally identifiable information about a student with someone outside of the education setting. The urge to share stories from the classroom is great, but you will need to exercise great care when you are talking about your students. This is true both in person and perhaps even more importantly, on any social media platform you use.

This concern for privacy can also go the other direction. In a small community, you may learn things about your students and their families that you should keep confidential. When Ann, one of the authors of this book, was a teacher, she worked at the local bowling alley bar on the weekends to supplement her teaching income. She would see many of her students' parents in the bar, occasionally in situations that were unflattering. Just as Ann was legally compelled to not share information about her students, she also knew that she should refrain from talking about parents' activities at school. These situations can become complicated very quickly, so it is important to remain as professional as possible.

In the end, we believe that the multiple, complex, and often close relationships of rural communities provide distinct advantages. In many rural communities, teachers are highly respected. Schools play an important role in the life of the community. The Friday night football game, or Tuesday evening basketball and volleyball games, bring the community together for social events. Families get to visit with one another when they come together for choir concerts or pancake breakfast fundraisers. Families often value the roles that schools play, and the teachers that provide education for their students. As you put down roots, and as you find the right ways to draw boundaries that protect everyone's privacy and your own personal time, you may feel very rooted in your rural community.

Living in, Commuting to

If you are able, you might want to try to live in the community where you are teaching. If you live in or near the community where you teach you will have opportunities to participate in community organizations, to become a member of a religious community, to join local groups, and to interact with community members over pancake breakfasts or the Friday night fish fry. Being nearby makes it easier to attend and participate in school events and form partnerships with local businesses and service organizations who might volunteer in your classroom or support your goals as a teacher. You will have more opportunities to become a rooted member of the community.

If you end up living away from the place where you teach—to be closer to family or friends or your partner's work, or for whatever reason—you may need to be more explicit about how you will learn about the community and make family and community connections. If you are commuting to the place where you teach, it is still important to take the time to attend out of school events, to come back on Saturdays to watch your students in the cross country meet, or to stay late on a Thursday for the band performance. These actions can help you feel connected.

For Discussion

How do you feel about living in a small place? What do you see as the pros and cons of living where many or all people know who you are and what you do?

Teaching in Rural Schools

Another advantage to teaching in a rural school is that, in general, teachers in rural schools report that they feel a greater sense of autonomy than in urban and suburban schools. On a day-to-day basis, rural teachers may feel a greater sense of control over what they do (Player, 2015; Cuervo & Acquaro, 2014). Teaching in a rural school may give you more control over the day-to-day and minute-to-minute decisions you'll make as a teacher, and there may be fewer classroom disruptions or behavioral problems in rural schools (Ballou & Podgursky, 1995). In a rural school, you may have more authority to decide what books to read or what topics to focus on than in larger urban and suburban districts where a district-wide pacing guide or a school-wide curriculum coordinator decide what should be taught when. Particularly in smaller schools, being the only third-grade or physics teacher in your school or district provides a lot of room to make decisions based on your expertise as a teacher and your students' needs. That sense of autonomy may not be found in every school, but it is often part of the reason that rural teachers express greater job satisfaction than their peers in other districts (Player, 2015).

Rural teaching may also give you increased opportunity for variety in your job. Rural teachers often wear many hats (Berry & Gravelle, 2013). You are more likely to teach different subjects than you are to repeat the same lesson several times in a day. A suburban teacher may teach six sections of the same Freshman English class every day. But a rural teacher may start the day with Freshman English, then supervise a study hall, teach a career exploration class, and end the day with a special creative writing class created in response to student interest. As a rural teacher, you may be called on to play multiple roles. You may have opportunities to lead before- and after-school clubs or play another role such as driving a bus or coaching a sport. Wearing multiple hats is not always easy. Duties on top of your daily teaching load can make for long working days.

.eed to wear multiple hats can make your work richer, but it can also make your work feel overwhelming. Try to imagine these challenges as opportunities that bring variety to the work that help keep things interesting and opportunities to shine and demonstrate your leadership ability.

For Discussion

The Rural Schools Collaborative has been working with its partners to tell the stories of amazing rural teachers across the United States. Each installment of their I Am a Rural Teacher series features an interview with a different rural educator. Visit the *I Am a Rural Teacher* website (https:// iamaruralteacher.org) and read the stories of several rural teachers. What do the teachers profiled there see as the advantages and challenges of rural teaching? What do these vignettes make you think about the work of being a rural teacher?

Rural Teachers Have a Big Impact

Rural places are diverse, and while many rural schools have plenty of resources to support your work as a teacher, some schools are faced with poverty and a lack of resources, and this can pose challenges for teachers in rural contexts. The harsh reality is that poverty rates are high in many rural places, particularly in the south and West. The Economic Research Service of the U.S. Department of Agriculture (2020) defines persistent poverty counties as counties where more than 20% of the population were living in poverty in each of the last three Census counts. Eighty-five percent of persistent poverty counties are also rural counties. Students who live in poverty often have needs that they bring to school that need to be addressed first before students can fully engage in learning.

Rural locations can also mean fewer resources for schools. As we discuss in Chapter 10, schools in the U.S. are funded by a mix of state, federal, and local funds. Local funding is primarily based on revenue collected from property taxes that are calculated based on a percentage of the value of the land in the school district. For many rural locations, property values are low. Open land that is not being used for industry or agriculture may result in limited tax revenue. State funding is often calculated on the basis of student enrollment, and per pupil funding may be limited in areas where student populations are small. All of these factors can mean that some rural schools do not have the same resources as more urban and suburban schools. On average, salaries for teachers are lower in rural districts than non-rural places. Although lower salaries may be offset by a lower cost of living (e.g. lower

Persistent poverty counties, 2015 edition

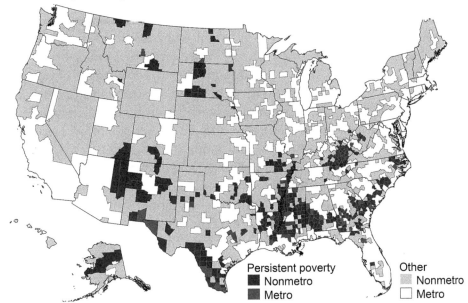

Persistent poverty counties are those where 20 percent or more of county residents were poor, measured by the 1980, 1990, 2000 censuses, and the 2007-11 American Community Survey.
Note that county boundaries are drawn for the persistent poverty counties only.
Source: USDA, Economic Research Service using data from U.S. Census Bureau.

remarkable understatement

rent and housing prices, lower costs for groceries and other goods), the salary differential can impact some teachers' decisions to stay and teach in rural areas.

Geographic distances may also mean that resources that are available in other settings may not be available in rural schools. Libraries, museums, and other educational resources may not be located near your school. This does not mean that there are not resources for teaching that can enrich your classroom, but it may mean that you need to be more creative and resourceful in finding virtual alternatives or identifying the community resources that support your teaching. Chapters 6 and 13 will provide you with strategies to identify, or map, the resources in your community and to design place-conscious instruction that helps you and your students identify and learn from the many resources in any rural community.

The challenges of poverty, funding, and access to resources are real. Chapter 2 documents some of the history of rural places that has led to long standing disenfranchisement and marginalization of rural people and places. Many rural areas of our nation have a long and continuing history of inequality. In places where there is a legacy of slavery, racism, immigration, or displacement, inequities and social challenges are real and impact the work of teaching. We do not want to diminish the challenges that you may face in a rural school. However, when you work in a rural district you can help students gain a greater understanding of how things have come to be in the place where they live, to study and understand the strengths and the challenges, and to learn about how their place can connect and contribute to the larger world. Rural schools play a crucial role in the lives and well-being of rural students. You will have an opportunity to help students think about their place in community and the world and prepare them for whatever comes next. You will also have an opportunity to be an advocate for students—to model how to welcome newcomers to the community who may be seen as outsiders, to support students who are exploring new ideas or challenging local traditions, to create a safe space for students who are gay, lesbian, bi, or transgender. Many teachers from rural communities talk about preparing students who can choose to stay and be contributing members of their rural communities and, at the same time, preparing students for the wider world should they choose to leave.

As a rural teacher, you have an amazing opportunity to enrich the lives of students and make a real difference (McCardle, 2019). In the next chapter, we describe rural teaching as an act of social justice. We believe that the role of teachers is to help prepare students to thrive, and to prepare students who can critique and work to change the systems that are barriers to equity. Teachers often become educators out of a desire to help grow and guide children and shape the future generation. As an educator, as an advocate, as an adult who cares about children, you have a real opportunity to make a difference for students.

If you are becoming a teacher because you want to make an impact, rural teaching might be the right choice for you. If you teach in a rural community, you may have real opportunities to see the impact of your work over time. In a small district especially, you are likely to be able to watch your students' progress as they move from your classroom to the next, and to be able to celebrate their accomplishments over time. Teaching in a rural community can also be an advantage because, on average, students "do better" in rural schools. By some measures, children and families in rural communities have better outcomes than those living in more urban and suburban areas. This is especially true for children growing up in low-income families. Research conducted by Raj Chetty and Nate Hendry at Opportunity Insights (see https://opportunityinsights.org) shows that, compared to similar families in urban areas, children in rural places may be less likely to go to prison and more likely to get married and start families, among other outcomes (Bishop, 2019).

Steve Druggan grew up in one of the small rural schools in Pennsylvania. After traveling and teaching all over the world, he's now back in his hometown, teaching. He said:

> *Growing up rural can be a privilege and a curse. I was privileged to attend the same school for 13 years and the teachers cared about us. Of course, I didn't think that at the time, but later it became clear and that is what I have taken with me. No matter how big a knucklehead I was, and I could be a pretty big one (just ask my mom), the teachers in that smallest of small schools kept trying to help me make better decisions. That is what I have taken with me: We have to care. Kids know it and deserve it.*

For Discussion

What is your "why" for becoming a rural teacher? What difference do you want to make when you are working with students in classrooms? What kind of a difference do you want to make in a rural community? Which of these (or other) advantages of rural teaching seem the most important and most likely to help you achieve your purpose?

A Book to Help You Thrive as a Rural Teacher

This chapter does not describe all of the advantages and challenges of teaching in a rural community. You will find that any of the places where you consider teaching present their own set of unique circumstances. In your field experiences and in your first years of teaching, you can explore how the community and the school's administration handle issues like isolation and resources, support teachers who are wearing many hats, and provide opportunities for new teachers to become members of the community. Other sections of this text will provide you with concrete strategies that you can use to ensure your success as a rural teacher and to provide you with a sense of satisfaction in your life and work in a rural community. We hope that, like us, you also agree that the advantages of teaching in a rural place far outweigh the challenges, and that you will develop strategies and plans to help you thrive wherever you end up teaching.

References

Anttila, E., & Väänänen, A. (2013). Rural schoolteachers and the pressures of community life: Local and cosmopolitan coping strategies in mid-twentieth-century Finland. *History of Education*, 42(2), 182–203. doi: https://10.1080/0046760X.2013.766267

Ballou, D., & Podgursky, M. (1995). What makes a good principal? How teachers assess the performance of principals. *Economics of Education Review*, 14(3), 243–252.

Berry, A. B., & Gravelle, M. (2013). The benefits and challenges of special education positions in rural settings: Listening to the teachers. *The Rural Educator*, 34(2), 1–13. doi: https://10.35608/ruraled.v34i2.400

Bishop, N. (2019, August 13). Rural news roundup: If rural life is so awful, why is it so much fun? *The Daily Yonder*. www.dailyyonder.com/rural-news-roundup-if-rural-life-is-so-awful-why-is-it-such-fun/2019/08/13/

Cuervo, H., & Acquaro, D. (2018). Exploring metropolitan university pre-service teacher motivations and barriers to teaching in rural schools. *Asia-Pacific Journal of Teacher Education*, 46(4), 1–15. doi: https://10.1080/1359866X.2018.1438586

Economic Research Service. (2020). *Rural poverty and well-being*. U.S. Department of Agriculture. www.ers.usda.gov/topics/rural-economy-population/rural-poverty-well-being/

McCardle, E. (2019, Summer). The middle of somewhere: The unique strengths of rural communities and why more teachers should consider working in them. *Ed. Harvard Ed. Magazine*. www.gse.harvard.edu/news/ed/19/05/middle-somewhere

McGranahan, D. A., Cromartie, J., & Wojan, T. R. (2010). Nonmetropolitan outmigration counties: Some are poor, many are prosperous. *USDA-ERS Economic Research Report*, (107). doi: https://10.2139/ssrn.1711309

National Center for Victims of Crime. (2014). *Urban and rural crime*. https://ovc.ncjrs.gov/ncvrw2016/content/section-6/PDF/2016NCVRW_6_UrbanRural-508.pdf

Player, D. (2015). *The supply and demand for rural teachers*. Rural Opportunities Consortium of Idaho. http://www.rociidaho.org/wp-content/uploads/2015/03/ROCI_2015_RuralTeachers_FINAL.pdf

Reininger, M. (2011). Hometown disadvantage? It depends on where you're from: Teachers' location preferences and the implications for staffing schools. *Educational Evaluation and Policy Analysis*, 34(2), 127–145. doi: https://10.3102/0162373711420864

Turner, J., Finch, K., & Uribe-Zarain, X. (2019). Three Midwest rural school districts' first year transition to the four-day school week: Parents' perspectives. *The Rural Educator, 40*(1), 1–15. doi: https://10.35608/ruraled.v40i1.529

Ulferts, J. D. (2016). A brief summary of teacher recruitment and retention in the smallest Illinois rural schools. *The Rural Educator, 37*(1), 14–24. doi: https://10.35608/ruraled.v37i1.292

Wille, A. M., Maher, M. K., Cornell, S. R., Kim, A. C., Reimers, B., & Hess, R. S. (2019). It starts with us: Including refugees in rural schools and communities. *The Rural Educator, 40*(2), 33–42. doi: https://10.35608/ruraled.v40i2.850

2

Social Justice and Rural Communities

You are likely reading this book because you have an interest in what it means to live and teach in rural communities. Maybe you are not exactly sure what "counts" as a rural school. *Rural* in this book is broadly defined as an interaction between geography, culture, and social characteristics. Rurality represents a space of educational inequality in which 8.9 million (or one in six) U.S. children live and learn. Rural communities across the United States share many characteristics related to population density and proximity to urban centers. Many grapple with issues such as isolation, access to resources, poverty, and teacher shortages. Rural communities across the United States are also remarkably diverse. Communities considered rural may rely on farming or food processing, resource extraction such as mining or logging, tourism, or may be transitioning from rural to suburban communities. Rural communities may also be located in areas with a legacy of inequity such as the South or Appalachia or may have high concentrations of Native people or immigrants. There are many different kinds of rural communities. In this book, we hope to challenge and expand your thinking about what rural might be by demonstrating the diversity and complexity of rural schools and communities.

Perhaps you are like most rural teachers in that you have grown up in a rural place and plan to stay there or you plan to teach in a rural school that seems similar to your own. Maybe you are one of many rural teachers who end up teaching in the very same school district or building that you attended as a child. Or, less commonly, life circumstances or an academic interest may have brought you to rural teaching. No matter your connection to rural schools and communities, you probably have some awareness of rural schools as places that don't always compare favorably to suburban or urban schools. For example, you may think that rural schools lack diversity. You may assume that rural students' standardized test scores are lower than students in suburban and urban schools. You may wonder if rural schools have broadband internet and up-to-date technology. While your knowledge and experience of rural schools will shape your understanding of these issues and others, you want to understand and probably have a desire to improve the school experiences of your rural students. You know that most rural communities are marginalized in a variety of ways, and like most urban communities, are places where change is needed to foster more just ecological and social outcomes.

Policy follows public perception and while rural places are indeed diverse, the social status of rural people is captured in the variety of derogatory terms that perpetuate limited thinking about rural places. For example, words like white trash, cracker, hick, redneck, and hillbilly are commonly used pejoratives with deeply rooted historical contexts. Notice, however, the assumptions in all of these pejoratives that rural people are White. No matter how racially or ethnically diverse your classroom, these words demean the kids in your rural classroom. If what it means to be rural was just about how far someone lives from an urban place, these names would not exist. The names illustrate that rural is a social difference, an often *stigmatized* social difference. The negative stigmas are often attached to rural places today originated in the early history of the United States. They are the outcome of social and economic circumstances of colonial America. The stigma attached to rural is not just a negative idea but has tangible outcomes in the form of what scholars refer to as "marginalization." To be marginalized means to be ignored, pushed aside, or seen as inferior. How do we know that rural is often a marginalized space? Consider the following questions:

- Why do fewer rural students than suburban or urban students enroll in and graduate from colleges and universities?
- Why do rural schools struggle to recruit and retain classroom teachers and school leaders?
- Why is it still socially acceptable in many contexts to use pejorative terms like white trash?

What other questions can you think of? Solving the challenges facing rural schools and communities requires working toward more equitable and socially just outcomes for rural children. The answers to questions like these require big-picture thinking that goes beyond the specific character-istics and history of any particular local community. And that's where you come in!

Rural communities, like urban communities, have particular challenges and affordances that can be traced to complex interactions among histor-ical, political, economic, and social influences. Understanding rural com-munities and their schools calls for an understanding not only of how each of these dimensions play out in contemporary rural life, but also how each dimension—political, economic, and cultural—is rooted in historical cir-cumstances. We start here with some historical context of rural as a cate-gory of difference in order to understand how the questions above are relevant, but not often enough asked, in a country that claims to be based on equity principles.

Any history is a story that is crafted by the author's choices about what to emphasize, ignore, or repackage in order to fit the intended perspective. This particular story about the origins of rural life in the United States is no dif-ferent. This story emphasizes the history of land ownership, of who had access to property and who did not. It explains, in part, how the early history of what is now the United States connects to the current political, economic, and cultural disadvantages experienced by rural people, schools, and com-munities today. The story does not ignore, but is incomplete in its treatment of, the experiences of Native people and enslaved people. It ends around the 1860s when the patterns that are still in place today were established. Important regional differences are collapsed into a shared history of early land ownership because that particular history has some power to explain the current challenges and strengths and demographics of rural communities today. Its purpose is to offer another way of thinking about rural commu-nities beyond a "that's-just-the-way-it-is" explanation of rural places.

The story starts at the early days of European settlement of what would become the United States. Read on to understand the strengths, con-temporary perceptions, and stigmatization of rural people and commu-nities. Following this section, we introduce a way to think about your teaching as a way to work toward dismantling the barriers and negative stigmas that have produced inequities in rural places.

A Story of Rural Land Ownership

People who arrived on the shores of what would eventually become the United States arrived under various circumstances based on their social class, culture, or race. Unfortunately, colonial history is mostly taught to children as a romantic and exciting tale. Freedom, adventure, and opportunity are central themes. Early slavery is often only a footnote. While colonization and westward expansion, for some, was undoubtedly experienced as freedom, adventure, or opportunity, the mythologized stories conceal a much more complicated narrative. Inspirational narratives about freedom, adventure, and opportunity obscure a foundational history of brutality and exploitation that has explanatory powers for contemporary injustices, for Native people and African Americans, and for people living in rural communities.

In most of British North America, colonization was a business venture. It was an "all hands on deck" type of project that required people with a variety of skills and freedoms to be successful. Many colonies were set up by joint-stock corporations, and English investors and landowners could not make a profit in the so-called "New World" without low-cost labor and free land. The only thing *new* about the New World, however, was the arrival of large numbers of European settlers. The world was not new, but stolen from millions of indigenous peoples who had lived there for centuries.

The Need for Labor in the Colonies

Early in British colonization, the colonies were sparsely populated. There were not enough people to do the work that needed to be done. There was vast demand for physical labor to clear trees, build farms, and work the land. As settlement expanded into the North American countryside, cheap manual labor was increasingly needed. At first, this need was met by indentured servants and the very poor. Britain had a large pool of (nearly) free labor in the form of vulnerable and expendable adults and children. In short order, destitute adults and children of England, Wales, and Scotland, and in some cases, prisoners, were transported to the North American colonies in an arrangement that benefited powerful people in Britain and the North American colonies.

Recruiters looking to meet the need for labor in the colonies frequently recruited people who could not pay their own passage and had no choice but to contract as indentured servants. They agreed to seven years of labor exploitation in lieu of payment for their voyage. The arrangement was intended to free Britain from what the wealthy class saw as the negative social influence and financial burden of care for the "excess" population by turning their labor into a resource for the British colonies.

The indentured servants, though not slaves, were considered to be a financial and social burden to Britain. The social status of the indentured servants and enslaved Africans who followed are key to understanding rural communities today.

From the very beginning of colonial life, land ownership, much as it is today, was influenced by race and social class. Any Briton who could pay for their own passage received a land allocation as incentive to come to the British colonies. At the beginning of the "headright" system, enslavers amassed acreage, 50 acres per person, for Africans brought against their will to the colonies. The indentured servants who could not pay for their passage worked off their fare, and also forfeited their land allocation to their sponsor. Sponsoring indentures and enslaving people from Africa were of tremendous benefit to the wealthy, specifically, as a means to increase their land holdings.

Claiming Land on the Outskirts of the Colonies

Black Americans could not own land until recognized as U.S. citizens in 1866. This was *200 years* after the first White people came to the colonies in the 1600s. Indentured people had two options for land ownership. Less desirable low-cost land could be purchased on credit or formerly indentured servants could squat, illegally, on legally unclaimed land on what was then the rural outskirts of the colonies. Either option pushed formerly indentured servants toward less fertile and mountainous acreage, positioning them not only toward the geographic, but also the social margins of the colonies.

Squatters had complete disregard for the Native people living on the outer edges of the colonies and considered any land unsettled by Europeans free for the taking. For about 150 years, the British government paid no attention to the squatters or to the Native people from whom the "free" land was stolen. Later, despite using military force and enacting land ordinances, the British government was mostly unsuccessful at removing the squatters, even from the territory of allied Native tribes. The squatters, the first individuals who lived in the most rural and remote areas of the colonies that were the most difficult to farm, were poor, disadvantaged, and mostly White. This, along with the outright denial of land ownership to formerly enslaved people before 1866, set the stage for the political, economic, and cultural disadvantage that persists today.

1619: Enslaved Africans in the Colonies

By the early 1600s, indentured servitude became inadequate to support the growing economic success of the colonies. As it became harder to find indentured servants in Britain, poor immigrants from Europe and Ireland were recruited. More labor was still needed. The first enslaved Africans arrived from the Caribbean and Africa in 1619. As the colonial economy grew, owners of large estates increased their profit with the free labor provided by large numbers of enslaved Africans. By the late 1600s chattel slavery was spreading across the south.

> *The New York Times'* "The 1619 Project" features essays, poetry, and fiction that move the story of slavery from the margins to the center of American history. https://www.nytimes.com/interactive/2019/08/14/magazine/1619-america-slavery.html

While U.S. textbooks may advance the romantic narrative that coming to the colonies was a virtuous adventure anchored by the Puritans' quest for religious freedom, the reality is far more complex. Of those who survived the journey and the first years of life in the New World, many were not adventurers in search of a new life, but arrived enslaved, exploited, or otherwise powerless. For nearly all who came willingly to the New World, the promise of a new life with opportunity for a better life through land ownership and social mobility would not be realized. Old World social positions were intentionally reproduced in the social hierarchy of the colonies. Our brutal history of African slavery has created persistent and grievous institutional racism that can be seen today in deeply disproportionate numbers of imprisoned Black and brown people, persistent opportunity gaps in schools with high populations of students of color, as well patterns of land ownership.

Rural Life as Ideal to Rural Life as Backward

In the late 1700s, in the decades after the Revolutionary War, Jeffersonian and Jacksonian democracy and westward expansion repositioned most rural former colonists from poor, lawless outcasts to people integral to the growth and character of the new nation. Small family farms were now foundational to the national character and the most fundamental American enterprise. Farmers were morally superior, hardworking, adventurous, and self-sufficient. These were the qualities of an ideal citizen. In 1784, just one year after the end of the Revolutionary War, Jefferson wrote: "Those who labor in the earth are the chosen people of God, if ever he had a chosen people, whose breasts he has made his peculiar deposit for substantial and genuine virtue." In the late 1700s, farmers were special people living the ideal (rural) life in service to the fledgling nation.

By the 1840s, the Industrial Revolution, particularly in the Northern United States, was starting to call young people off the farms and to urban centers in search of economic security, status, and an easier way of life. The best way of life was now an urban way of life, and those who could migrate east to the cities did so. Accordingly, people who clung to rural ways of life were seen as ignorant and backward because they didn't move to city centers and/or were slow adopters of agricultural technology, or as lawless, an idea still attached today to Appalachians. This is in spite of the fact that then, as now, urban places can only exist with water, minerals, and food from rural America. In spite of this, the isolation and hardships of rural places, and the people who lived there, were seen as incompatible with the urbanized progress of the Industrial Revolution.

Westward expansion of the 1860s created widespread, largely White settlements, pushing Native peoples further onto reservations and funneling landless Black migrants to the North, mostly into cities. As the extraction economies (logging, mining, and timber) and small and mid-sized farms faltered throughout the twentieth century, many rural communities were unable to compete with multinational corporations despite a history of multiethnic labor organizing.

> The West Virginia mine wars was not only the bloodiest labor conflict in American history that you've never heard of, but was also perhaps the most diverse. As early as 1910, the United Mine Workers of American (UMWA) required as an oath that members not discriminate by "creed, or color, or nationality." The 10,000 miners who organized were Black, White, and immigrant. The "Redneck Army" wore red bandanas to identify each other in battle. See more at: https://www.theguardian.com/us-news/2018/apr/14/redneck-pride-west-virginia-protests-strikes

While some communities have reinvented themselves as arts centers or have been designated as Opportunity Zones for tech startups, other rural communities continue to struggle with the same kinds of issues—poverty, educational attainment, addiction—more commonly associated with urban communities. History has shaped, and continues to shape, the rural places where you might live and work.

> **For Discussion**
>
> Can you find evidence of a Native American presence on the land where your community is currently located? What can you learn about the Native American presence in your community? Keep following the thread and see what you can learn about the Europeans who "founded" your community. Where were the founders from and what brought them to what is now your community? The Community Walk activity in Chapter 6 may help you find answers to these and other questions you may have.

The history of who had the option and financial means to own land (all stolen from Native people) in more rural or less rural areas of the British colonies gives you a way to understand a bit more about the racial and economic trends of contemporary rural communities. The story about who could live where also gives some context for the social positioning of rural people in the twenty-first century. Now that you know that rural places are connected to histories that don't just exist in the past, you can consider how that history continues to impact day to day life in ways that are not always positive or just.

A Three-Part Approach for Social Justice for Rural Schools and Communities

What do you think of when you hear the term "social justice"? Social justice is often understood as a means to address racial inequality. The term is so common that it hides the ways in which "social justice" means different things to different people. In this book, we take a broad view of social justice. Our broad view considers how categories of disadvantage such as gender, sexuality, race, and socioeconomic status (see, in particular, Chapters 5, 8, and 16) intersect with rurality. This view is also appropriate because rural schools and communities have been systematically disadvantaged economically, culturally, and politically. Education in rural schools *is* a project of social justice and, like the complexity of racial injustice, no one category tells the whole story.

There are a variety of frames for thinking about social justice such as Marilyn Cochran-Smith's frame for social justice within racially diverse urban schools (Cochran-Smith, 1997) and Derman-Sparks and Olsen Edwards's anti-bias education (2020). The social justice frame used in this book is based on the work of Nancy Fraser (2005; 2009). Fraser defines social justice as parity of participation. By parity of participation, she means that every person is of equal moral worth and is therefore entitled to justice. For Fraser, justice is a social arrangement that enables parity of participation in everyday life. By Fraser's way of thinking, to work toward social justice is to work to dismantle three main impediments to parity of participation. She argues for (1) economic justice, (2) cultural justice, and (3) political justice. The questions provided for each type of justice we will review are useful in breaking down the big concept of "social justice" into specific ideas and actions. The questions are sample questions to get you thinking about what social justice could look like and what actions in schools, classrooms, and communities could bring about more equity in rural schools and communities.

Economic Justice

Economic justice has to do with financial resources and how they are distributed. It is related to the socioeconomic impact of policies. Economic (or socioeconomic) injustice is plainly identifiable in rural communities in forms such as the exploitation of human and natural resources, economic marginalization that produces a lack of long-term living wage jobs, and high rates of child poverty, addiction and disability as compared to urban communities.

For more statistics about economic justice, see: https://www.ers.usda.gov/topics/rural-economy-population/rural-poverty-well-being/.

Questions for thinking and action about resource distribution include:

- How much inequality is just?
- How much funding is needed to restore economic equality?
- How will we decide who gets what and how much?

Economic injustice is closely associated with larger economic structures that are created by policies. Economic structures are why some communities are rich and some are poor. Economic structures are unjust when

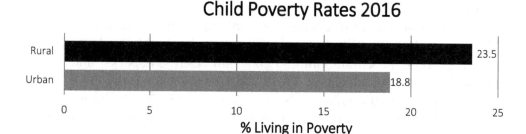

Child Poverty Rates 2016

they impede what Fraser calls "participatory parity" in peer interactions. Participatory parity is the extent to which a person or group can interact with peers and participate in decisions. Although economic disadvantage and cultural disrespect are distinct paradigms of injustice, they are intertwined and mutually constitutive.

Cultural Justice

Cultural justice is about the recognition of how cultural differences impact a group's social status. While economic justice is about economics and how income disparities produce lower, working, middle, and upper "classes" of people, cultural justice is needed to counter the idea that some groups of people are not seen as worthy of equal respect. Recognizing or tolerating difference is not enough. Struggles over cultural recognition and justice are about how particular groups are devalued by who those identify with White middle-class culture. Cultural justice is closely connected to economic justice.

Questions for thinking and action about cultural recognition justice include:

- What kind of differences matter between people and when do they matter?
- How can differences be recognized and valued?
- What groups are seen as having the intellectual potential to use innovative thinking to solve problems?

Rural people are unique to the extent to which they suffer misrecognition so openly. Twenty years ago, noting the struggle of rural people relative to other groups, Howley and Howley (2000) wrote,

> *The rural is emblematic of the most entrenched status quo and therefore represents—in contrast to the potentially transformative positioning conferred by other contexts (e.g. race, gender, ethnicity)—a hopelessly regressive condition. Even critical educators equate the rural with machine politics, inbreeding, and racism.*
>
> (p. 75)

The struggles for recognition of rural difference happen within large systems of economic inequality. Rural people are frequently represented as "less than" in arenas as diverse as federal policy, children's and young adult literature, textbooks, and popular culture. The history reviewed earlier in this chapter argues that failure to value rural difference is as old as the United States itself. Rural people and resources have generally been useful only to the extent that they can help others. Rural places are where we train and get many of our military recruits, house our prisoners, and dispose of our garbage. Especially in the media coverage of the 2016 presidential election, rural people and places are portrayed as backward and unimportant, and often racist.

Political Justice

Political justice is about who is included and excluded in decision-making processes and how those decisions are made. Political justice is about having a political voice (representation) in decision making. Not all people have the same access to political representation. Equal access to representation is needed in the political decision processes about how resources should be distributed. Representative justice is about who will decide how much will be distributed and to whom. Representative justice is about political representation.

Questions for thinking and action about representative justice include:

- What groups are included or excluded in policy making about how resources are distributed? Who is left to decide?
- Do the rules and policies provide access to equal voice in public deliberations and fair representation in public decision making?
- How can all rural residents have equal opportunity to participate in political decisions at all levels?

Political justice is about who gets to be on the political "stage" where fairness is debated. It's also about the process of making the rules that guide how things get decided in politics. Broadband policies, for example, favor suburban and urban spaces over rural (Eppley & Shannon, 2017). Lack of broadband is an impediment to equal access to participation in state, national, and global policies. As we discuss in Chapter 10, local school boards function under a number of local norms and policies that do not necessarily create equitable opportunities for participation in decision-making processes. Likewise, school boards also fall under the jurisdiction of state-level policies that do not necessarily work well for rural school districts. Representation justice is needed for equitable access to decision making at all levels.

Barriers to Social Justice in Rural Schools

You were likely already very familiar with concerns about economic justice for rural schools and communities. Economic justice includes issues about what resources a school can offer, and also, how and to what extent the students are able to take advantage of what is offered. While this book aims to make clear that rural schools serve many functions, one function is to prepare students to support themselves economically. We know that there is work to be done by communities and schools in this area. Evidence of this need can be seen in rural students' access to advanced science courses, world languages, and Advanced Placement (AP) courses (Gagnon & Mattingly, 2016), as well as rates of early school leaving (Strange, 2011). Inequities in these areas can place students at a distinct disadvantage after graduation. Refer to Chapter 10 for a discussion of policies meant to alleviate economic inequity.

However, we know that all groups of students do not experience the same access to funding. Racialized differences are easy to spot, and there are strong associations with racial diversity and urban schools. However, according to the National Center for Educational Statistics (2013), racial disadvantage is not unique to urban schools. The following statistics show a breakdown of the percentages of rural students by race who attend high-poverty rural schools in remote rural communities. (A school is considered high-poverty if at least 75% of its students qualify for free and reduced lunch.)

- 59% of Black students
- 57% of American Indian/Alaska Native
- 29% of Hispanic students
- 19% of Pacific Islander
- 21% of students of two or more races
- 10% of White students

The \ graph on the next page shows differences in poverty rates by race and ethnicity.

As you can see, rurality intersects with culture, race, and ethnicity in ways that underscore the idea that social justice is not only multi-dimensional (economic, cultural, political), but also has a strong spatial component. Who you are in school matters, but so does *where* you go to school.

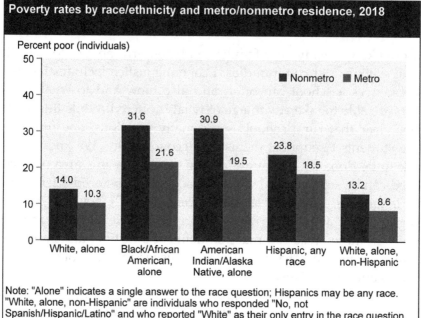

Poverty rates by race/ethnicity and metro/nonmetro residence, 2018

Percent poor (individuals)

■ Nonmetro ■ Metro

Race/ethnicity	Nonmetro	Metro
White, alone	14.0	10.3
Black/African American, alone	31.6	21.6
American Indian/Alaska Native, alone	30.9	19.5
Hispanic, any race	23.8	18.5
White, alone, non-Hispanic	13.2	8.6

Note: "Alone" indicates a single answer to the race question; Hispanics may be any race. "White, alone, non-Hispanic" are individuals who responded "No, not Spanish/Hispanic/Latino" and who reported "White" as their only entry in the race question. Source: USDA, Economic Research Service using data from the U.S. Census Bureau, annual American Community Survey, 2018.

Who gets to make decisions about how schools will work, who they will include, and how they will be funded encompasses economic and cultural dimensions of justice. In nearly every context, decisions tend to be made by those who hold power, often at the expense of others. In the United States the voice of the White urban and suburban middle and upper class is disproportionally present. This, as we argued earlier, is a historical legacy, but is underscored by the uneven distribution of rural communities across the United States. For example, 80% of schools in South Dakota are rural, compared with 7% in Massachusetts. Rural interests are varied and dispersed geographically, but more often than not, they are politically less powerful.

Your thoughts about your preparation to teach in rural classrooms are no doubt focused on meeting the individual and collective needs of the children you will teach. You might also be aware of the potential of your classroom to be a place enabling of your students' development as local, regional, and global citizens. How might rural teachers play a part in working toward more just rural schools and communities? In this book, we share some strategies about how you might think about your rural classroom as a place not only where content is learned, but also where children are prepared to make decisions about their community. This goal cannot be realized without awareness of the histories of rural places and forward-thinking, innovating teaching couched within a social justice agenda.

where is the defense of this argument ...? (handwritten margin note)

References

Cochran-Smith, M. (1997). Knowledge, skills, and experiences for teaching culturally diverse learners: A perspective for practicing teachers. In. J. J. Irvine (Ed.), *Critical knowledge for diverse teachers and learners*, pp. 27–87. American Association of Colleges for Teacher Education.

Derman-Sparks, L., & Olsen Edwards, J. (2020). *Anti-bias education for young children and ourselves*. National Association of Education of Young Children.

Eppley, K., & Shannon, P. (2017). Practice based evidence: Intelligent action inquiry for complex problems. *Literacy Research: Theory, Method, and Practice, 66*, 1–17. doi: https://10.1177/2381336917719685

Fraser, N. (2005). Reframing global justice. *New Left Review, 36*(36), 69–88.

Fraser, N. (2009). *Scales of justice: Reimagining political space in a globalizing world*. Columbia University Press.

Gagnon, D. J., & Mattingly, M. J. (2016). Advanced placement and rural schools: Access, success, and exploring alternatives. *Journal of Advanced Academics, 27*(4), 266–284. doi: https://10.1177/2381336917719685

Howley, A., & Howley, C. (2000). The transformative challenge of rural context. *Journal of Educational Foundations, 14*(4), 73–85.

National Center for Educational Statistics. (2013). *The status of rural education*. Washington, D.C.: National Center for Educational Statistics. https://nces.ed.gov/programs/coe/pdf/coe_tla.pdf

USDA, Economic Education Research Service. (2020). *Rural poverty and well-being*. https://www.ers.usda.gov/topics/rural-economy-population/rural-poverty-well-being/#demographics

Strange, M. (2011). Finding fairness for rural students. *Phi Delta Kappan, 92*(6), 8–15. doi: https://10.1177/003172171109200603

3

Understanding Rural Places

Each reader of this book is likely to bring unique ideas about rurality based on their personal experiences. What comes to mind when we hear the word "rural" is shaped, in part, by our experiences, but also by what we have learned socially from sources such as school, pop culture, and the media. For many people, the word "rural" tends to suggest images of low-income, White-majority communities. Television shows, such as *Duck Dynasty* or *Hart of Dixie*, portray writers' and producers' versions of rural life in the Southern United States. Other shows and movies, such as *Fargo* or *Brokeback Mountain*, depict a version of life in the West. An especially problematic representation of rural life in central Appalachia is shown in the book and movie of the same name, *Hillbilly Elegy*. Rural places as they are shown in the media are mostly imaginary in the sense that they are created with a particular message in mind. With the exception of *Hillbilly Elegy*, none claim to be accurate pictures of what rural life is like in the places shown. What you picture in your mind when you think of "rural" is better called a "rural imaginary" because your vision is based on the representations you've seen and the experiences you've had, rather than any objective truths. Each of us has different rural imaginaries.

Whether a rural imaginary includes the distressed Appalachian coal miner or the pioneering, American Gothic midwestern farmer, it often positions rural communities as imagined relics of a simpler time or, conversely, as deeply entrenched in addiction, racism, or homophobia. Neither of these extremes, of course, is true. American Indian, Latinx, or African American communities challenge the idea that rural communities are White, in the same way that pockets of rural economic prosperity challenge the idea that all rural communities are poor. Knowing what rural *is* is difficult because each rural community is made up of unique geographic, economic, and social aspects. This chapter will give you a frame for understanding individual rural communities and for making some connections across rural places.

For Discussion

What images first come to mind when you think of rural? Sketch your vision, describe it in writing, or tell a partner. Do you picture a midwestern family farm? The Mississippi Delta? A New England village? Central Appalachia? An American Indian community in Arizona, Utah, or New Mexico? A large-scale California farm \? The mountainous West? Who are the people who live there? What do they do for a living?

Identify the life experiences, learning, or images you think contributed to your understanding. Then, brainstorm some possible implications of imagining rural as limited to the geography you imagined. Who does your vision include and exclude?

As you read in Chapter 2, what we understand about rural with our "common sense" has roots in the earliest days of colonial America. For a time in United States history, rural people were celebrated as the American ideal. Modern common-sense understandings about rural people have changed pretty dramatically since colonial times. Today, we no longer hold up Thomas Jefferson's salt-of-the-earth farmer as the ideal American citizen. The oversimplified idea from Jefferson's time, a thin story about rural farmers' role in growing the nation, has been replaced with a modern narrative that rural people are backward, not very smart, and live in White-majority rural communities that are mostly the same everywhere. One oversimplification has replaced another. Our contemporary understanding of rural is equally inaccurate.

Any rural community is made up of a combination of geographic, economic, and social characteristics. A complete understanding of any one rural community is possible only with full consideration of each characteristic as well as the interplay among the three. Differences among people, the geographies in which they live (plains, mountains, desert, etc.), and economic factors converge to create great variability from one rural community to the next. Though rural schools are both unique and connected, no two rural communities are the same. Understanding the wide variation among rural schools and communities is critical for a nuanced understanding.

Geographically: What Is Rural?

One aspect of a definition of rurality must, of course, have to do with geography. Rurality has something to do with the land, and the number of people living on that land. But even then, rurality is hard to define. In fact, the federal government has over a dozen definitions of rural. What the definitions share in common is that they define the geography of places based on the density of the population and the distance from areas where many people live close together.

A key set of definitions is based on U.S. Census Bureau data. The U.S. Census definition of rural is: "all population, housing, and territory not included within an urbanized area or urban cluster." According to this definition, rural is "residual" or what is left over after determining what places are urban. The National Center for Education Statistics (NCES) worked with the Census Bureau and developed a locale classification system, breaking rural down into three categories: rural fringe, rural distant, and rural remote. Details about the classification are available at https://nces.ed.gov/surveys/ruraled/definitions.asp.

Urban-Centric Classification System	Distance from an urbanized area with less than 50,000 people	Distance from an urban cluster with 2,500–50,000 people
Rural Fringe	Less than 5 miles from an urbanized area	Less than 2.5 miles from an urban cluster
Rural Distant	5–25 miles from an urbanized area	2.5–10 miles from an urban cluster
Rural Remote	More than 25 miles from an urbanized area	More than 10 miles from an urban cluster

Communities considered "rural fringe" are less than five miles from an urbanized area or are less than two and a half miles from an urban cluster of 2,500 to 50,000 people. Distant rural communities are more than five miles but less than 25 miles from an urbanized area or are between two and half miles, but less than ten miles from an urban cluster. Rural remote communities are more than 25 miles from an urbanized area or are more than ten miles from an urban cluster.

For Discussion

Go to the NCES Search for Public School Districts website where you can look up every school district in every state: https://nces.ed.gov/ccd/dis trictsearch/. Choose a rural school district. Choose one you know, if possible. In the District Details, you can find the locale designation. You may be surprised to find that your impression of a rural community does not match its official designation. To what extent are the rural places you know appropriately matched with the correct official designations? What might the implications of a rural designation (or lack of designation) be? Now, check all of the schools within the district. Do they have the same classification as the district? What are the possible implications of this scenario?

Rural Places Are Geographically Diverse

Every state and territory in the United States (except Washington, D.C.) has rural schools and communities. And that's where the similarity ends. Some states, like Alaska, Texas, and Montana, have more square miles of rural land than other states. In some states, such as Maine, Vermont, and Mississippi, about half of students live in rural areas. In other states, including Rhode Island, Utah, and Nevada, fewer than 5% of public school students are rural (Showalter et al., 2017).

Within and across the states, the geography of rural places varies—from mountains to prairies, from forests to farmland, from inland lakes and coastal communities to deserts and the tundra—the geographic features, the plants and animals, the distances between places, the resources, all vary greatly. This matters because the geography of rural communities, in part, makes the place what it is. For example, the distance between a rural community and the nearest suburban and urban communities impacts the day-to-day life of people in the rural community in multiple ways, from the availability of goods and services such as broadband to the likelihood that people travel out of the community for work. In the case of extraction-based communities, the geography of a place can be central to its current or past economic support of a community. For example, a commercial fishing-based community will have different needs and priorities and will differ socially from a Central Appalachian community supported by mining.

Representations of rural places, such as the farm-themed decorations you might see on the walls of your local grocery story or the rural places shown in movies and popular culture, fail to capture the geographic diversity of rural communities in the United States. The geographic diversity of rural communities tends to be collapsed into common representations of rural communities located either in Central Appalachia or, more often, in the midwestern regions of the country. Given that 80% of people in the United States live in suburban or urban places and therefore lack significant firsthand experience with rurality, the representations of rural that we see in our daily lives have an outsized effect on how rural is understood. The typical midwestern or Appalachian representation of rural works as a set of codes that hide the actual variety of rural geographies and reinforces a limited imagery about rural communities.

Generalizations of rural geographies, and sometimes official definitions, distort the multiple realities of rural communities. Rural schools can be located in profoundly dissimilar settings with profoundly dissimilar populations, from exclusive ski hamlets in Colorado, to rural parishes in Louisiana, to remote Yup'ik villages in Alaska. If we wrongly learn from the representations around us that rural geographies lack diversity, we could likewise "learn" that rural people lack diversity as well. In reality, distinct rural communities exist in every region in the United States.

Economically: What Is Rural?

A second facet of rurality has to do with how economic factors shape rural communities. Although it may be tempting to slip back into thinking that rural places are mostly separate from suburban and urban places, economics is a powerful reminder that this is not true. Thinking back to what you read in Chapter 2 about economic justice, you will remember that there is much to consider about how decisions are made about how financial resources are distributed to and across rural communities, and also who decides how much financial inequality should be tolerated. However, understanding how rural communities are made up economically also requires understanding of how rural economies are intertwined with other economies, in an arrangement that often disadvantages rural communities. At least since the Industrial Revolution began in the late to mid-1700s, rural communities have provided natural resources, goods, and workers in support of more urban economies in the United States, and later, a globalized economy.

The effects of economic globalization began between WWII and the 1980s and have generally not been favorable to rural communities. One immediately obvious effect of globalization on rural economies is the rise of agribusiness. Patents on seeds, powerful political lobbying, as well as "factory farming" all fall under the umbrella of agribusiness. Factory farms are multinational corporations (with brand names you would likely recognize) that operate huge professionally managed operations with expansive acreage and output. Many employ migrant and undocumented workers with sub-standard wages. Particularly when animals are involved, the sheer size of the operations, their water consumption and amount of animal and chemical waste are ecologically devastating for the surrounding communities. Smaller, family-run operations often simply cannot compete. A fraction of the family farms exist today as compared to the numbers before the early 1970s. The replacement of small- and medium-sized farms echoes the somewhat recent arrival of large multinational corporations such as Walmart, fast-food restaurants such as Burger King, and even chains exclusive to the United States such as Dollar General. These businesses profit from economies of scale and inexpensive land on which to build new stores. Lacking purchasing power, local businesses are at a distinct disadvantage and often cannot compete.

Extraction-based industries, such as logging, fishing, and mining, are another kind of economic anchor to many rural communities. These industries continue to be socially and economically relevant to rural communities, but most industries operate at a fraction of their previous level, if they are still in business at all. Some communities continue to be precariously supported by extraction, such as the logging town of Roseburg, Oregon. A previously booming railroad town, Thurmond, West Virginia, is promoted as a "ghost town" that attracts over a million visitors a year to Thurmond and two adjacent state parks. While tourism rarely replaces the loss of an industry, as in the case of Thurmond, tourism is an important source of economic viability. National parks, on the other hand, are often an economic anchor to their communities. In fact, outdoor recreation is the biggest growth sector for rural economies.

The growth of mountaintop removal, hydraulic fracking (unconventional gas development), and expanded factory farming are relatively new economies that often place rural communities in tenuous economic and ecological relationships with companies that do not necessarily have either a social or economic commitment to the rural communities in which they are located. For example, there is important research on hydraulic fracking that suggests a significant negative financial effect on rural schools (Schafft & Biddle, 2014) to say nothing of the devastating health and ecological effects from water source contamination. Rural communities are frequently exploited in the process of extracting natural resources such as fresh water, natural gas, coal, or timber. Modern exploitation follows Indigenous histories of violent removal and colonization. Pipelines installed on tribal lands are a recent example of resource exploitation. Rural communities are not economically isolated, but are intertwined with regional, national, and global economies. They not only provide food, fiber, and natural resources, but also provide human capital when young people, in the search for economic opportunity, migrate from economically vulnerable rural communities to suburban and urban hubs.

For Discussion

Access the most recent *Why Rural Matters* report (Showalter et al., 2019) at the website of the Rural School and Community Trust (http://www.rura ledu.org). Locate your state's results on the list of state-by-state results. Consider questions such as:

- Where does your state fall in the priority ranking?
- What factors led to your state's priority ranking?
- What do you learn by comparing your state with others?
- What surprises you about your state's results?
- What facts does the priority ranking miss about your state?
- What would you like readers of this report to know about the rural statistics reported about your state?

Rural places are generally under-resourced—add to this a lack of recognition of difference and a relative lack of political power—resulting in a trifecta of barriers to social justice (see Chapter 2). This multi-perspective view challenges the idea that rural people are undeserving of economic justice because rural people have *chosen* their own situation. This kind of thinking might lead someone to ask (aloud or silently), *Why can't rural people just make better choices about their health? If there are no jobs, why don't they just move somewhere else?* Within this view, the struggles of rural communities are not a result of systemic inequities, but rather a series of poor life choices made by people lacking the smarts and discipline to be successful in modern life. We hope to challenge this position in this book.

Socially: What Is Rural?

If you are reading this book, you probably are familiar with the stereotypical representations of rural people. If you grew up in a rural community, you likewise may know that people living in rural communities, like any other, have a wide variety of personal experiences, jobs, moral and ethical stances, and political positions. The authors of this book strongly believe that as a rural teacher, you are obligated to assume a stance of intellectual curiosity about the community members living around your school. This means that you are compelled to find out about and listen to children, families, and community members in order to understand their histories and beliefs. You must firmly resist the urge to fall back on the use of assumptions or stereotypes to explain behaviors, and you must call out others who disparage individuals or families. We will give you some tools with which to do this in upcoming chapters such as Chapters 5 and 6.

As a new teacher, it is important to know that across the United States, rural America is 80% White. Latinx, a gender-neutral category that refers to people from Latin American countries, are the fastest growing ethnic group in rural communities. Rural communities benefit from the strengths and contributions of Latinx people. Their social and cultural contributions equal the importance of their support of economic revitalization with contributions to agriculture, restaurants, and food processing industries. While rural communities average 80% White, there are many rural communities with a higher percentage of White students and others with a lower percentage. (See Chapter 15 for a more in-depth discussion of the diversity of rural places.) For example, according to the Rural School and Community Trust's 2018–2019 report, *Why Rural Matters* (Showalter et al., 2019), if you were to randomly choose two students from a rural school district in the United States, there is a 32% chance that the two students would identify with two different racial and/or ethnic groups. For example, there is a 32% chance that one child would be White and one Latinx. According to the report, if you were to repeat the exercise in the following states—Delaware, North Carolina, Oklahoma, and Nevada—more likely than not (at least a 50% chance), the randomly selected students would have different racial and/or ethnic identities. There is a 99% chance, however, that two randomly selected students in Tornillo Independent School District in Texas would *share* an ethnic identity because all but two of the 1,133 students enrolled in the district identify as Hispanic (official school documents often use the very broad category "Hispanic"). Tornillo, therefore, has a very low rural diversity index. Racial and ethnic diversity is highly variable in rural schools and communities. Linguistically, recent trends in states such as Florida indicate increasing numbers of non-Spanish speaking Latinx students who speak indigenous languages such as Mam and Kaniobal. Terms like Hispanic or Latinx can potentially obscure important within-group differences.

As these few examples show, "80% White" doesn't tell a complete story about racial and ethnic diversity in rural communities. You should also know that the ethnic and racial diversity of your community will not necessarily be obvious. Likewise, it may not be apparent, at first, if tensions exist, or how the experiences of some community members differ sharply from others. It may take some investigating on your part in order to understand who the community is and what their histories are.

Social norms are unofficial rules about behavior. Every group has a set of social norms or accepted behaviors that its members (usually) follow. You can see social norms in action in a shared office, when riding public transportation, or eating lunch in the faculty room at school. Social norms in rural schools and communities sometimes mask important differences among groups and individuals (Chavez, 2005). Values influence social norms, but values are beliefs about what is important. Values are connected to culture, tradition, religion/spirituality, and families.

Whether or not you grew up in the same community in which you hope to teach, you may subscribe to some of the community's social norms and values, but not others. It is important, however, that you recognize what those norms and values are and how they include and exclude groups and individuals. In thinking about social norms, the unofficial rules about behavior, it is important to understand that there is not a uniform "rural culture." *Each* rural community will have complex histories and ways of being that influence those social norms. In that way, the very idea of rural is one that is constructed by these social norms—norms influenced by the members of that society. For example, what students do after graduating high school is connected for various reasons to what the social norms and values are common to a particular community.

For Discussion

Use the rural district you researched on the NCES website or another district with which you're familiar. Using the district website, other sources, or your familiarity with the school, what evidence can you find that your rural school and community values postsecondary education? (For example, what percentage of students take the SAT?) If you are personally familiar with a rural school, do most college-going students move away from home to attend college or do they live at home and commute? What might be the reasons for either? What evidence can you find that your rural school and community values students' contribution to the local economy by entering the workforce immediately after graduation?

Finally, it is important to note that not every person who considers themselves "rural" actually lives in a place that might officially be defined as rural. Some people who identify as rural live in suburban and urban places. Economic decline, environmental disasters, and other forces may force people to move to more urban areas. For example, 46% of American Indians and Alaska Natives live in urban and suburban communities (First

Nations Development Institute, 2017). Students and their families may still feel very connected to the places and the social norms of the places they have recently left. Likewise, not everyone who lives in a place that is geographically defined as rural would describe themselves in that way. Devon, one of the authors of this book, lives in a town of about 28,000 people in Mississippi, about 3 hours from the nearest Target. Her friends in Chicago cannot imagine living in such a rural place. Her friends in town feel like they live "in the city" because they have access to coffee shops, bookstores, and an escalator. Rural is relative because it is a social construction.

Difficult Questions about Difference

There is no doubt that a complex understanding of rural communities requires engaging with some characteristics of some rural communities that we would rather ignore. The social makeup of rural places is an especially slippery idea and one that cannot be separated from demographics, social norms and values, and economics. Not only can social demographics differ significantly from community to community, but each community is unique in its social norms and values. Regardless of these differences, rural places tend to be understood as places unfriendly or even hostile to differences of race, ethnicity, language, gender, and sexuality.

These issues are uncomfortable terrain to navigate for any teacher. We want to emphasize that not all communities share these values and norms, and, especially, that even in a community in which these views are common, not all people associate with racist or anti-LGBTQ sentiment. An example of this is the Black Lives Matter protests in white majority rural communities related to the murder of George Floyd. Cultural norms are shifting in part due to demographic changes in previously rural communities, particularly in the Midwest where the growth of young Black and Latinx families is outpacing the growth of older whites. We acknowledge that this is an extraordinarily difficult topic that is likely to evoke strong feelings. Throughout this book, we hope to engage you with a number of difficult topics that are necessary for you to grapple with. Just as important as it is to vigorously defend against the painting of all rural places with a broad brush as places where racism and anti-LGBTQ sentiment are accepted parts of daily life, it is equally important to engage with the problem of discrimination and racism in rural (and any) communities.

Many scholars who write about racism as it connects to schools and communities often take what is called a "sociological view." To take a sociological view of "rural racism" (Chakraborti & Garland, 2011, p. 2) means to understand that an individual's views or even a group's views about race are a social issue rather than a personal failing. This means that the role of the individual is not ignored, but an individual's views are considered within broader social, cultural, and economic histories and networks. In other words, a person's beliefs do not develop in a vacuum.

Thinking about rural racism in this way requires an interrogation of the *whys* and *hows* of racist discourses as they are enacted in rural places. This wide-angle view also takes into account diversity between rural communities in terms of their differing histories, economies, and norms. As you read earlier, knowing that 80% of rural communities are White-majority does not help us to understand very much about an individual community. Thinking about racist views as connected to history, economies, and norms is a good approach to move beyond a "that's just the way they are" view. It took Karen, one of the authors of this book, many years to begin to understand how people who she knew and loved in her own rural community could associate with racists views. Effectively challenging the bias, discrimination, and exclusion of individuals with anti-racist and anti-bias pedagogy begins with a more complete understanding of the problem as it manifests in a group or community.

Rural racism is still racism. In many respects rural racism manifests the same ways in rural communities as it does in White suburban communities. Unique to the rural context, however, is the idea that rural areas are somehow a "breeding ground" for racist ideas. Understanding the whys and hows of rural racism requires acknowledgement that there are characteristics of rural communities that influence how racism is perpetuated and experienced. For example, in White-majority communities, African Americans and members of ethnic minority groups have more heightened visibility than in more ethnically diverse communities (Pugh, 2011). In these communities, the relative numbers of African American and ethnic minority community members increase the potential for social isolation within White-majority spaces (Pugh, 2011).

Many ethnicities and identities place one at risk of discrimination in rural communities. Discrimination on the basis of race, culture, or ethnicity is not equally distributed from community to community or even within a community. Differences in an individual's social standing and income, for example, are two relevant within-community factors that can impact the extent to which an individual or group might experience discrimination differently in the same community. We discuss the intersection of identities further in Chapter 15.

For Discussion

Think of a rural community you know well. Identify the ways in which the community might unevenly accept people who fall outside the cultural and social norms in important ways. Who might be excluded? Who would not? Why? What might any exclusion look like? Find similarities and differences between the rural communities identified by your peers. How might you explain both the exclusion within a community as well as any differences in how people might be excluded from community to community.

Conceiving of rural places as simple and problem-free places where everyone gets an equal chance at happiness and prosperity is not only a myth but is deeply problematic. Problems that are not acknowledged cannot be intentionally mitigated. Racism and anti-LGBTQ sentiments in rural places neither can be assumed nor understood outside of a specific community context. Racism and anti-LGBTQ sentiment in rural places are just two of the ways that people are discriminated against or marginalized, and they are always connected to place-specific factors. Boundary maintenance, class identity, social and economic policies, histories of White land ownership and slavery, as well as geographic and social isolation, are possible contributing factors. We encourage you to listen carefully to the students in your classrooms and the families in your community in order to begin to understand their points of view so that you can more effectively implement anti-bias and anti-racist pedagogies in your rural classroom.

Teaching toward the Future in Rural Places

In 1781 philosopher Immanuel Kant posed three questions: *What can I know? What ought I do?* and *For what may I hope?* More than 200 years later, Kant's questions are useful as a guide in thinking about how rural schools and communities are made up of geographic, social, and economic characteristics (see Guyer & Wood, 1997).

What you can know after reading the three sections above about how rural places are geographically, economically, and socially diverse is only the beginning of what you can know about teaching in rural school. As is true with every piece of writing, and especially so for a book as ambitious as this one, as the authors, we had to make decisions about what to include and what not to include. As you read through this book, we want you to think of it as a springboard for what you can know about rural teaching.

good discussion !

Kant's second question is *what ought I do?* As a new teacher you might feel powerless to effect change in your school and community. We hope this book will help with that. While we respect and acknowledge your feeling that perhaps as a new teacher you are poorly positioned to advocate for change, we suggest that advocacy is an integral part of your role as a teacher in the twenty-first century. Teaching is political work. (See Chapters 10 and 19.) While we don't feel it is your responsibility to single-handedly and fundamentally alter a school and community, at the same time, we do feel that you should work within your sphere of influence to effect change. We hope your satisfaction from doing so will be among the many ways you will thrive in your rural teaching position.

Rural communities' collective negotiation of possible answers to social and economic challenges requires equal parts science and developed human potential of students to bring about more equity and social justice in rural communities. Your careful preparation for a rural teaching position is a significant step in this direction. It is what you can do right now. Ultimately, your students' informed democratic engagement with local, regional, state, national, and global issues is what will enable their participation in decision-making processes about what should be remembered, restored, conserved, changed, or created (Greenwood, 2013) for their lives, their communities, and their world.

Kant's last question is *for what may I hope?* Despite very real material and social disadvantage in most rural places, there is a lack of understanding of "spatial inequity" as a category of disadvantage in the same way that we understand disadvantages related to gender, race, ethnicity, or sexual orientation. Instead, rural disadvantage is attributed to individuals' personal failings rather than understood as connected to geographic, economic, and social factors. This is not just harmless and uninformed public opinion. About Appalachia, Fraley (2007) wrote:

> *Historically, stereotypes have been wrapped up in efforts to dominate and oppress—to take land and resources—through dehumanizing a group and eroding their dignity. In this way stereotypes are tools for oppression, and subordination of a particular group, and the establishment of lasting power structures.*

(p. 367)

Understanding the variability and complex histories of rural places and your plans for action when you get in the rural classroom is rural advocacy. Working toward higher test scores is not enough. As discussed in Chapter 2, your work as a rural teacher is a project of social justice because you want your work to enable full and equal participation for the rural residents you teach.

References

Chakraborti, N., & Garland, J. (2011). *Rural racism*. Routledge.

Chavez, S. (2005). Community, ethnicity, and class in a changing, rural California town. *Rural Sociology 70*(3), 314–335. doi: https://10.1526/0036011054831224

First Nations Development Institute. (2017). *Research note—Twice invisible: understanding rural Native America*. First Nations Development Institute.

Fraley, J. (2007). Appalachian stereotypes and mountain top removal. *Peace Review: A Journal of Social Justice, 19*, 365–370.

Greenwood, D. A. (2013). A critical theory of place-conscious education. In R. B. Stevenson, M. Brody, J. Dillon, & A. E. J. Wals (Eds.), *International handbook of research on environmental education* (pp. 93–100). Routledge.

Guyer, P., & Wood, A. (Eds. & Trans.) (1997). *Critique of pure reason*. Cambridge University Press.

Kant, I., & Smith, N. K. (1929). *Immanuel Kant's critique of pure reason*. Bedford.

Pugh, R. (2011). Responding to rural racism: Delivering local services. In N. Chakraborit & J. Garland (Eds.), *Rural racism*. Routledge.

Shafft, K., & Biddle, C. (2014). School and community impacts of hydraulic fracturing within Pennsylvania's Marcellus shale region, and the dilemmas of educational leadership in gasfield boomtowns. *Peabody Journal of Education, 89*(5), 670–682. doi: https://10.1080/0161956X.2014.956567

Showalter, D., Klein, R., Johnson, J., & Hartman, S. L.(2017). *Why rural matters 2015-2016: Understanding the changing landscape*. Rural School and Community Trust.

Showalter, D., Hartman, S., Johnson, J., & Klen, B. (2019) *Why rural matters*. The Rural School and Community Trust.

4

Why Place Matters

Amy, one of the authors of this book, writes:

When I was a little girl, we spent our summer weekends on the Shenandoah River in Virginia. My Mom would pack the cooler full of ham, bologna, pimento cheese sandwiches, and sodas. We'd park our small camper near my parents' friends on the river's edge. By day, the adults would fish, play cards or horseshoes, and tell stories that seemed to grow even taller as the day wore on. We kids were given to our imaginations, creating games often won by the most impressive backflip off the tire swing, tied high to a tree growing from the bank of the river. Where I grew up, everyone had a story about the river—sneaking out for late night parties, losing a high school friend who drowned, or stories of fishing and boating. Our river stories united us, as stories tend to do, with the river as a unifying symbol that we were from this place.

But when summer ended, so too did my education on the river. We never studied it in school. We never learned about its relationship to tourism and how it supported the economy of our tiny town. Our expansive firsthand knowledge about its flora and fauna and role in the valley's changing ecosystems was never made relevant to what we were learning in school. Likewise, we never studied the displacement of the 450 families, many of whom were forcibly removed from their homes by the establishment of the Shenandoah National Park in the 1930s. While my peers and I knew the stories about the power of the federal government and the residents' resistance to the park, we never learned more about the multiple processes that preceded the establishment of the park—nor did we learn about how the rural citizens, some of whom were family members, resisted the loss of their properties.

When my cousin graduated from high school, he sang the traditional folk song, "Oh, Shenandoah," at the ceremony. It was an appropriate choice, marking the transition to adulthood with a song that meant something about a particular place—our place. While the Shenandoah Valley and its river never showed up in the official curriculum, it figured prominently in our out-of-school learning.

This is the case for many rural kids who experience place in tangible and valuable ways outside of school, but then come to find an official school curriculum completely disconnected to their knowledge and experience. While I had a rich, lived experience and deep knowledge about my river, I knew little of its history, importance, or how I might protect it. The river was simply a backdrop to the "important" stuff I needed to learn in school.

Why Place Matters

The curriculum in many schools has become almost entirely standardized, commercialized, and devoid of place and local contexts. In this chapter, we will consider why it is important to think about place, the relationship between place and identities, and how context can influence and shape understanding. Here we ask: How can *context* influence *content*?

For Discussion

Take a place inventory. Think about places that are important to you. Often, strong place attachments develop in childhood, but you likely have also developed more recent attachments to places in your adulthood. Your university campus may be one example. Think of a physical place that is important to you, either a recent one or one from your childhood. When you reflect on this place, what do you see? Who are you with? How does the memory make you feel? Can you think of other places related to your culture or religion? Do others in your family also have attachments to the same places?

A Sense of Place

Why do some places hold special meaning and how is place relevant to teaching and learning? Thinkers from a range of disciplines beyond education (psychology, geography, anthropology, and sociology) have considered this question. Each discipline has a different perspective on the question and the possible answers. What we can take from this wide body of work is that place ought to be important in the school curriculum because our place attachments, built on meaningful experiences in place, are a part of how we understand ourselves as people. Said more simply, place ought to matter in teaching and learning because place matters to people.

An individual's sense of place is multidimensional (Jorgensen & Stedman, 2001). A sense of place is made up from beliefs about who we are in relation to a particular place, our feelings about that place, and the unique ways we behave in that particular place (Scannell & Gifford, 2010). Because place identity is multidimensional, not all people in the same place develop the same place attachments. Personal experiences, families, schooling, community events, and other factors can influence connections to place.

The vignette at the start of this chapter is a good example of how a sense of place can be developed: A belief about the importance of the Shenandoah River, feelings and memories about why the river is important, and the unique experiences afforded by that particular place. Place attachments and identities are informed by our feelings and memories, and the attitudes and beliefs in a place. While not all rural students will have a strong sense of place, many will. Therefore, a sense of place can be a powerful influence in students' lives and can inform the ways they approach content and learning.

For Discussion

Use the opening vignette to consider what types of place-based connections you could make relevant in the subject area or grade levels you plan to teach if you were teaching in this place. What are the instructional opportunities and how might learning about the Shenandoah River engage with what students already know in order to make new connections? For example, how could a STEM teacher use the river to teach concepts related to volume, ecosystems, and/or climate change? How could the history of the region and the role the river played in the Civil War be connected to social studies content? How could students' stories about place be useful for teaching memoir or other narrative genres in English language classrooms? Then, ask the same types of questions about a place that matters to you.

A Critical Pedagogy of Place

The learning opportunities above are place-based but now we want to take your thinking one step further. A critical pedagogy of place prioritizes learning connections between the local, regional, national, and global contexts, *while also* considering power and privilege. The word critical as used in this way does not mean to be critical or to criticize, but rather to consider the role of power. In a critical pedagogy of place, local learning that leverages students' lived experiences and place attachments, like those above, extend beyond the classroom to consider the broader systems in which we all live.

Students' learning about their ecological environments is important but it is not enough. If students are to learn how to participate in decision making about the role of the river in their community in terms of its economic, social, and environmental impact, a broader view is needed. Not only how does the river shape the community, but also how does the river connect to regional, national, and global systems? In classrooms that enact a critical pedagogy of place, localized learning, such as a river study, spirals out from local contexts to regional, national, and global understandings. This spiraling is where power becomes relevant. The river is not neutral. It has different purposes and meanings to different groups in and outside of the community. But not all "readings" of the river are equally valued. Some people have more voice than others about the river and its impact on humans. This is an example of how places are made by people as much as people are made by places (Gruenewald, 2003).

The Shenandoah National Park, for example, was made by people, but also in very real ways *made* the people who once lived there. The park has a historical and political past—a *text*—and paying attention to that text and to power (critical) is needed to think through why and how places might influence people and how people with varying positions of power influence places. This is necessary work if our students are to be informed, active participators in democratic processes.

As we argue in Chapter 3, teaching is a political act. By that we mean your work as a teacher is grounded in social, cultural, and economic realities and histories. There is no escaping this. No matter how appealing it might seem, teachers cannot simply "close the door and teach" because every decision, every text, and every child and teacher are connected to larger systems as well as working within ongoing and past histories. Critical pedagogy embraces this reality by engaging students in the questioning, exploring, and investigating of hierarchies or dominant systems that impact all of our social, cultural, economic lives.

This type of head-on and informed thinking connects rural teaching with the social justice framework described in Chapter 2. With a focus on how students can understand and critique systems, a critical pedagogy of place lends itself well to social justice inquiries about the interconnected nature of poverty with other injustices such as race and class.

How does a critical pedagogy of place change what we do in school? Implementing a critical pedagogy of place requires a paradigm shift in thinking about what schooling is for and what it can do. Contemporary schooling is focused on workforce training so that the U.S. economy can retain its power on the global economic stage. In 2011, President Obama summarized this position clearly: "A world-class education is the single most important factor in determining not just whether our kids can compete for the best jobs but whether America can outcompete countries around the world" (as cited in Mechaber, 2011, para. 2).

From this point of view, ranking and sorting students according to their future contribution to the economy is logical. In contrast, a critical pedagogy of place asks students and teachers together to consider how we might live in a place that is distinct from as well as connected to other places.

A critical pedagogy of place goes beyond our current focus on school as a place where children prepare for different kinds of jobs relative to their academic abilities. For example, a water quality study is important, but adding an examination of the possible impacts of local industry, and environmental policies, along with the economic impact of the industry on the whole community, gives a richer, more complete, and complex understanding of the water quality results. A critical pedagogy of place engages students with the project of living well, economically, *and* with each other as citizens in a democracy.

Take a look at the table below and notice how the first column gives examples of place-based questions. The second column, however, deepens and expands the questions with a critical framing.

Place-based education	Critical pedagogy of place
What local event, situation, or history would interest students?	What can we learn from studying the past history of a current place, problem, or person?
What stories can we tell about the community?	Who decided on the policies that impact this issue or characteristic of the community?
What service projects can we do to help our community?	Why did this happen, and what does it mean for the future?
Where can we visit in the community to see something firsthand?	How is what's happening here connected to other places?
What is happening in the community?	Who is or was harmed by this situation? How can we change what is happening?

Questions to Enact a Critical Pedagogy of Place

Reflect on Chapter 2 and our discussion of teaching for social justice and parity of participation. Can you see how these questions in the table connect to issues of economic, political, and cultural justice? Asking questions about policies that impact rural communities can help students understand their rural economies as they interact and intersect with global markets. Asking questions about who decided those policies and who might be harmed or helped drives at issues of political justice and how rural people are or are not represented in decisions affecting their communities. Questioning why something happened, by whom or for whom, allows for critique and cultural justice, examining how cultural differences are recognized and embraced in rural places. A discussion of these questions allows students to engage in critical thought about those key issues regarding rural places—what should be *remembered, restored, conserved, changed, or created* (Greenwood, 2013).

While a critical pedagogy of place is not specific to rural communities, its critical lens is well suited to rural contexts. As we discussed in the two previous chapters, rural communities frequently serve outside interests. Rural places often provide water, minerals, food, recreation, and human capital to suburban and urban communities. Older students in particular are well aware of this relationship. Age appropriate understanding of this provides an opportunity to consider how one's rural community may have been disrupted and injured, and importantly, who has experienced those injuries. This lens provides a wide-open space for investigations of inequality in all forms, including histories of Indigenous people.

For Discussion

Look back to your previous brainstorm about teaching from the Shenandoah River (or another place you chose). How could you extend your ideas from "place-based" to include a more critical stance? For example, the name "Shenandoah" is a Native American word of unknown origin (possibly Algonquian). A critical inquiry could consider how the region was colonized, whose stories remain untold, and why. Thinking economically and socially, how does tourism serve local economies in regions that have not been served well by extractive industries such as logging and mining? How and why are community resources exported to more urban places? What questions address economic, cultural, or social justice about these places?

Resisting the Rural Imaginary

In your work using place critically in the curriculum, it is important to think through how you will engage with stereotypes about rural places. While the word "stereotype" suggests negative representations, the term "rural imaginary" captures the imaginary rural in our minds—those stereotypes as well as images of romanticized rural communities (refer back to Chapter 3 for more on the rural imaginary). In pop culture, the media, and perhaps in our own minds, we sometimes have the tendency to believe the "best" or "worst" of rural places.

Because it is impossible to separate people from place, you can see the same conflicting views of the places where rural people live. Teachers can engage in community asset mapping (see Chapter 6) and engage students as curricular investigators or makers of place as one way to resist these almost myth-like representations of rural. Find more instructional strategies about using place in Chapter 13.

Context matters. Paulo Freire (1970) wrote a powerful critique of the traditional educational system in what he coined as the "banking model" where all-knowing teachers "deposit" information into passive learners. He critiqued this model because it implies that students come to a learning situation devoid of their own knowledge. In many ways, a standardized curriculum that ignores place reproduces the banking model of education. It assumes that a common or globalized education is the "important" content and that the context is irrelevant. Using place critically is an opportunity to make the common curriculum more responsive to the local context. Importantly, we can use a critical pedagogy of place to examine our own communities in order to work toward dismantling economic, cultural, and political representation barriers to equal participation in decision-making processes.

References

Freire, P. (1970). *Pedagogy of the oppressed.* (M. B. Ramos, Trans.) Continuum.

Greenwood, D. A. (2013). A critical theory of place-conscious education. In R. B. Stevenson, M. Brody, J. Dillon, & A. E. J. Wals (Eds.), *International handbook of research on environmental education* (pp. 93–100). Routledge.

Gruenewald, D. A. (2003). The best of both worlds: A critical pedagogy of place. *Educational Researcher*, 32(4), 3–12. doi: https://10.3102/0013189X032004003

Jorgensen, B. S., & Stedman, R. C. (2001). Sense of place as an attitude: Lakeshore owners attitudes toward their properties. *Journal of Environmental Psychology, 21*(3), 233–248. doi: https://10.1006/jevp.2001.0226

Mechaber, E. (2011, July 18). *Staying competitive through education: The president and American business leaders announce new commitments* [Weblog post]. https://obamawhitehouse.archives.gov/blog/2011/07/18/staying-competitive-through-education-president-and-american-business-leaders-announ

Scannell, L., & Gifford, R. (2010). Defining place attachment: A tripartite organizing framework. *Journal of Environmental Psychology, 30*(1), 1–10. doi: https://10.1016/j.jenvp.2009.09.006

Part Two
Thriving in Rural Communities

5

Rural Literacies

The first time Amy, one of the authors of this book, realized she had an accent was in college. Amy says:

> It was the first week or two of my freshman year, and I said something that made everyone laugh. It was probably my use of "greazy" to describe the dining hall's pizza. I remember a friend of mine from Philadelphia corrected me, saying, "It's greasy"—emphasizing the /s/ sound. Another time, a friend seemed surprised that I said "ink pen" instead of "pen" or "sliding board" instead of "slide."

Accents, regionalisms, colloquialisms, and dialects are good examples of how language and literacies are shaped by place and culture. But the influence of place and the ways we come to know our world go far beyond word choice, intended meaning, and accents.

For Discussion

Take a moment to think about a place where you grew up or have spent a lot of time. Can you think of specific words or phrases that you feel might be unique to your community? (Karen's grandmother, for example, said "warsh rag" for dishcloth. Devon grew up in lower Michigan, where "Up North" is both your vacation destination and a state of mind.) Do you know how any of the words or phrases originated? Have you ever had an experience like Amy where you experienced a mismatch between your ways of using language and the norms of a new place or group?

As part of a research project many years ago, Amy met an elderly man from her hometown who grew up and has lived all his life in a "holler" (a *hollow* or narrow valley between mountains or hills). "Mr. Fox" (a pseudonym) agreed to be interviewed because he knew and trusted Amy's Dad who at the time worked with Mrs. Fox at a local factory. After inviting Amy into their small trailer, Mr. and Mrs. Fox held hands while seated at their kitchen table. While he talked about his life—that he grew up very poor with eight siblings and left school in seventh grade to help support his family—he would stop and shake his head or wipe away a tear. He admitted that he struggled in school, was bullied for being poor, and confessed that he couldn't read or write. Mrs. Fox looked up and said, "He's not stupid." No, Mr. Fox was certainly not stupid. A lifelong and skilled carpenter, he took Amy on a short walk to show her the two-story home he built for his daughter. But, by nearly any definition, Mr. Fox is functionally illiterate, meaning he lacks the necessary reading and writing skills to complete everyday tasks such as filling out an employment application or a medical history at a doctor's office. Mr. Fox wondered how learning to read and write might have changed his experiences. He thought perhaps he would have his own construction company.

For Discussion

Mr. Fox said that some people who grow up in his community have it the "hard way" while others have it the "easy way." What do you think Mr. Fox meant?

Think about Mr. Fox's assertion that he can't "read or write." In building his daughter's home, he might have needed help with permits and other official documents, but he demonstrated his proficiency with blueprints, lists, catalogs, directions, labels, and invoices—not to mention his spatial thinking and mathematical abilities! Few people have the skills to accomplish what Mr. Fox accomplished. Yet, Mr. Fox was not successful with reading and writing in school, despite staying in school until seventh grade.

Mr. Fox went to school a long time ago, and it is difficult to say now how his schooling experience failed him. We do know, however, that he brought an impressive literacy skill set to the building of his daughter's house (and to the countless other carpentry jobs throughout his career). In the process, he also likely continued to develop his skills as he navigated the range of literacy tasks needed to complete the job. His literacy learning was not limited by age nor by the seven years spent in formal schooling.

Although not proficient in school based literacy tasks, Mr. Fox is a lifelong literacy learner.

Mr. Fox and Amy grew up in the same community, but they had vastly different experiences as literacy learners in school. Importantly, Mr. Fox's parents were also unable to read and write, and due to their financial circumstances, contributing to his family's welfare trumped the importance of continuing his education, difficult as it was. We know you are likely reading this book for a college class, and Mr. Fox's decision might seem impossible to understand. Yet, as teachers preparing for jobs in rural schools, we (Amy and the other authors of this book) need you to know that you will likely teach a young Mr. Fox. Will you be ready for him? How can you make your classroom a place where Mr. Fox knows he belongs?

These questions are important for thinking about the relationship between literacies and rural communities and schools. This chapter addresses the complexities of literacies in terms of how rurality shapes literacy. We work from the idea that the teaching of literacy is situated in a place. We provide examples of what we mean by "rural literacies" and how rural literacies can inform teaching and learning in the rural classroom. This chapter asks: How does recognizing, valuing, and teaching from students' rural literacies support the teaching and learning of school-based literacy learning?

What Is Literacy?

Before we can unpack what we mean by rural literacies, we need to define what we mean by literacy. The way we use the word "literacy" in this book refers to more than the interpretation of print and one's ability to write in a way that others will understand, an outcome of the mental processes that happen in the mind of the reader and writer.

We want to challenge you to think of literacy more broadly. A more expansive view of what can be read and who is counted as literate has very real implications for literacy learning in school. Imagine literacy classrooms where not only are children like a young Mr. Fox regarded as literate (and told they are *able*), but also where outside knowledge is brought into the classroom and used as a tool for in-school literacy learning. Classrooms where literacy is thought of this way are inclusive spaces for literacy learning because out-of-school literacy learning is as valued and relevant as in-school literacy learning. Importantly, recognition of Mr. Fox's success at using texts for out-of-school purposes suggests that he was likely capable of learning ways to use texts in school. An inclusive, broad understanding of literacy provides the conditions for learning in two important ways:

1   Teachers recognize a child's previously obscured ability to make meaning from texts. The child is repositioned at school as a thinker, producer, and user of text.
2   Understanding that learning progresses from the known to the new, recognized out-of-school literacies offer teachers a repertoire of strengths and interests on which to base new literacy learning.

Literacy learning is far more difficult without these two conditions. But what, exactly, do we mean by literacy? Simply, literacy is a tool with which one can do things. It is also social, cultural, and political in nature. To unpack that idea, we use theorist James Gee's (1989) conceptualization of literacy *as the mastery of secondary discourses.* Your primary discourse is the discourses into which you're socialized at home. All other discourses are secondary.

Mastery of Secondary Discourses

Discourse when used within the context of literacy should not be confused with "discourse" as a synonym for conversation. As defined by Gee (1989), discourse means, "a socially accepted association among ways of using language, of thinking, and of acting that can be used to identify oneself as a member of a socially meaningful group or 'social network'" (p. 18). In this way, discourse refers to a theoretical concept related to literacy, *an identity kit.* You have a primary discourse and have already learned and acquired multiple secondary discourses—and these multiple discourses make up, in part, how you understand yourself as a person. For example, you are in a teacher preparation program, perhaps focused on preparation for rural teaching. Your teacher education program has norms of language use and behavior to which you usually adhere, as well as shared values and points of view and particular texts that you read and write. As a member of this discourse group, you know how to talk and act to be recognized as someone who is studying to be a rural teacher. Although there might have been some bumps along the way, you have mastered the future teacher discourse as well as other discourses: basketball player, college student, gamer, or vegetarian. Science learner is a discourse and so is "reader." These discourses are all examples of what Gee (1989) means by "secondary discourses." Remember that literacy is the mastery of secondary discourses. A secondary discourse refers simply to a discourse that you learned and acquired outside of your immediate family.

This is key: The more discourses you have mastered, the more tools you have to navigate life. Command of multiple discourses prepares you to interact appropriately in a variety of situations because you can think and speak from the perspective of the relevant discourse as well as use its texts. As you might suspect, certain discourses afford you access to money, power, and status in mainstream society in ways that others do not. Different discourses are valued differently in different situations. As teachers, you are in the discourse building business. The more discourses your students master, the more literacies they can master in the future. Your work is to *add* discourses, not replace or subtract.

For Discussion

In addition to your teacher education program, what are some other discourse communities to which you belong? With a partner, brainstorm what it means to be a member of that social group. What are the symbols, expectations, values, or ways of communicating that indicate membership in that group?

Now that you know that literacy, a tool with which one can do things, is the mastery of secondary discourses, let's discuss rural literacies.

What Are *Rural* Literacies?

As you read in the section above, literacy is a social practice. We read the world from the perspective of our discourses, and our discourses contribute to how we understand ourselves. Because literacy is the mastery of discourses, the mastery of discourses associated with rural life can be understood as *rural literacies.* Understanding the idea of rural literacies is essential for a critical understanding of rural places and sets you up as a teacher to recognize and value your students' rural literacies and their abilities with text inside and outside of school.

A pile of corn in an agricultural-based rural midwestern community serves as an example for this idea (see Edmondson, 2003). The corn was used as a symbol of protest. Over a period of months, a pile of corn by the train depot grew. And grew. New piles appeared. To the residents of Prairie Town, the corn was a text that could be read using their rural literacies. It would not make sense to someone who was not a member of this discourse group. To the community, the piles represented the enactment of farmers' rural literacies. The corn, a text able to be read by people in the community, was a symbol of the farmers' collective refusal to sell at an unfair price. The farmers used rural literacies, in this case, their advanced understanding of agribusiness and farm policy, as a tool with which to negotiate the agricultural market so that they could be fairly compensated for their product.

Rural literacies can be an important part of a person's identity, which is why we have this chapter in a book about rural teaching. Students' membership in a rural community and their rural literacies inform their understanding of the world. This becomes important in the classroom across all grade levels and disciplines as students learn other secondary discourses. These rural literacies shape identities. They acknowledge the ways rural communities need to ensure the sustainability of rural places. Recognizing and teaching from rural literacies in your future students is a way of teaching for social justice in a rural classroom.

The pile of corn as text and the community members' ability to read what the pile of corn means for the rural community pushes on two ideas about literacy that you may not have considered before:

1   Literacy is more than reading and writing print.
2   Literacies are multiple.

Literacy Is More than Reading and Writing Print

Only community members or others who share discourses about farm policy and markets could accurately read the piles of corn. To anyone outside these groups, the corn perhaps symbolized the farmers' foolishness for not selling the corn before winter or perhaps the piles suggested that the corn was not fit to sell for some reason. Each person's reading of the corn happens through a lens of the discourses of which they are members. This explains, in part, how literacy is a social practice, and also (as we will discuss in the section below) how literacies are multiple rather than singular.

You could likely imagine how, as a teacher who was not in the know about farm policy and markets, the meaning of the corn would be completely incomprehensible to you. An informed reading of the corn would require rural literacies that you, as the teacher of the farmers' children, may or may not possess, but, likely, that your students would. While the farmers undoubtedly read long, complex documents before deciding to sacrifice the corn as an act of protest, the documents were just one kind of text on which they based their decision. The rural literacies they enacted included multiple texts:

• Their individual family's values and financial situations
• Goals, values, and identities shared and negotiated with the community

- Collective community decision making processes
- Understanding of and discussions about the stated and unstated goals of federal farm policy
- And, importantly, close consideration of the future economic sustainability of small and mid-scale farming operations.

It is probably safe to say that in the process of making this decision, the community used rural literacies to learn about their histories, culture, and values (Shannon, 2003). Rural literacies enabled their actions to wrest some level of power over their economic conditions. While print was clearly involved in many of these aspects, the literacy practices enacted went beyond the writing and the decoding of printed documents. The community members read the *word* as well as the *world* (Freire, 1987).

Literacies Are Multiple

As we have said, literacy is the acquisition and learning of secondary discourses. Discourses are social identities (NFL fan, gamer, musician, farmer) and everyone has membership in many discourse groups. It follows then that literacy should be thought about as plural, not singular, because literacy is embedded in the social interactions between people. As we have discussed, literacy is practiced differently by different groups who share particular discourses that are not equally valued. "Farmer," for example, is differently valued depending on the context and circumstance. This is why literacy cannot be understood separately from social justice. All discourse groups have norms (agreed upon ways) about the use of print-based texts as well as non-print based texts such as language, values, interests, and beliefs. There is great variability across people and discourses. Literacy cannot mean one thing across groups and is therefore *multiple*.

Your thinking about literacies cannot be separate from the specific geographic, cultural, and social characteristics of a place. Any techniques or methods that you employ inside your classroom are connected to life outside the four walls of your classroom. Your job as a rural teacher is to support children's learning and acquisition of additional literacies in your classroom. Old ideas about school as a place to learn to write and decode print are insufficient preparation for globally connected, technology-driven modern lives. Think back to the farmers' corn protest and the literacies they used. Reading and writing print was needed, but was not enough in order for them to take control of their product.

Rural communities are intertwined with each other and with sub-urban and urban communities. The idea of rural communities as isolated and separate from the rest of the nation and world is a myth. While rural literacies are required to prepare and empower children to make decisions about what they want to preserve about their community and what they want to change, rural literacies also require an opening up of children's thinking beyond the local. We, all of us, need educated rural literacy learners who can participate in the decision-making processes that impact not only the terms of daily lives in rural communities, but, especially, the terms of rural communities' relationships to local, regional, state, national, and global places. This means that rural literacy teaching and learning ought to be a project of democratic and global citizenship. In a globalized world, the sustainability and growth of rural communities requires connected thinking. See Chapter 4 on a critical pedagogy of place.

Mr. (and Mrs.) Fox

A few years ago, Mrs. Fox was in a life-threatening car accident that required multiple surgeries and a lengthy recovery. In addition to worrying about her health, Amy often wondered if Mr. and Mrs. Fox struggled to navigate health insurance and hospital bills. Would the church pastor or a neighbor be willing to assist in those tasks? Although it's unclear what went wrong in Mr. Fox's education, something clearly did. We want to return to the questions we asked at the end of the story about teaching a young Mr. Fox: Will you be ready for him? How can you make your classroom a place where Mr. Fox knows he belongs?

We might also ask: What is the purpose of literacy learning in rural schools? Or, to another question asked at the beginning of this chapter: How does recognizing, valuing, and teaching from students' rural literacies support the teaching and learning of school-based literacy learning?

In considering these questions, think about the interrelated concepts of culture, identity, and literacies. Culture has characteristics shared by a social group, such as beliefs and values. Culture also has shared features such as dress, food, music, and language. There can be many cultures within a place. In Appalachia, for example, there are many cultures having to do with histories and traditions (e.g., coal mining and music), with recreation (e.g., hunting and NASCAR), and ethnicities and race (e.g., Affrilachia and Mexilachia)—and there is also Queer Appalachia as well as youth cultures and urban cultures.

For an example of how culture, identity, race, ethnicity, and literacies interact, look at the work of author, educator, and Affrilachian Poet Frank X. Walker (www.frankxwalker.com/) and the Mexilachian music of the Lua Project (http://luaproject.org/mexison).

These diverse cultures are made of many discourses. For example, Appalachia has 25 million residents, so it does not have a monolithic culture. Many people think of the South or "out West" as one place with one discourse. However, just as cultures can be diverse and varied in a place, so too are our identities. Our cultural identities represent our sense of belonging to a culture. Discourses are the bridge between these cultures and our internal sense of belonging. They represent the ways of knowing and communicating that culture. They are rich with symbols and vocabulary, print and non-print texts, and gestures. We express cultural identity, our membership to a social group, through our multiple literacies and discourses. Students' rural literacies can be a powerful expression of their membership in a rural community.

References

Edmondson, J. (2003). *Prairie town: Redefining rural life in the age of globalization.* Rowman & Littlefield.

Freire, P., & Macedo, D. (1987). *Literacy: Reading the word and the world.* Taylor & Francis.

Gee, J. P. (1989). What is literacy? *Journal of Education, 171*(1), 18–25.

Shannon, P. (2003). Hog farms in Pennsylvania. *The Reading Teacher, 56*(7), 688–691.

6

Understanding Strengths and Assets in Rural Communities

Like many, my initial impressions deemed Hamilton City as a desolate rural community with nothing to offer. In fact, I would often regard it as a small town with a three-block radius. I was oblivious to the types of businesses and the individuals that inhabited this rural town. Moreover, my initial impressions were dismantled after exploring the town and conversing with the community members. It was the El Toro Loco market that made me recall the flavors and spices needed for a community to flourish. It was the carnitas from El Patio that were responsible for the many recommendations I have made thus far urging my friends to visit Hamilton City. But above all, it was the community members who were eternally humble and proud of their rural town that ended my initial impressions.

The vast amount of information that I have acquired through the exploration of Hamilton City has ultimately impacted the ways in which I think about teaching in this community. As mentioned before, my first impressions of Hamilton City were negative. Like many, I had several misconceptions about this rural community. However, taking the time to submerge myself within this community allowed me to foster a sense of appreciation. The community in itself is welcoming, supportive, and passionate. Such positive characteristics exhibited by the community reinforce my desire to implement a place-based approach in my teaching. Essentially, the ultimate goal is to have students be appreciative and proud of the rural community they too call home.

Cecilia Romero-Robles, rural student teacher
Read more about Cecelia at https://iamaruralteacher.org

This chapter provides a way for you to explore and consider your beliefs and assumptions about what it means to live and work in a rural setting and teach K–12 students. You may be getting ready to teach and live in a community that is completely new to you, or you may be preparing to become a teacher in your hometown. Either way, this chapter will introduce you to a series of steps you can use to explore and learn about the community, document what you discover, and consider how you can use this knowledge to more fully understand your students and enrich your work in the classroom.

Assumptions about Rural Places: Examining and Challenging Preexisting Ideas

Just as Cecilia described, it is a normal human experience to enter into new situations with some preliminary ideas or impressions about the people and places you are about to encounter. Over the course of our lives we come to depend on these preexisting ideas to help us understand what we are seeing and to help us make choices about our actions and interactions with others. Some experts call these preliminary ideas cognitive heuristics—mental shortcuts we use to help us process information quickly. While they are useful in a lot of situations, unfortunately, they are not perfect. In fact, sometimes our preexisting ideas can be incomplete, and other times they can actually be inaccurate (for further discussion about stereotypes and assumptions see Chapter 2 and 15).

If our preexisting ideas or assumptions are incomplete or inaccurate, then it seems like it would be a wise thing to change them, right? The funny thing is, changing our preexisting ideas is not as easy as it sounds. This is because we tend to have two types of beliefs or assumptions that influence our actions and feelings. Some of our preexisting ideas are explicit; this means they are fairly easy to recognize, evaluate, and adjust if needed. However, some of our preexisting ideas are implicit, or tacit, beliefs. These are unspoken ideas and they can be more difficult to detect; they tend to hover just below our conscious awareness, and thus, they can be a bit more challenging to identify, evaluate, and adjust. Our preexisting impressions tend to be very tenacious and even when they are wrong they can be resistant to change.

And if that wasn't complicated enough, changing our ideas is made harder due to a psychological process called confirmation bias. This term refers to our human tendency to notice or interpret information in a way that supports our existing beliefs, while at the same time interfering with our ability to process evidence that does not line up with our beliefs. For example, can you think of a time when you were headed to a class or even a party and you went in expecting it to be boring? What did you notice? And what did you fail to notice? Chances are, you noticed a lot of things that agreed with your ideas about "this is going to be boring" and you missed things that were happening that might have been interesting.

For Discussion

Can you recall a time when you experienced confirmation bias in your own life? What was your original belief? What did it cause you to notice in the situation? What did you fail to notice in the situation? What were the consequences for you?

When you think about rural communities, if your preexisting idea is that rural places are out of step with modern life, then you may tend to notice the things that agree with that belief but fail to notice the things in the community that point to some of the modern and cutting-edge aspects of the community. Confirmation bias is a fascinating puzzle of human perception and it reveals how our preexisting beliefs and assumptions can shape what we are able to see and what we fail to see.

What does this mean for our everyday lives? And what does it have to do with your preparation for being a rural teacher? Basically, it means that you have three big tasks to tackle in every important learning process. As you prepare to be a rural teacher, you first need to do the work to uncover your preexisting beliefs and stereotypes about rural people and places. Then, second, you also need to be thinking about how those beliefs may be "filtering in" information that easily connects with your existing ideas while at the same time "filtering out" information that does not easily fit with what you already think you "know."

Finally, once you've got those processes underway, then you need to do the work to refine or revise your understanding about rural places and rural teaching. Experts refer to this effort as "engaging in conceptual change" or "knowledge modification" where, after you recognize and own your existing beliefs, you can start to revise them by either adding some new concepts that extend or enrich your current knowledge, or by choosing to embrace a new set of ideas that more accurately represent the current context of rural schools and communities.

One of the challenges we all encounter when we experience the conceptual change process is the temptation to rely on shortcuts such as our heuristics and confirmation bias, which allow us to ignore conflicting information so that we end up maintaining rather than changing our existing beliefs about rural schools and communities. To avoid this pitfall, one of the best approaches we can take is to engage in direct experience with rural people and places, document our new observations and insights, and then share them with others who can provide helpful guidance and feedback. This process can result in important growth in our beliefs and understandings.

Getting to Know a Rural Place

As you read in Chapter 2, each rural community is a unique assemblage of people, history, culture, economics, values, and perspectives, and thus, it's just not possible for one simple narrative to capture the full complexity of what it means to live and work in a rural place. For example, some people describe rural communities as hopeless, backward, or dying, while others depict rural living as the epitome of a peaceful and idyllic life. Since neither of these extremes fully represents the complex and nuanced make-up of rural communities, it is really valuable to examine your own preexisting assumptions and beliefs about rural life and also explore some new understandings of what it means to live and work effectively in a rural setting.

One approach to developing a more complete understanding of rural people and places is through the use of a tool called Asset Mapping. This tool "maintains that strengths and resources exist in all communities and that those elements can be identified, encouraged, and leveraged to advance the various aspirations of the community" (Downey, in press). Various types of professionals have used the Asset Mapping process to discover and create an inventory of the various strengths, assets, and resources present across all sectors (e.g. residents, businesses, organizations, and institutions) of a specific community (Flora et al., 2016).

Developing an inventory of the places, organizations, people, and programs that contribute to the strengths and assets of your rural community can help you develop a rich understanding of the resources available to your school and classroom and give you great ideas of ways to enrich student learning and connect with your students and their families.

Explore Your Rural Community with a Rural Community Walk

One effective way to map the various assets in a rural community is by doing a Rural Community Walk (RCW) (Downey, in press). The RCW provides you with a simple structure to *explore, document, reflect, and respond* as you build your understanding of what it means to work and thrive as a teacher in a rural community.

Before You Walk

Explore Your Ideas

Since preexisting beliefs and assumptions can filter or shape what we are able to see and understand, it is important to try to figure out what some of those beliefs and assumptions are. Some of these beliefs may even be grounded in your own experience of living rurally (in Chapters 15 and 19 we ask you to reflect again on this). Effective educators explore their assumptions together through adopting what is referred to as an *inquiry stance*, where they work together in a community to generate new understandings through discussion, collaboration, and interpretation (Cochran-Smith & Lytle, 2001). See Chapter 18 for further discussion of the value of taking an inquiry stance.

For Discussion

A great way to get started establishing your inquiry stance is to consider how you would answer the following: What does rural mean to me? What images come to mind when I think about rural schools and communities? What words would I use to describe a rural community? What words would I use to describe a rural school? How do I feel about rural schools and communities? As you share your answers with your classmates, listen for how your answers are similar to, and different from, your classmates' answers.

As we noted in Chapter 2, there are a lot of different ways to answer these questions. Some preservice teachers have described rural as far away, old-fashioned, backward, out-of-date, middle of nowhere, traditional, conservative, etc., while others have described rural people and places as resilient, resourceful, adaptive, responsive, innovative, etc. As Sara, a rural student teacher in California, said:

I think I came very quickly to understand that there are different types of rural experiences. I grew up in a very small rural farming community. We didn't have a stoplight; everybody went and hung out at the store on the corner after school. My experiences are that nobody in my community struggled with money issues, we didn't have the poverty I see now in the community where I teach. I was walking into that rural place with a different perspective or different lens; it was eye opening.

With the construction of your inquiry stance underway, go ahead and create some questions you would like to ask as you explore your rural community. You may have some topics that you would like to discuss with community members such as school board members, community leaders, business owners, teachers, parents, students, senior citizens, etc. Some questions you could ask include: What do you see as the strengths of the community? What is your view of the importance of the school? What are the ways the community supports the school? What are your hopes for the youth of the community?

Explore Digital Information

You can learn a lot of valuable information about a rural community and its school by exploring digital tools and databases. One way to start is to open Google Earth and take a virtual tour of the community's physical spaces. Then dive into various online databases and documents to see if you can get a sense of the strengths and assets of the community through its history. If they have a local museum, check out the stories of families and efforts to build the community over time. If they have a local newspaper, explore current aspects of the community such as social activities, upcoming events, local leadership and governance, student accomplishments, community initiatives, etc. State websites can also provide information about housing data, crime, and available resources and institutions, and this digital information can provide some preliminary data to support or challenge your ideas and assumptions identified above.

Ideas for Online Databases to Explore

- *Rural Health Information Hub* provides a wealth of information about health services in rural communities: https://www.ruralhealthinfo.org
- *Am I Rural?* provides an interactive map revealing how different places are classified: https://www.ruralhealthinfo.org/am-i-rural
- *Rural Data Visualizations* provides a host of ways to explore rural demographics by year or by state: https://www.ruralhealthinfo.org/visualizations
- *Social Vulnerability Index* is sponsored by the Centers for Disease Control and examines stresses on communities related to health, disease, and disasters: https://svi.cdc.gov
- *Social Capital Project* ranks geographic areas based on the presence of social capital: https://www.lee.senate.gov/public/index.cfm/scp-index
- *Broadband Now* provides information about your state and county's broadband access: https://broadbandnow.com

- Your state's Department of Education (to find state-wide student achievement data)
- Your community's website(s)
- City or county government, tourism boards, Chamber of Commerce, etc.
- *National Center for Education Statistics District Search Tool* can be used to find the locale designation for your school district and schools: https://nces.ed.gov/ccd/districtsearch/
- Your school's website data dashboard for local student achievement

Explore with a Drive

The digital information you have collected will start to come alive when you take a preliminary drive around the rural community. Your digital survey of the area might point you to some specific areas of interest— resources, amenities, neighborhoods, parks, etc.

Go for Your Walk

Explore with a Walk

After you've taken a brief drive to get an overview of the community, now's your chance to get a closer view by actually walking through the various areas you noticed. If you are going to be teaching in a smaller rural community, take time to walk through the entire town. And if you're going to be teaching in rural area with multiple schools, choose a portion of the community closest to where you'll be working or living, and focus your exploration there. If you can, invite a knowledgeable community member to walk with you as a guide and interpreter—another teacher, the principal, a parent, or a local business member. An effective guide can really be key to more fully understanding a rural community and will be able to describe the history of the community, share its stories, explain the connections, and provide important insights about the sometimes unseen strengths, assets, hope, and evolving nature of the community.

Here are some of the things you can look for as you walk and talk with your community guide. Take notes about your observations and questions regarding:

1 Businesses—retail, coffee shops, bookstores, barber shops/hair salons, restaurants, grocery stores
2 Organizations—churches, associations, nonprofits, libraries, museums
3 Healthcare—medical, dental, mental health, clinics, hospitals

4 Civil service—government, mail, fire, police

5 Economy—what residents produce and consume in the community

6 Education—schools, county extension offices, post-secondary education

7 Cultural engagement—art centers, community theaters, museums, sports facilities, newspapers, radio, community directories

8 Facilities—buildings, housing, land, recreation facilities, for sale signs

9 Infrastructure—condition of roads, bridges, lights, sidewalks, water, parks, recreation, community gardens, bike paths

10 Transportation—public, private, school bus routes

11 Community leaders—skills, experiences, capacities, passions, contributions

12 Community stories—defining elements of community life and history

As you walk, you will encounter lots of fascinating information about the community, its people, and its history. Some of the information will fit with what you were already thinking while some of the information could be new and enlightening. But some of the things you see—political messages, homes in need of repair, boarded up businesses—could also make you feel uncomfortable, or sad, or even upset. In these moments, embracing your inquiry stance can be really helpful and give you a chance to explore your experiences together with your guide. This is a great point to ask questions and hear your guide's perspective on things you're seeing, learn more about the history of how these things came to be, and understand how different members of the community are dealing with these issues today.

After Your Walk

Document Your Discovery

After gathering all your information from the digital sources and your observations, conversations, and notes, draw a map that captures your key insights. Provide as much detail as you can to represent what you've learned about the community, its people, its features, and its unique combination of strengths and assets. You can use whichever type of media works best for you—from paper and pencil like the example in Figure 6.1 to digital story maps using tools such as ArcGIS (https://www.youtube.com/watch?time_continue=88&v=Kl-J9GjieYM&feature=emb_logo) or Explorer for ArcGIS https://www.esri.

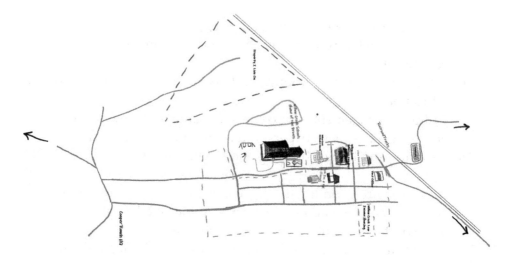

Figure 6.1 Map from a Rural Community Walk

com/en-us/arcgis/products/explorer-for-arcgis/overview or Google Tour Builder https://tourbuilder.withgoogle.com.

Through doing all this important work to *Explore* your rural community and *Document* its features, strengths, and assets on your map, you have discovered and created an inventory of the various strengths, assets, and resources present across various sectors (e.g. residents, businesses, organizations, and institutions) in your community. Now, your last two steps are to *Consider* the meaning of your new insights and plan your personal *Response* to this new information.

Consider Your New Insights

In order to bring together all your new insights, revisit your first set of questions and think about how the findings from your inquiry, and especially the items you chose to include on your map, challenged or affirmed your preexisting beliefs and assumptions about your rural place and its people. A useful tool that supports this type of productive professional reflection is known as: *I used to think… and now I think…* This research-based tool is referred to as a core thinking routine and was first developed by researchers in the Harvard Graduate School of Education (Harvard Project Zero, 2015).

This tool can be beneficial to you because it can help you identify when you have *replaced* an old idea with a new one, and it can also help you recognize when you have *extended* or *enriched* your understanding by adding new realizations to existing understanding. Furthermore, it can help you see when your previous ideas have been completely *revised* due to encountering new information. Thus, this tool is an effective method by which you can document and consolidate your new insights, explain how and why your perspective has changed, and strengthen your growing understandings.

For Discussion

Start by finishing the sentence stem, *I used to think…* by writing down some of your early assumptions and your explicit and implicit beliefs about rural schools and communities. Once you've finished this, you can follow it by completing the And now I think… sentence stem, capturing your insights and understandings. Share your insights with your peers.

Develop Your Response

The final step in this rural community Asset Mapping exercise is to design your response—the adjustments or changes you would like to make in your professional and personal life in light of your new learning. As a result of this community mapping exercise and the strengths and assets you discovered in this rural community you might ask:

- How can I incorporate some of my new understandings into my work as a rural teacher?
- Since connections to place are essential to allow rural students to see themselves in their own learning (see Chapter 13), in what ways can I incorporate my new understandings into my work with students and my lesson planning?
- What do I want to learn more about that I could discuss with students, families, or colleagues?
- How can I contribute to this rural community's strengths and assets?
- How do I want to respond to the aspects of the community that don't feel like a strength or asset?

Teaching with Your Community's Strengths and Assets

Johnathan Imhoff is a teacher who learned about his community, identified its strengths and assets, and leveraged those to support his students. When Johnathan started teaching in the mountain town of Weaverville, CA, the music program was in dire straits. Over the past five years, Johnathan has dedicated himself to resurrecting the program. Johnathan said:

> *The opportunity [to restart the music program], it's kind of like soul-affirming. I get to provide this thing that wasn't really offered before. I remember my first year there was a senior who was really thankful, they wrote a letter afterwards like, "You know I had real doubts whether or not they were ever gonna get the music program back, so thank you..." There's no way to do this program successfully if you can't build relationships. You have to be invested in these kids' lives. You can really build a relationship that you can't really in an urban school. You have these fun intergenerational opportunities between students and members of the community, and they can support each other. We have community members come through. They'll come in and sit in the pep bands. That sort of opportunity happens all the time, whereas in cities there are a billion things community members may be distracted by.*
>
> Read more about Johnathan at https://iamaruralteacher.org

Did you imagine as a teacher you would be participating in community events or leading local activities? Just like Johnathan, many new teachers don't think about the importance of building relationships outside their classroom. But as you can see from Johnathan's story, building relationships with students' families and community members is actually a very important part of being an effective rural teacher.

The insights gained through this community asset mapping exercise can be the start of an exciting journey of personal and professional growth and new opportunities, as happened for Johnathan. In this chapter, you have been introduced to some new ways to recognize different types of local resources and considered how those resources could be used to support learning in your school and classroom. You've also started to see how various aspects of rural communities can contribute to your own sense of place-consciousness—an understanding of what it means to know and care for a place, to value its local context, and consider its connection to the rest of the world. This growing sense of place-consciousness will be critical to your long-term effectiveness in the classroom and to your ability to thrive as a rural community member (for further discussion of place-conscious teaching see Chapter 13).

Your willingness to adopt an inquiry stance—a choice to pause, recognize you don't know everything you need to know, and be curious to learn more—will also help you thrive as a rural teacher. As you engaged in the community asset mapping process you may have identified some of the various assumptions and stereotypes you held about rural people and places. As we discussed at the beginning of this chapter, it's quite normal for all of us to enter into new situations with some assumptions in mind because they help us process information quickly. And while they can be useful, they are not perfect, and sometimes they can actually be problematic. Assumptions and stereotypes can trick us into thinking that we know more than we actually do; they create a false sense of security about the accuracy of our ideas, particularly when it comes to our beliefs and our worldview. A powerful way to guard against this false security is to practice cultural humility.

Cultural humility is an attitude—a set of feelings, actions, and beliefs—that recognizes that other people, their cultures, and their ideas are just as important as your own. It is a recognition that your own beliefs, values, and worldview while they are important, are not superior to others. When you practice cultural humility, you seek to be open to hearing and trying to understand the beliefs, values, and worldviews of others. It's helpful to remember that being open to hearing other ideas doesn't mean you have to agree with them. Rather, openness simply means you are *willing* to listen without judgment for the purpose of understanding someone else's views. And in addition to actively listening to others, an attitude of cultural humility can also help to shape how you express your own positions to others. Cultural humility can help you to present your own ideas in a non-offensive manner and listen to alternative ideas from a position of respect and empathy. In this way, cultural humility can make a significant difference in building mutually respectful relationships with your students, your colleagues, and community members in rural schools and communities, or wherever you may be (for further discussion see Chapter 15).

References

Cochran-Smith, M., & Lytle, S. (2001). Beyond certainty: Taking an inquiry stance on practice. In A. Lieberman & L. Miller (Eds). *Teachers caught in the action: Professional development that matters.* Teachers College Press.

Downey, J. (in press). The rural community walk: A structured learning experience for understanding place. In P. Roberts & M. Fuqua (Eds.) *Ruraling education research: Connections between rurality and the disciplines of educational research.* Springer Science+Business Media.

Flora, C., Flora, J., & Gasteyer, S. (2016). *Rural communities: Legacy and change*. 5th ed. Westview Press.

Harvard Project Zero. (2015). *I used to think..., now I think...: A routine for reflecting on how and why our thinking has changed*. https://pz.harvard.edu/resources/i-used-to-think-now-i-think

7

Families as Partners in Rural Communities

A few years ago, a small, rural Mississippi school used funding from a federal grant to operate an afterschool program. The Promising Readers program focused on improving literacy skills for students in grades K–3, but it had a more important purpose—to create opportunities for meaningful partnerships with families. Classroom teachers and family members worked together to plan and implement each day's activities. Three times a week, K–3rd grade students would eat a snack and play outside for a few minutes after school and then come back into the classroom to rotate through a variety of centers focusing on reading, writing, and art. Each center was staffed by one of the students' family members. One day, Davonte's mother led a read aloud of one of her favorite picture books in the reading corner and then supervised while students drew pictures in response to the text. Aisha's aunt and Raven's grandmother worked in the writing corner, listening to students read their drafts aloud, helping them with spelling, and celebrating great illustrations. At an activity table, Byron's aunt squirted out shaving cream, and kindergarten students practiced writing their letters in the foam. Each of the family members received a small daily stipend for their work in the afterschool program. The stipend wasn't much, but it offset the cost of transportation and childcare for younger siblings and communicated that the family members played an important role in the program.

Family members valued the program. They learned more about reading instruction happening at school and started spending more time on literacy at home. They became more comfortable at school and began attending Parent Teacher Association (PTA) meetings and school events more regularly and even started showing up early to volunteer in classrooms before the program began. One mother was hired as a teaching assistant, and another went on to complete her teaching degree. Teachers also valued the program, appreciating the ways Davonte's mother read aloud with so much expression and Aisha's aunt's skill at resolving conflict. Teachers appreciated extra support for classroom instruction and help from volunteers. Teachers also found that family members offered important insights about their children (they knew who could work together in a group and who might not) and helped to brainstorm and problem solve about student behaviors. The Promising Readers program was a true partnership between the school and families, and it had long lasting benefit for both.

This chapter will give you the opportunity to explore your responsibilities as a rural teacher related to building positive relationships and collaborating with a variety of rural families in order to support teaching and learning in the classroom. To get started, take a moment and think back to the time when you were considering possibilities for your career path. What kinds of things did you picture yourself doing? Maybe you could see yourself in all kinds of different roles or maybe you always saw yourself as being a teacher. Either way, when you considered the possibility of becoming a teacher, you probably pictured yourself in a classroom, working with students, and having a lot of fun engaged in interesting learning experiences with them. Did you also picture yourself working with your students' family members?

For Discussion

What do you think families should do to support their student's learning? How have these ideas been shaped by your past personal observations and experiences of family involvement? How might your ideas be culturally biased?

As you describe your answers to the first discussion question, you are starting to identify some of your preexisting beliefs and expectations regarding the role of families and the nature of your relationship with them. When you answered this, did you find yourself viewing your students' families as your friend or foe? Enemy or ally? Silent supporters or engaged partners? And then, as the second question would indicate, it is also important to think about where your ideas and expectations may have originated. Your expectations about the family's role in their child's education, and your beliefs about how family members should relate to teachers, are often shaped by personal experiences—both good and bad.

Determining the aspects of your own life and culture that influence your frame of reference about family engagement is an important first step. Different experiences and beliefs about the "right" way for families to be involved may lead to significant missed opportunities for you to support student learning (Purcell-Gates, 2002). For example, if your mother volunteered in your elementary classroom on a regular basis, this might shape your expectations for how you think families should be engaged in your classroom. However, it also means that you will also want to be on the lookout for some of the other ways families can be involved with their child's schooling that might be different than what you have experienced in the past.

Rural Families as Allies

We know that family involvement in schools makes a significant difference in students' achievement. Research has consistently shown us that a high level of involvement by parents, stepparents, grandparents, aunts, uncles, guardians, and community members is one of the features of high-performing schools (e.g. Mayer et al., 2000). And the good news extends one step further; when family and community involvement is high, students are more likely to achieve higher grades, have regular attendance, have better social skills, graduate on time, and pursue postsecondary education (e.g. Cox, 2005). However, here is an important take away for rural teachers: Studies have shown that family involvement alone does not account for the increased student achievement; rather, it is *teacher outreach to families* and *the quality of interactions between teachers and families* that lead to increased student learning, especially in reading and math (Padgett, 2006). In other words, you will need to be ready to take concrete steps to connect with your students' families and community members and build relationships that will support the teaching–learning process.

As you prepare to be a rural teacher, it is really important to view your students' families as key allies in student learning. As you begin think about interactions and outreach with families it is important to not make assumptions about your students' home life, their family members, or the ways they live their lives. You need to get to know each rural family for who they are, and learn about their uniqueness in structure, size, and background. Families want to know that they can trust you to care about their child's well-being and success and to treat their child fairly and compassionately. In addition, family members want to feel respected; they want to know that you value their knowledge and insights about their child and are willing to work with them in an inclusive partnership based on trust.

Families know their children the best and have important insights and knowledge to share that can contribute to learning in your classroom. Finally, family members want you to respond and communicate with them as partners in their child's learning and development. With these foundational understandings in place you can begin to build meaningful partnerships with your students' family members.

Building Trust with Rural Families and Community Members

As teachers, our primary work is building relationships and at the core of every healthy relationship is an authentic sense of trust. Trust is not a naïve or blind faith; rather, real trust is a willingness to risk being vulnerable with another person based on the knowledge that the other person is safe, reliable, honest, open, and competent (Tschannen-Moran, 2014).

Five Facets of Trust (Tschannen-Moran, 2014)

1   Benevolence—demonstrating care and respect
2   Honesty—being accurate
3   Openness—sharing information freely
4   Reliability—being dependable
5   Competence—being skilled

Your job as a teacher is to focus on being a trustworthy person and actively building trusting relationships with students and their families. The exciting outcome of this effort is that these types of healthy relationships with students and families characterized by trust and integrity can have a long-lasting positive impact in students' lives. The ultimate goal is to create a school and classroom environment where parents and families feel welcome and wanted so that teachers and parents can collaborate together in the best interests of the students. This type of strengths-based collaboration encourages a focus on problem-solving and a sense of shared responsibility to create positive outcomes for all students.

Beginning with the first day of school (or even before school starts), demonstrating trust, goodwill, and genuine concern for students and their families is important. We can build trust across a rural school and community when we take deliberate action to reduce others' sense of vulnerability and help them to feel safe and secure. However, this process takes time and it depends on good communication. A common mistake for a lot of teachers is simply not communicating enough or contacting family members only when a student is experiencing a problem. As one rural high school teacher shared:

> *Consistent and regular communication with our rural parents and caregivers is what builds trust. Ongoing dialog about a student's progress helps to establish trust and relationships. And then any emotional or academic concerns can be addressed more proactively, rather than waiting for a crisis to arise.*

When trust is weak or absent, the classroom and school environment tend to be marked by negative thoughts and feelings such as blame, judgment, criticism, and/or defensiveness. In these environments of low trust, people tend to feel that they are not cared for, heard, or valued. These are environments that lack respect and psychological safety. However, when schools and classrooms are on their way to developing high-trust environments, the signs are very clear. The environment is marked by a sense of positivity, energy, enthusiasm, communication, responsibility, and integrity. These are the types of trusting environments where students and teachers thrive. There are three critical steps you can take as a teacher for *starting, supporting,* and *sustaining* a foundation of trust with rural families and community members.

Starting Steps

Because you hold the professional role of teacher, the expectation is that you will take the initiative to get the relational ball rolling. It is your responsibility to make the first move and it's really important not to sit back and wait for family members approach you. The best thing you can do is to reach out and connect with family and community members in a warm and respectful manner as soon as, or even before, school starts. As you reach out, it is important to share a little bit about yourself, but the majority of your time should be dedicated to asking good questions and listening actively to their answers. For example, use some of the insights you gained from your Rural Community Walk (in Chapter 6) as a springboard and ask family members to tell you more about something you noticed—a local statue, a particular store, the library that was once the one-room schoolhouse, etc. Your goal with these first steps with families is similar to your goal with students—you want to get to know them so that you understand their perspectives, cultural backgrounds, questions, concerns, and goals and respond in personal and meaningful ways. This may mean inviting family members to school, or, as one rural Superintendent shared, it may mean going to the places where families are.

> *I have a few parents who consistently do not have working phone numbers or access to the internet, so an email is also out of the question. Obviously, mail can take a few days and in today's culture, that's not very efficient. So I am lucky that I have time and I can go to their house and connect with parents personally.*

The key to getting started is initiating communication by the teacher. As one rural teacher shared,

> *I created a short video to introduce myself, set expectations, and tell parents that they are welcome to contact me and give me feedback. Through this first contact, I hope to show parents that I am open and looking forward to working together with them.*

With all of these forms of communication, you want your message to be organized, concise, and accurate so that it will be easy for parents to understand and respond to if they have questions.

All families have important insights to offer about their child, and all have contributions they can make to your classroom. As one rural kindergarten teacher shared,

> *It's really important to me to learn about students' cultural, religious, family, intellectual, and personal experiences and resources for use in instruction. I like to reach out and have these conversations with families about their cultural beliefs and personal experiences. In kindergarten, students often do not know their beliefs or have much personal experience that influences learning. So involving parents or guardians can help me expand on these skills. This helps me draw out the differences in students' backgrounds and learning differences, therefore enhancing my lessons and instruction to meet learning needs for all my students.*

Encourage families to participate and share their strengths. These kinds of efforts will take time and energy, but the investment will make a tremendous difference in your work with your students and their families. With time and practice you will be able to build your skills of initiating trusting partnerships with families and community members and supporting your students' growth and development.

Supporting Steps

Once you have established some initial connections of trust with your students' family members, your next step is to support the ongoing development of trust. Deliberately continue to initiate conversations with them in a consistent, warm, and respectful manner with a focus on sharing positive aspects of their child's learning and growth. This will also be a very important to time to listen and really hear their perspectives about what is and is not working for their child.

Trust between you and your students' families will grow as you take their concerns seriously and respond to them in a welcoming and non-judgmental manner. As several veteran rural teachers recommended, when you talk with families, frame your comments and suggestions in ways that focus on describing rather than evaluating behaviors, concerns, or areas for growth. "Aubrey got out of the desk seven times during reading" and "Skylar wrote three pieces for our school newspaper" communicate more specifically and concretely than "DJ was a problem during reading" and "Keisha is really smart."

Trust is fostered when there is reliability and predictability in a relationship. One of the most important things you can do is to be as consistent as possible in how and when you communicate with families over time. And as one rural parent shared,

> *When I think about some of the positive things I have seen some of my kids' teachers do, one is an app that allows the teacher to post pictures, big assignments, and other things from my child's classroom. One of my kids has a teacher that regularly posts what they are working on in their class. It is nice knowing what projects they are working on. It may be a bit of work for the teacher, but it does help keep the parents more in the loop about what their kids are doing at school.*

Since one size does not fit all when it comes to parent–teacher communication, it's important to ask parents which communication tools they would prefer in order to stay connected. Some parents might say, "Email me if my kid was troubled today or if they're missing homework," but that might not be the case for all families. As one rural teacher shared, "A recent survey of our school's parents found that parents wanted less communication from the school. Daily emails were overwhelming, so the principal committed to bi-weekly emails instead."

The effort to support the growth of trust can sometimes feel a bit over-whelming at first, but over time you will build your active listening and communication skills, the positive outcomes will be noticeable. Through respecting the perspectives of families and community members, and genuinely empathizing with them, you will earn their trust and students will reap the benefits both academically and personally.

Sustaining Steps

A high-trust environment also needs to be cultivated and sustained. There are three key factors that will help you to nurture a foundation of trust with rural families and community members over time: purpose, integrity, and shared responsibility. The first factor, purpose, is focused on being clear about your reasons for building trust—you need to know your "why." It's so important to be clear in your own mind about why connecting with families is important for your students' growth and development. Keeping students' well-being as your focus leads to opportunities to really listen to their perspectives, celebrate individual successes, accept and deal with frustration openly, as well as maintain their confidentiality to the extent allowed by law.

The second factor that helps to sustain trusting relationships over time is integrity—actually being who you say you are. This means that teachers who demonstrate integrity are fully present for their students and keep their word. These are the teachers who are careful to use humor appropriately and they say what they mean and mean what they say. They don't promise the moon but then fail to follow through. Teachers with integrity are also willing to admit their mistakes and respond to constructive feedback, as well as provide feedback to others when needed in a caring and constructive way. The key is communication—including calls and visits and written communication (a class newsletter, a class-to-home notebook, email, texts, automated reminders, or even traditional report cards) that is consistent, and contains positive information about students' academic progress, social emotional skills, and interpersonal skills.

The final factor that helps to sustain trusting relationships with families over time is the development of a sense of shared responsibility and influence for student outcomes. Rather than working in isolation, trusting, respectful relationships are key to creating the time and space needed for all parties to work together and contribute to positive outcomes for students. Effective family engagement is not a one-way street. Trust is not sustained when teachers simply report information to families or tell them what to do. Family engagement activities must be culturally appropriate, accessible, relevant, and value family members as key partners with valuable expertise (Brenner et al., 2003).

> **For Discussion**
>
> Think back to when you were a student—how did your teachers start, support, and sustain trust with your families? Or, if you are a parent, what have you observed about how teachers build and sustain trust with your family?

Rural Realities

Just as it is crucial to understand the importance of trust with families and the steps you need to take to build and sustain trust over time, it's equally important to understand that there are a variety of factors that shape the ways in which rural families are able to be involved and engaged with their local school. In this section, we will explore some of the ways a rural context could impact and shape how and when families are able to connect and engage with the school and its teachers. We'll also consider what this could mean for your professional practice.

Think about important rural elements such as transportation, distance, and time; consider how these factors interact to impact rural families' lives. For example, some rural families may live fairly close to the school, so distance might not be a major factor shaping their involvement. However, that could change if the family did not have access to reliable transportation. It's important to recognize that even smaller distances can become a significant obstacle for school engagement when reliable or public transportation are not readily available. Then there's the situation for some rural families who may live a significant distance from town and the school. This means that not only do they need access to reliable transportation, they also need to have enough time to travel these major distances. Driving long distances can be very time consuming, and this can be particularly true if the roads are not in great condition or the weather is prohibitive. These challenges are then compounded if the family does not have access to a safe or reliable vehicle.

A different, but still related factor is family employment. Some rural families, such as farmers, do work that is weather-dependent. They must work when the weather allows and, unfortunately, suitable weather doesn't always fit with the school schedule. Other rural family members may have inflexible work schedules, such as shift work at a mine or a mill or at the local Dollar General. You may need to schedule conversations or school visits around the realities of their work lives, or find other ways to keep communication channels open and build trust. Knowing the job responsibilities family members have can help you to make appropriate arrangements for meetings and engagement.

Another rural reality has to do with access to the internet, and, sometimes, cellular service. An increasing number of schools are turning to various platforms to manage communication with families. Schools send text messages about snow days and school events or use platforms to share students' grades and assignments. These tools can be very helpful—when they work. However, if some families do not have access to internet, or reliable cell service, the tools can end up as barriers for families who might otherwise stay engaged.

Addressing Barriers to Trust

As you get started building trust with families, you may find that there are barriers you need to address. Some adults may not have positive feelings toward schools, remembering their own childhoods or times they have felt dismissed or intimidated by a teacher or administrator. School can feel like a hostile place, particularly for minority or low-income students (Edwards et al., 2003; Purcell-Gates, 2002). Parents who dropped out—or were pushed out—of schools may not feel comfortable interacting with teachers.

Family members, especially newcomers, may not know how or when to access school information—particularly as schools move to sharing school news via websites or other technological platforms. Cultural and linguistic differences can also shape how family members interpret school policies and expectations. For example, some family members might appear uninvolved in their children's education due to their belief that the school knows what is best for students. Some families believe that their role is to entrust their children's education to the teachers. Families may not attend school events because their cultural expectations are that visits to the school occur only when their children are in trouble. Teachers who lack cultural understanding may interpret these families as uncaring or uninvolved, when in reality these are people who are making decisions from a place of caring and a cultural definition of what it means to be a good caregiver or parent.

Finally, it is also important to recognize that some families may experience serious difficulty or disruption such as serious financial losses, illnesses, injuries, deaths, natural disasters, or chronic problems such as alcohol or opioid addiction. These situations significantly impact a family's capacity to be involved with the school.

Understanding these factors can help you to have accurate expectations for family engagement. This does not mean that you settle for low expectations; rather, it allows you to set strong expectations and develop appropriate, positive, supportive avenues to reach those expectations. It may mean that you need to be more explicit about inviting parents to school events, or it may mean you need to reach out to family members around the issues that matter most to them as you build trust. This can be important for your own well-being as well. Unrealistic expectations can lead to high levels of frustration and discouragement. However, as you build accurate and appropriate expectations for family engagement, the better it will be for all involved.

For Discussion

How might families think and feel about working with you as their child's teacher? What skills will you need to develop in order to be effective in your work with families? What are some of the different ways that rural families might think and feel about the process of schooling? How might mismatches in beliefs and practices represent missed opportunities for you to support student learning?

Building Successful Rural School–Family Partnerships

As you build trust and engagement with your students' parents and families, you will be able to draw on the various strengths of rural schools and communities. For example, in many rural communities the schools serve as a hub for the social connections within and across the community. This type of community interconnectedness can provide a lot of opportunities to see both your students and their families outside of the school setting. You can get to know your students' lives outside of school, where and how their families work, and have opportunities to learn about the things that are important to them. As one new rural teacher shared,

> *My rural school has a lot of events that encourage parents to show up to support students. Most of these are athletic in nature, but some like the spelling bee, battle of the books, Science Olympiad or the geo-bee are more based in academics. These extracurricular activities offer parents a chance to see what their children are doing beyond homework. Even more helpful is that many teachers serve as coaches and advisers to these activities. This offers parents a chance to see teachers involved in students' education and well-being, building trust between teachers and parents. By offering a way*

for parents to be involved in students' extracurricular activities, especially when the teachers are involved in a capacity, it allows parents to meet and see their children interact with the teacher, and vice versa. When both parties see the interactions as calm and positive then that strengthens trust, and that really helps the students. It also allows parents and students to see teachers committing to something beyond the classroom. It helps strengthen that relationship because it shows that teachers want their students to succeed outside of the classroom.

In a rural community, it can be common for adults to serve in a variety of community roles and so your positive relationships with students' families will extend to your relationships with the community. One student's father may be one of the church leaders in town and a soccer coach. Another student's grandmother might be the branch librarian and head of the high school booster club. These interconnected relationships can be intimidating, but don't let them scare you. Instead, embrace the opportunity to know your students' families in rich and interconnected ways, and bring that knowledge to the classroom to support your students.

References

Brenner, D., Jayroe, T., & Boutwell, A. (2003). Building on the strengths of families: The Promising Readers program. *Language Arts, 80*(4), 275–283.

Cox, D. D. (2005). Evidence-based interventions using home-school collaboration. *School Psychology Quarterly, 20*(4), 473–497. doi: https://10.1521/scpq.2005.20.4.473

Edwards, P. A., Pleasants, H. M., & Franklin, S. H. (2003). *A path to follow: Learning to listen to parents.* Heinemann.

Mayer, D. P., Mullens, J. E., & Moore, M. T. (2000). *Monitoring school quality—An Indicators Report.* National Center for Education Statistics, U.S. Department of Education.

Padgett, R. (2006). Best ways to involve parents. *Education Digest: Essential Readings Condensed for Quick Review, 72*(3), 44–45.

Purcell-Gates, V. (2002). "… As soon as she opened her mouth!": Issues of language, literacy, and power. In L. Delpit (Ed.), *The skin that we speak: Thoughts on language and culture in the classroom* (pp. 121–141). The New Press.

Tschannen-Moran, M. (2014). *Trust matters: Leadership for successful schools.* Jossey-Bass.

8

From Here or Away
Relating to Students

I was raised in a small rural town in Virginia. When I got my first teaching job in a rural school elsewhere in the state, on day one I realized I was naïve about how growing up in one rural community prepared me to teach in another. My new community was not only in a much more rural area than where I was raised but was far more diverse. I had several students for whom English was not their first language and there were significant differences among the children in terms of their economic situations. I learned that first year how to communicate with parents and students and teach the children differently from what I was taught in college. In my teacher preparation program, I somehow managed to get the idea that place doesn't matter much in teaching.

In the classroom, I learned that kids need to be loved before you can teach them anything. And did I ever learn that! From little Jasmine who sat right in front of me every single time I read aloud and rubbed my sleeve with her sweet hand, I learned that some kids engage their senses in the learning process. From James, I learned that meeting the needs of some children means helping to keep them safe so that they can better manage their emotions. I understood James more when I visited him at home. I learned that he had no electricity. There were dirt floors in his home, and he had no bed. I also learned that drug dealers had used him as a runner. I struggled with the idea that James was supposed to learn content even though his basic needs weren't met. From Kevin I learned that sometimes, you're just wrong and the kids are right. When I asked Kevin in my polite and loving first-grade teacher voice to please get off the floor because it was dirty, he replied: "Miss Price, God made dirt and dirt won't hurt." I had to agree.

That year I learned that each child needs to be taught from wherever they are and whatever they know. But, first, they need to know you love them each individually. It might seem there is little parent or administrative support. You might be tempted to think no one cares. In the community where I worked, parents worked at jobs with odd hours leaving kids, out of necessity, alone in the evenings. The parents cared deeply. As a staff, we worked together to meet the kids' needs at school. We co-taught and did cross-grade learning, which was innovative at the time! We learned to be creative and to advocate for what was best for our students. We worked together to provide food for kids or take them to a movie or buy them clothing and shoes. However, even then I knew that my efforts weren't enough or sustainable. There was only so much I could do. This was heartbreaking for my 23-year-old self because I really did think I could save the world. But I wasn't a savior—and that's not what they needed anyway. The kids were resilient and whip smart, sometimes even under the worst conditions. And yet—they wanted to come to school and learn. School for many of them was a safe haven. That's what they needed from me—a safe haven where they could learn. Their rural was so different than my rural, but this fact became irrelevant the more I learned about them and their lives and invested in their learning. What I learned from that first class, and still use every day in my classroom three decades later, is to make sure my students know I love them.

Lori Price Snidow, first-grade teacher, Virginia

How do we know what we know about rural places? Lori was surprised to discover that being from one rural place did not prepare her very well to understand another. Like Lori, your identification as urban, rural, or suburban will act as a "lens" through which you see your rural community. This chapter addresses being "from here" or "from away" or somewhere in the middle. It looks at how your place identity, experiences, and values are relevant to your teaching.

Let's begin with the idea of being either an insider or an outsider. An insider might feel like they belong to a place, have friends and a sense of community in a place, or feel like they know and understand the place where they're teaching. A teacher might feel like an insider if they are from the same community that they are teaching in—or, like Lori in the opening vignette, they might initially feel like an insider because they are from another rural community. An outsider, on the other hand, might feel new or that they do not yet belong to or fully understand the place, or have a community of peers in a place. Outsiders might not yet understand the history, traditions, and what is important to people who live in a place.

There are multiple ways to feel like an insider or an outsider. Feeling like an insider or an outsider in a place but does not necessarily have to do with whether you are from there or how long you have lived there. In fact, some teachers can feel like outsiders even in the same schools and places where they grew up. Any community has its affordances and limitations that are obvious or less obvious, and any individual teacher will be comfortable or challenged by a variety of factors that are, to be honest, difficult to identify in advance.

That said, anyone's transition to a new rural community might have some predictable place-specific challenges such as a lack of access to certain amenities like a gym or big box stores. But there are many advantages to teaching in rural areas, like smaller class sizes and community support, that—for a lot of people—outweigh the disadvantages. It can be what you make of it. Still, we acknowledge there can be real challenges to relationship building if you are a newcomer, no matter what kind of community you grew up in. Particularly if you are from a non-rural place, a rural community could seem strange and alienating. As Jenny, a preservice teacher said about her field experience in a rural school, "I'm not rural, I don't know how I will relate to the students" (Azano & Stewart, 2016). Amy, one of the authors of this book, who grew up in a rural community, describes when she first began teaching in an urban high school and how she worried about connecting with her students:

> My students had grown up in the city, and I was from a remote rural area of the state. They would casually tell me about taking public transportation (by themselves!) and laughed when I said I was 20 years old before I had ever used a city bus. Yet, when we read Steinbeck's Of Mice and Men, we all found characters with whom we connected. As we started writing about those connections and the things we valued—the people we love, our histories, our hopes for the future—we learned that we weren't really all that different.
>
> I remember one of my students wrote about dinner at his grandmother's house after church on Sundays. I shared that my family did that, too—that, no matter what, we were all expected to pour into Nanny's house by 1 pm to sit together at the dinner table. Even though we were from different places—theirs as one of the most densely populated areas of the state and mine with its one mile Main Street and lone traffic light—we were able to find common ground in our families. But, of course, it's different in rural areas when those community–school boundaries are less clearly defined. When I taught in the urban community, it was rare that I would bump into a student or their family members outside the school day. There were numerous places to shop or be social, and I enjoyed the anonymity

when I left the school building. By comparison, in the rural community where I grew up, it was common to bump into teachers wherever you were in the community. For rural teachers, going to the movies on a Friday night means you will likely see a student, a parent, or colleague. On football Fridays, however, you may find that your presence is expected at the stadium.

But even for teachers who grew up in the same community in which they are now teaching, long-standing relationships and familiarity can be challenging. You may very likely find the names of your own classmates' children on your class lists.

Welcome, Newcomer!

> ### For Discussion
>
> Think about a time you were a newcomer. Did you move around as a young child? Did you attend summer or sleep away camps? How about when you first arrived on your college campus? On a sheet of paper, make two columns and write down the ways that you felt that you "fit in" and, in the other column, the ways you might have "stood out." With a partner or in a small group, share what you wrote.
>
> Next, discuss how you navigated both the situation and the feelings you had. What did you do to manage your emotions? Whether you enjoyed the situation or not, how did you meet people and make connections? Did you ever transition from "outsider" to "insider," and—if so—how did this happen?

Being a newcomer to a place can be challenging. As you discuss being a newcomer, you might find that some people enjoyed being in their new situations, but for others, the new situation produced anxiety and insecurity. Some people navigated the transition to insider, and some did not. These are important conversations to have to better understand your own response to new situations and, importantly, to learn that you are not alone in your response. If you tend to feel a bit anxious about being in a new environment, then that is likely to be true wherever you begin your teaching career—and not necessarily because you are in a rural school. Focusing on strategies you used in the past to successfully manage those feelings sets you up to do so again.

If you are a newcomer to a place, whether you identify as suburban, urban, or rural, there are many reasons to make an effort to build out-of-school relationships and become a member of the community. Deeper connections to the community can help you feel welcome and help you build relationships that turn into friendships. Connections to the community and families can also help you understand your students and their needs, and the needs of the community, and make you a better teacher. Even if you become a teacher in your home community, activities outside of school can help you see your community from a new perspective and understand your students and their families. Here are three categories of actions you could take to enable new connections in a new community.

Action	Connections
Join a club or coach a team in the community	• Volunteer to assist (or coach) a sport in the community. (Especially at the younger levels, a willingness is often the only prerequisite.) • Volunteer to be a 4-H leader. • Volunteer to work in the concession stand at home football games. • Join (or, if it doesn't exist, launch) a club related to a hobby or interest you have—bird watching, cycling, hiking, sewing, soccer. • Join a social, political, religious, or other organization in your community that meets regularly.
Attend school events	• Attend your students' after-school events—take tickets, supervise, or just sit in the stands. • Divide your time equally between sports and the arts. Drama performances and year-end concerts are extremely important to the participating students. • Chaperone prom and/or other school dances. • Football will facilitate many interactions, but all sports are equally important. Is the cross-country team struggling? Support them!
Participate in school activities	• From technology to parent communication, there will be no shortage of committees at school for which you can volunteer. • Special events at school tend to be planned by the same core group of teachers. Join them. • Consider initiating a GSA (Gay Straight Alliance) if your school doesn't yet have one. • Step up when a school group needs an advisor.

Johnathan Imhoff (the music teacher from Chapter 6) was a newcomer. He made deliberate decisions that helped him put down roots in his community.

He started by joining a trail-cleaning group, hiking the many beautiful trails around Weaverville. Then he joined the community band and even played a role in a local theater production of *Mary Poppins*. He says, "That's the thing, rural towns allow you to do things you wouldn't necessarily be able to do in bigger places." Sometimes, getting involved just meant having coffee with his colleagues or saying hello to the parents of a student. Johnathan said,

> *I know it's hard, especially when you're first starting; you're treading water, there's paperwork and all these other things, and it's like, "Oh now I'm gonna go volunteer." It's probably like the literal last thing you want to do, but your life will improve if you do. My life improved a lot doing community band.*

Now, Johnathan is the director and conductor of the community band. He's been able to meet many friends and mentors through his local community involvement (see https://iamaruralteacher.org).

These actions signal to students and families that you are invested in your rural school and its community. Involvement with families in the community is an excellent opportunity to get to know people and to have them get to know you. As well as community-based activities, look for professional opportunities where you can get to know faculty and staff beyond your building, department, or grade level.

For Discussion

These ideas are just a start. What additional ideas can you think of? What clubs or activities (in and out of school) were you involved in as a K–12 student or at college?

Where Are You From?

> *In our community, there are the "been-heres" and the "come-heres." Newcomers to a rural area need to be open to the culture and the diversity that is already present. We still have lots to offer even though sometimes it might look like we don't. Immerse yourself into those basketball games, the Sunday morning worship services, or even the fundraiser down the street. All of these things show the community, students, and their guardians how invested you are in them.*
> Britinie Fitzwater & Chris Riley, Page County Public Schools, Virginia

"From Here," "Not from Here," "Local Boy/Girl," "Been-here," "Come-here," "Blow-in," "From Away," "Flatlander," "Person from Away," "Leaf Peeper." These are just a few of the expressions we have heard people use describing themselves or others who are from "somewhere else." We've also heard words like "yooper" and "tarheel"—words that identify a group of people *from* a specific place. While we suspect that rural places might be especially fond of labeling residents in this way in order to keep track of who is who, it is not an uncommon practice in non-rural places. After living in New York City for three years, a friend said she could call herself a "New Yorker" because she knew the grid pattern of the streets and avenues! Others claim it takes ten years to be a New Yorker, and still others swear you need to be born in New York to be a bona fide New Yorker.

The former superintendent in Amy's rural hometown school district worked in the district for more than 20 years. She started as a classroom teacher, moved into administration, and eventually became the superintendent. Approaching retirement, she jokingly asked when she would finally be a legitimate *from here*. Amy laughed and told her it might take some more time. Many regions have words that are used to name people who are from somewhere else.

For Discussion

What words like these are used in your community? How might they work to include or exclude others? With a partner, discuss how you think the names reinforce boundaries. Why do people use them to separate and designate? Might people have the feeling that they own or belong to places? What role might the names play in that process?

It is important to give this some thought whether you are from a rural place and intending to teach in one, or you are from places that are more urban or suburban. If you have always lived in a rural place and your community struggles to recruit teachers, then bringing attention to the ways these descriptors might make newcomers feel unwelcome, no matter the intent, is warranted. If you are called one of these names, you might consider finding an opportunity to share with others about where you are from and what brought you to teach in the community. In the classroom, in fact, you can even emphasize this difference. Use it as leverage to let students *teach you* about their community.

We're Different. We're the Same.

Where do you go to church? Do you believe in God? Are you married? Do you think gay marriage is okay? Do you like the president?

Even in a community that seems "tight-knit" and homogenous, individuals have important differences from one another. It is never a good idea to assume that you understand someone's political views, values, experiences, religion or spirituality, or personal relationships. But this can be especially tempting to do in some rural communities where difference is not obvious. The same is true of the people who are new to a community: Assumptions cannot be made.

But what if, as a new teacher, it seems that your values are different from the majority of those living in the community? What if issues about your values come up while you are teaching in a rural school? (We get this question a lot.) For any teacher, navigating our students' interest in our personal lives can be challenging. In rural schools, these questions can be especially difficult due to more fluid boundaries between your students' lives and your own. All the same, you should expect questions! In our experience, we have had to do the most thinking specifically about how the expression of our gender or sexuality, and political and religious views impact our relationships with the children in our rural classrooms and schools.

Politics

Whether you are from the community or are an outsider, students will make assumptions and ask questions about your political beliefs. This can be uncomfortable for any teacher. The extent to which you feel like you belong in a community can make these discussions especially uncomfortable. We all want to be accepted and fit in.

One way to think about this is to remember that teaching isn't really about *you* (Though it sure feels that way!). Your opinion on a topic, any topic, matters much less than what your students know and believe about that topic. Part of your job as a teacher involves a commitment to critical thinking and to challenge students to consider *why they think the way they do.* When you are teaching during an election year, for example, students will want to know which candidate has your vote. Remember, teachers hold enormous power that can influence students. An endorsement of one candidate could be an affront to a student's belief system. An endorsement for another might align you with some students, while alienating others. Be careful not to assume that students' (or their parents') political views are the same as yours. One strategy to sidestep the question is to, instead, talk about your decision-making process, the election cycle, and the issues being debated. You might share with students the following questions that help to guide political decision making:

- Do I trust the candidate to make decisions about matters close to me (education) and more distant from me (foreign policy)?
- Are the candidate's proposed solutions workable?
- Does the candidate not only have my interests at heart but also is committed to protecting the interests of vulnerable communities and groups?

Your questions, of course, might be different. The intent is to support students in self-reflection about how they might decide which candidate or initiative to support. What do they value and why? Why are some issues important to some people and communities and, perhaps, less so to others? What are the connections between our local issues and global issues? Most importantly, you can stress the importance of political participation.

Religion and Spirituality

In rural communities, it is not uncommon for people to be very forthcoming about the importance of faith in their lives. Others consider their faith a private matter, or do not participate in organized religion at all. This difference is often influenced by the extent to which churches emphasize the importance of evangelizing. Some churches teach that it is not only acceptable but necessary to share one's beliefs. In this case, when students share their beliefs in class, or ask you about yours, they are fulfilling a spiritual mandate.

Keeping this in mind, when asked about your faith in the classroom, you still must consider carefully how your answer might affect your relationship with students, as well as your personal comfort level. Will your answer make students feel included or excluded? Ultimately, it is your right to share as much or as little as you want. If you attend services in the same community in which you teach, you will almost certainly see students there from school. In this case, they will know this part about your out-of-school life. Likewise, if you grew up in the community, you will likely know the religious affiliation of some families. In some especially small communities, your students may very well know how you spend your weekends or Wednesday nights without your having to tell them whether you attend services or not. If you don't attend services (for whatever reason), you could say, "I'm not a member of any congregation. What do you like about your church?" If you are comfortable sharing your religious beliefs, you might consider saying, simply, "I was raised in a (Catholic, Jewish, Muslim, Buddhist, Protestant, Baptist, or other type of) family. How about you?" Or maybe your feelings about faith and spirituality are more complicated, and you are uncomfortable talking about religion. In that case, maybe you'll say, "It's something I think about. Have you always been a member of the ____ church?"

> *A Teacher's Guide to Religion in the Public Schools* can provide you with more information and guidance about what is, and is not, constitutional, and how to talk with your students and teach about religion. The guide was published by the First Amendment Center and has been endorsed by numerous school administration and religious organizations.
> See https://www.religiousfreedomcenter.org/wp-content/uploads/2014/08/teachersguide.pdf

These moments can be difficult and almost always come up unexpectedly. It can help to think about some possible responses in advance so that you are not caught off guard. It is difficult terrain to navigate—your right to share and your right to privacy versus your students' rights to feel heard and welcome in a safe and inclusive classroom. Whatever you decide, it is important to recognize that your history in the community may influence your interactions with your students.

Sexual Orientation and Gender Expression

Closely related to religion and spirituality, issues about gender roles, sexual orientation, and gender expression are also likely to come up in rural classrooms. In some rural communities, there may be strict expectations about appropriate roles for women and men. Some teachers might believe that only boys should help move furniture or be in charge of student government. In some places, girls are discouraged from pursuing higher education or careers that may take them out of the community. Sometimes these norms and expectations are expressed in dress codes at school. Consider how dress codes enforce or allow for gender expression (see http://neatoday.org/2018/07/24/when-school-dress-codes-discriminate/).

When you are asked or when students bring up issues of gender roles, you can ask questions that affirm that you value students' and families' ways of being and, at the same time, encourage students to reflect and consider other ways of thinking. Even just asking, "I wonder why we have that tradition?" can encourage students to reflect.

You may get asked about your own sexual orientation or gender identity, or have students who are questioning their own. You might have teacher friends who talk about their same sex spouses so regularly that students quickly lose interest. Other friends or colleagues may, for a variety of reasons, feel less safe sharing details about their personal relationships. These concerns are not only related to same sex partners. In especially conservative communities, some divorced women or single parents are uncomfortable sharing these kinds of details. But, again, if you are from the community, or if you live in the community, your students are likely to know these things about you—and you about their families in turn.

The advice here is to know the norms of your community, be reflective about and maintain appropriate boundaries and, above all, *be professional.* It is rarely appropriate to speak with your students at length about your adult relationships. When they inquire, take some pleasure in knowing that they are likely asking because they want to get to know you better. Like conversations about religion, share only what is appropriate to the situation and feels comfortable. When you are active in your rural community, you will almost certainly see students outside of school. While we are careful not to fall into the trap of suggesting that it is the responsibility (or burden) of underrepresented groups to educate others, we are saying that representation matters. Additionally, you should not assume the people in a rural community will not be open to accepting you as you are. Rural places are often thought to be politically conservative and, sometimes, that is indeed true. However, even within the most conservative rural communities, many people respect people with differences. Consider the students who don't identify with the dominant ideas in the community. For them, school is an opportunity to see a successful, caring professional embodying difference in their community.

Other Questions

There will be other topics that arise—ones neither you nor we can anticipate. As we say throughout the book, teaching is a political act. Your stance on vegetarianism, vaccines, gender equality, high school football—any of these issues could pose opportunities and also stumbling blocks in your relationships with your students. Our takeaway is to be cognizant of your community, to be empathetic and open to diverse thoughts, and to practice cultural humility (see Chapter 6).

We want to highlight here with our discussion of politics, religion and spirituality, and sexuality and gender that no one is either an insider or outsider every day in every situation. Your sense of belonging in your community is more helpfully understood as a continuum rather than a binary: As opposed to insider *or* outsider you are, to greater and lesser degrees, both insider and outsider in any given community. If you are someone who grew up in the same rural community in which you hope to teach, you are an insider in many ways. However, you have also had experiences and have perhaps developed beliefs that now mark you as an outsider and set you apart in certain ways. If you are new to a rural community or, like Lori (from the opening vignette) grew up rural but teach in a different rural community, you might be an insider in some ways but fall squarely on the outsider end of the continuum in other regards. We encourage you not to rely on what you think you may know about any rural community, and, instead, commit to learning and relationship-making.

Even if you *could* be an "insider," this is not necessarily an advantage and being an "outsider" is certainly not a foregone disadvantage. In either case, you'll need to make an investment in your rural school and community in unique ways once you become a teacher. You might get asked, "Where are you from?" Many of us have been asked this question countless times because of the way we speak, look, or dress. The truth is we can be from many places. Identities are complicated, and assuming the identity of a rural teacher is no exception. The important thing to remember is that we are not just *one thing*. We close with a simple activity to prove the point.

For Discussion

Complete the following statement: Just because I _____ doesn't mean I _____. Think of a label or category that applies to you, but where you defy stereotypes about that category in some way. For example, just because Devon is a vegetarian, doesn't mean she loves eggplant. She doesn't.

Addressing ideologies and how communities influence them can be a vibrant aspect of your classroom. Returning to the vignette that opened this chapter, based on what Lori learned, if she were completing this activity, she might say: Just because I'm from a rural place doesn't mean I know *your* rural place.

Reference

Azano, A. P., & Stewart, T. T. (2016). Confronting challenges at the intersection of rurality, place and teacher preparation: Improving efforts in teacher education to staff rural schools. *Global Education Review*, 3(1) 108–128.

Part Three
Thriving in Rural Schools

9

Building Professional Networks in Rural Schools

Tracei is a high school English teacher in Mississippi. Early in her career Tracei participated in the summer program of the National Writing Project. She spent a month meeting with other teachers to think about the teaching of writing and to improve their teaching practice. She shared the ideas she was learning with her colleagues in her high school, and together they started a before-school writing club. Once a week, the two teachers met with a small group of interested students to work on poems and other writing projects of their choosing. The writing club turned into a collaboration with a professor at the local university. Dr. Cutts gave the students feedback on their poetry and attended their poetry reading. She also invited students to campus for a poetry event.

A few years later, Tracei participated in a summer program at The Olga Lengyel Institute for Holocaust Studies and Human Rights (TOLI). What she learned had a powerful impact on her teaching, but, even more importantly, she developed a network of colleagues committed to teaching for human rights and to fight injustice. Tracei described her network:

We came from all walks of life, grade levels, personal experiences, and religious beliefs, and somehow we managed to find an unbreakable love for one another. The Memorial Library was an actual home. The home of Olga Lengyel, a Holocaust survivor who lost all of her family in Auschwitz. Before she died, she left her home and belongings to be used as a place to teach teachers how to teach about what happened during the Holocaust, she believed that Never Again began in the classroom. We spent twelve days together. Days that blended together into a series of memories. When we were all finally back at home, we started a GroupMe. We started a Facebook page. We started writing letters to one another. My ninth graders in Louisville exchanged writing with Amber's kids in Wisconsin, and then Amber and her kids came down to Louisville to shadow my students. I recently lost my best friend, Stan (my cat), and when I posted on FB that he'd gone on a walk and not returned, TOLI sisters from Texas, Arizona, New York, Wisconsin, Kentucky, North Carolina, Indiana, and Montana were sending messages to make sure I was holding it together.

Yes, it's good to have a support system as a teacher, but it's even better to have a family of teachers from all over the world who love you and lift you up. We also support one another in our work as teachers. We share lesson plans, we plan together, we write together, we read one another's proposals and drafts of random important stuff—I've read two book drafts from two different TOLI sisters. They truly are my badass teacher friends. We help one another stay focused and on track, and we listen to one another when the focus is gone and we've run way off the track.

Tracei teaches in a small school in rural Mississippi. Sometimes, the work is challenging, sometimes it is overwhelming. But Tracei is thriving in her rural classroom because she has worked deliberately to build a network of colleagues—people to collaborate with, people who support her when the paperwork and bus duty get to be too much, people she calls friends. You will find colleagues all around you if you know where to look. These colleagues are likely to be fellow teachers and administrators who work in your building, but they can also be your friends and neighbors and leaders in the community who share your expectations for educational achievement and community vitality, and educators from all over the country who share your vision for teaching. This chapter will help you think about how to develop connections to others who align with your purpose and goals as a teacher, leading to better educational outcomes for students and a thriving community for you.

Building Collegial Relationships in School

There are many reasons to develop collaborative relationships. Studies suggest that teachers are happier in schools where they make friends and feel supported by their colleagues (e.g. Coburn et al., 2012). Relationships with your colleagues benefit students as well. Students do better when teachers work in collegial, supportive environments (Kraft & Papay, 2014). Developing relationships with colleagues will be important for your success. You will want to foster relationships with peers who teach nearby who can watch your class while you run to make a copy or use the restroom. Colleagues can also help you be a better teacher. They might listen to your teaching ideas and give you feedback or just help you understand where to park when you come back for the homecoming game.

It is important to have a strong support network of educators. Some schools have formal teacher inquiry communities who come together to analyze student data and plan instruction accordingly, or a formal induction program that will provide you with a mentor to support you during the first years of teaching. In other situations, teachers work together to share resources, collaborate on planning, think about a challenging student, or just be a friend who covers your class if a flat tire makes you late for work. If you are currently enrolled in a teacher preparation program, it is quite likely that many of your professors ask you to work in groups on your course assignments. That group work is meant to prepare you for the important task of building a professional network of mentors and colleagues who can support your success when you are teaching (Coburn et al., 2012).

Be a Good Colleague

In order to build collegial relationships, you need to be a good colleague yourself. Being present and positive at faculty meetings and other formal and informal school events will help you build relationships with other teachers. Of course, following through on your commitments and assignments is also part of being a colleague—volunteering to help with the book fair, being on time for bus duty, fulfilling your promise to write grade level lesson plans—all of these types of actions show that you are dependable and helpful. And of course, building collegial relationships means being willing to help others as they help you (including front office staff, cafeteria workers, custodians, bus drivers, and other key personnel that make up a school community). No matter where you teach, but especially in a small community, how you treat your colleagues will impact your ability to make friends and to find peers willing to lend you their stapler or take your misbehaving student for a time out when you need a break. Finding peers to support you means being supportive of your peers—which often includes being a good listener. Sometimes teachers just need someone to bounce ideas off of just long enough to puzzle through a challenging classroom situation.

In bigger schools, your closest colleagues might teach the same subject or grade that you teach. You might have a common planning time or after school meetings that bring you together on a regular basis where you build relationships. However, if you teach at a smaller school, you might find yourself as the only teacher of your subject or your grade. For example, you may be the only math teacher at the middle school, or the only third-grade teacher in the elementary school. If you are the only teacher of your grade or your content area in a rural school, you may feel like a "lone wolf," alone in the wilderness with little support. Even if you are not the only one who teaches your content area or grade level in your building, you may still feel professionally isolated if your teaching philosophy is different from that of your colleagues. The experience of feeling like a "lone wolf," the feeling of being alone without colleagues to collaborate with, is one of the concerns that some rural teachers express about their positions. We want to offer some strategies that can help you feel connected to a community so that you succeed no matter how many colleagues are in your school.

For Discussion

As you interact with your classmates and peers, what kinds of interactions do you find helpful and supportive? What interactions lift you up and make you a better teacher (or student)? And what kind of interactions do you find draining or unhelpful? What do you do (or can you do) to seek out peers who are supportive and thoughtfully challenging and to find colleagues who help you be a better teacher?

Interdisciplinary Collaboration

One strategy you can use to develop collegial relationships is to collaborate with teachers outside your content area. Interdisciplinary collaborations can help you plan meaningful and engaging instruction for your students, help build a sense of community in the school, and support your own professional growth and feeling of connectedness in your work.

Interdisciplinary collaboration simply means working with teachers who teach other subjects to collaboratively plan units of instruction that involve more than one content area. When two or more teachers from different content areas work together, you both bring your expertise and knowledge of resources, and students benefit from seeing content presented from multiple perspectives (Eckert & Alsup, 2014). One way to engage in interdisciplinary collaboration is to work with your art teachers, or even local artists in the community. There are many ways to connect music or visual arts with other content areas. Learning about the music of a time period you're studying can bring it to life. Studying patterns in nature can reinforce the learning of scientific and mathematical concepts. Arts integration has been shown to boost learning in many ways (Eisner, 2002). Lessons can even be tied to career and technical skills needed in local industries.

Literacy integration is another key way to engage in interdisciplinary collaboration. Literacy and language arts teachers can collaborate with teachers in other content areas to integrate reading and writing across the content areas. In fact, state standards increasingly call for students to read and write both informational and argumentative texts, and standards for science, social studies, and mathematics call for students to be able to read and write in the disciplines. Literacy integration can support vocabulary learning and reinforce comprehension of content area texts (International Literacy Association, 2017). You can work together to plan writing assignments about the local history or plan a unit that involves writing persuasive letters about healthy behaviors in health education.

Developing interdisciplinary lessons can be a great way to learn from other professionals while developing a support system of peers. The flexibility to work collaboratively across disciplines, and in many cases with community members, is one of the advantages of teaching in rural school.

Cross-Grade Collaboration

Another way to build peer relationships is to collaborate and co-plan instruction with colleagues who teach different grades than you. Cross-grade teaching might include planning with the teacher who teaches just above or below the grade you teach. For example, the third and fourth-grade teachers might work together to plan a Women's History Month living history museum—with students doing research, writing speeches, and dressing like an important historical figure or presenting on prominent female leaders in their local community.

Cross-grade collaboration can also involve shared activities that involve older students with much younger students. A sixth- and a first-grade teacher might work together to plan regular experiences for middle school students to read with younger students—boosting reading fluency for the older students and providing one-on-one book time for beginning readers. Or tenth-grade biology and third-grade students might draft, revise, and share non-fiction books about local ecosystems (the forest, the desert) with different levels of detail consistent with their grade level science standards. A regular time to have your class connect with another class provides your students with special relationship opportunities and is a chance for you and the other teacher to see each other teach and learn from one another.

For Discussion

What examples of cross-grade or interdisciplinary collaboration have you seen in the past? What successes and challenges have you seen?

Building Collegial Relationships Outside of School

n her recent dissertation, Jordon (2019) talked to early career teachers in rural schools about their decision to remain in the profession. Many of the teachers she spoke to felt a sense of isolation in their schools, but they found mentors and peers outside of school, and those peer relationships were part of the reason they decided to keep teaching in years two and three. Similarly, you will likely want to find and build relationships with colleagues who teach in schools like yours, the same grade or content you teach, and/or who share your vision and purpose for teaching. A network of peers can keep you going when you feel overwhelmed and share your joys when things go well.

I am a Rural Teacher

Meet other rural teachers, watch their videos, and read their stories. Visit the I Am a Rural Teacher website at www.iamaruralteacher.org or follow them on Twitter at @iamaruralteach1

One way to build your peer network is to start now—in your teacher preparation program. As you work on group assignments and listen to your peers talk in class (or write on discussion boards) you will likely find others who think like you do or whose perspective you value. Keeping in touch with the friends you make during your teacher education program is one way to find peers in the same boat as you. You might all be figuring things out together over text messages or group chats or Sunday brunch during your first years of teaching. GroupMe or other text message platforms can make sharing messages (and memes) quick and easy. Make sure to get their non-school email address or phone number so you can stay in contact after completing your preparation program. Your peer network might also include family members who are teachers, which is not uncommon in rural communities.

If your mother, uncle, or cousin is a teacher with more experience, they might be a safe person to talk to about your teaching and they may enjoy learning the newest methods from you.

Meet Colleagues in Professional Organizations

One way to build your professional network is to become a member of a professional organization. Professional organizations bring together educators with the same interests or who share a professional role. There are organizations for specific kinds of teachers (e.g. teachers of English as a second language, teachers of young children) and people who teach the same content area (e.g. science, reading, or music). The National Rural Education Association (NREA) is the professional organization for rural educators. The box below contains a partial list of the many professional organizations.

Professional organizations can provide you with resources to support your practice. National organizations' websites often have amazing resources for educators. For example, the American Library Association provides resources for teachers who want to communicate with families about censorship, and the National Science Teaching Association provides lesson plans for teaching about agriculture and food, climate science, evolution, and many more topics. The Digital Library at the National Council for the Social Studies is a collection of classroom activities and teaching ideas. You may wish to use your organization's research summaries or position statements to communicate with parents or administrators about why you teach the way you do or to make changes that will improve outcomes for students. Research summaries may synthesize the latest research about an education issue or topic and often use friendly, accessible language to make recommendations about effective teaching strategies. Position statements generally summarize the organizations' point of view on a particular topic or provide a rationale for a specific aspect of teaching.

When you join a professional organization, you will often receive their journal or newsletter. You may read about other teachers' classrooms and schools that give you new ideas to try with your students or read about the latest research in your area. When Devon was teaching fourth grade in rural Michigan, she looked forward to receiving her copy of *Language Arts*, the elementary-focused journal of the National Council of Teachers of English journal every month. *Language Arts* helped her connect with a community of educators who were trying innovative practices. Hearing from other teachers about the ways they incorporated reading and writing in the classroom became powerful reinforcement for her own practice.

Professional Organizations
Professional Organizations for Content Teachers

American Council on the Teaching of Foreign Languages
American Library Association
American School Band Directors Association
Computer Science Teachers Association
Global Language Project
International Council of Sport Science and Physical Education
International Federation of Adapted Physical Activity
International Literacy Association
International Society for Technology in Education
National Association of Agricultural Educators
National Association for Gifted Children
National Association for Music Education
National Art Education Association
National Business Education Association
National Council of Teachers of English
National Council of Teachers of Mathematics
National Science Teaching Association
National Council for the Social Studies
Society of Health and Physical Educators
TESOL International Association

Professional Organizations for Teachers of All Subjects

American Council on Rural Special Education
Association for Childhood Education International
American Federation of Teachers
Association for Middle Level Education
Council for Exceptional Children
National Association for the Education of Young Children
National Association for Gifted Children
National Association for Multicultural Education
National Education Association
National Indian Education Association
National Rural Education Association

Professional organizations also have national and regional conferences that you may be able to attend. At conferences, you can hear from nationally known speakers and attend sessions by other educators who share successful ideas for the classroom and let you learn about education in other states. National conferences can be hard to attend if they are located far from your district in expensive locations. Regional chapters of national organizations bring together educators from a particular region of the country and might have meetings that are more accessible. For example, the National Association for Multicultural Education (NAME) has eight regional chapters and each of them typically has local conferences in addition to the national meeting (see https://www.nameorg.org/name_regions_states_chapter.php).

But perhaps the most important reason to join a professional organization is to build a network of educators who are doing the same or similar work as you are. You might meet colleagues at the organization's conference or by joining an online community sponsored by the organization. Member newsletters or blogs will connect you to others who are doing work in your area. Not every organization provides the same resources, but all provide you with an opportunity to connect with leaders, teachers, and beginners in your field and resources that can help you be a better teacher.

We suggest you join a national or regional professional organization. We also recognize that national organizations can be overwhelming—with tens of thousands of members (or more) and conferences in giant convention centers that bring together teachers from across the nation or the globe. There are two ways you can build a smaller and more focused network. One is to join smaller groups within a national organization. National organizations have smaller communities or groups for educators with a specific interest, passion, or role. Becoming a member of a special interest community or a focus group can help you connect with educators who share your interests or who can support you as a rural teacher. For example, the National Association for the Education of Young Children (NAEYC) has an "interest forum" for Rural Children, Families, and Early Childhood Educators that includes an online community where people can build relationships. The second way to build a smaller, more local network is to join a state-level professional organization.

State-Level Professional Organizations

Most national organizations have chapters or affiliates that bring together educators within the state or, sometimes, within a particular area or region of a state. For example, the National Council of Teachers of Mathematics has at least one and sometimes several affiliate chapters in all 50 states in the US, most provinces in Canada, and even in the Virgin Islands (see https://www.nctm.org/Affiliates/Directory/). The NREA has state level organizations in many states, and you are guaranteed to meet other rural educators through this organization (see https://www.nrea.net/State_Affiliates). Your state affiliate will likely name a rural teacher of the year every year—a competition you may enter and win someday! States also have chapters of the American Federation of Teachers and the National Education Association, the two main teachers' unions States may also have their own unique organizations.

State-level organizations can provide many of the resources and professional learning opportunities of larger national organizations, but they can also help you meet other teachers in your area. If you are the only educator in your subject area at your rural school, your state organization might be a good way to build your professional network. You might also find opportunities for leadership in your state organization if you are an active member.

State-level professional organizations also host local conferences and professional development opportunities. Summer and even school year professional learning opportunities can sustain your teaching and help you improve your practice. They also provide you with an opportunity to meet colleagues who are teaching the same grade or subject as you or who have the same interests as you.

It may take some trial and error to find the right professional organization, or combination of professional organizations, for you. If you are currently a student in a teacher education program, you might consider joining several organizations so you can get a sense of the benefits they offer for a cheaper rate. Most organizations provide a substantial discount for students.

For Discussion

Ask your professors and mentor teachers which organizations they have joined over their career and how membership in an organization has helped them succeed.

Use Social Media to Build Professional Learning Networks

Another way to build peer relationships outside of school is to develop an online professional learning network via social media. Especially if you play a unique role in your school (for example, you are the only science, art, or third-grade teacher), but even if you have supportive colleagues and peers in similar roles, it can be beneficial to build networks with educators over social media.

Whatever social media platforms you use (and they change pretty rapidly) there are educators who post or blog regularly about teaching. You can find other educators who teach your grade or subject and who think about teaching like you do on just about any platform, and many platforms have education-focused communities that you can participate in. Many teachers use Twitter to share resources and tell stories from their classrooms. Tumblr, Facebook, Instagram, and even TikTok have educator communities.

Finding other teachers is as simple as searching for lists of teachers you would like to interact with. The Twitter educator community is very large. A search for "history teachers on Twitter" nets a list of hundreds of teachers with #historyteacher in their bio. Or search your chosen platform for specific hashtags such as #4thgrade or #musicteacher. Closed groups limit membership to people who are educators and you may need to request to be allowed to join.

Sometimes the online teacher community is more social. As we write this, there are teachers on Tumblr who participate in a fall gift exchange and send small gifts to teachers they have never met (Tumblr Teacher Gift Exchange), post pictures of their outfits on Fridays (#fashionableteacher), and develop meaningful friendships (#educhums).

Social media communities also go way beyond the social—online teachers share lesson plan ideas, get feedback on how to prepare for interviews or mentor a student teacher, puzzle through how to handle a particular discipline issue, and share all kinds of support. The We Are Teachers HELPLINE! group on Facebook (https://www.facebook.com/groups/weareteachershelpline/) and the #edchat on Twitter have thousands of members who chat about teaching, and there are other, more specific shared groups you can join. There are educator communities focused on particular technology tools or platforms (e.g. Nearpod or Google Classroom) and communities focused on particular content areas or other aspects of teaching. On any given day, teachers may be joining together for Twitter chats by following a particular hashtag. You can join the weekly #RuralEdChat to connect with other rural teachers or find a calendar of Twitter chats at https://sites.google.com/site/twittereducationchats/education-chat-calendar.

For Discussion

With your peers, visit several social media platforms of your choosing. Find posts or communities relating to education and teaching. What do you see there? What kinds of things are teachers talking about? Do posts have a social or professional focus? Are they positive and supportive? Compare each platform. Which seems most useful for you as a beginning teacher?

Whatever social media platform you decide to use, there are several things to keep in mind:

1   *Be discerning.* You might find that a particular community or blogger is mostly negative, complaining about their work and students. Or maybe they make unprofessional posts. Don't be afraid to leave one group and join another if you find that a community is not helpful or does not share your values.

2   *Beware of the time suck.* Social media can provide you with a supportive community or helpful professional learning opportunities. Social media can also suck up hours of time. Keep track of how much time you are spending and whether or not that time is helping you as a teacher.

3   *Be professional.* Remember that no matter how tightly you lock down the privacy, social media is never really completely private. Teachers have lost their jobs because of posts on social media. There are steps you can take. One is to be sure to separate your professional and your personal social media accounts. A second is to make sure that you do not post anything that you would not want families or your administrators to see.

4   *Respect privacy rights.* Be sure to respect your students' privacy rights and be sure you have permission to share students' images and quotes online. Even if it's really funny to share a students' work, doing so without their permission is a violation of federal laws and can have dire consequences. You can arrange or crop your photos so that no faces or personally identifiable information are shown and still share your classroom décor and teaching successes.

Find Colleagues at Professional Learning Opportunities

As we described above, state and national professional organizations often host in-person and online professional learning opportunities such as workshops and conferences. We hope you will have many more opportunities to attend workshops and participate in other professional learning opportunities as you attend workshops, conferences, institutes, or fellowships hosted by your district, regional education agencies, non-profit groups, and many others. Whatever your interests and focus area, you can likely find professional learning opportunities to support your learning. Museums and libraries host workshops focusing on their collections or how to have a maker space in your classroom. Teach Plus and the Education Policy Fellowship Program provide year-long fellowships focusing on education policy. National non-profits offer workshops on everything from teaching materials science and engineering (ASM Materials Education Foundation) to family and community engagement (Institute for Educational Leadership). After your third year of teaching, you might decide to work on being certified by the National Board for Professional Teaching Standards, a year-long process that recognizes accomplished teaching practice.

You can build your professional learning network at workshops and professional development sessions like these. Well-designed professional learning opportunities will include time to get to know and build relationships with the other learners who are participating—the relationships can be as or more important than the content you are meant to learn. But even if you are attending just a one-day workshop, you can introduce yourself and get to know the other teachers who are participating. If you pay attention in order to find others who share your values and interest in rural education, if you share your contact information and stay in touch afterwards, you might find colleagues who become part of your network of colleagues. Tracei, as described in the opening example, participated in both the National Writing Project and the TOLI workshops. She built amazing relationships that collaborate around teaching and that sustain her as a teacher.

Find Your People (They Could be Anywhere!)

As you go about building your professional network, remember that civic leaders and volunteers in your community can also become peers and colleagues. Local business owners may be a good source of perspective as you consider preparing your students for work after school. Local non-profits may be good partners to help incorporate service learning into your curriculum. You might collaborate with local day care providers or arts and service organizations or churches or other organizations. Community members can be important allies.

In 2009 in Red Bluff, California, a group of community leaders began to meet to discuss their fears and hopes for the future of their small town. These business owners, social service employees, and educators who live in Tehama County expressed concerns about unsatisfactory high school graduation rates and low expectations for college attendance. They knew from the research that higher education levels in their community would contribute to more economic opportunity and better health outcomes. Out of these conversations, the group Expect More Tehama formed with the goal of increasing educational expectations for their youth. Members of this group recognize that in a rural community, traditional decision makers are not separate or untouchable because everyone is connected. They know that schools are the center of their community and everything they do should tie back into raising educational opportunities for their future leaders, so they collaborate with local teachers by promoting mentoring programs, arranging local internships, and supporting summer academic programs.

In any community, you can find colleagues who will help you achieve your goals in your classrooms, not to mention become amazing friends and mentors. Just be sure to respect your students' rights to privacy and follow guidelines from the Family Educational Rights and Privacy Act (the federal law that states that students and families have a right to privacy about educational records) when you are sharing information about your class with anyone outside of school.

Many different factors influence the type of professional network you will develop as a teacher, but also stay open to learning and contributing in many different contexts. Who are the peers who reassure you in your purpose and affirm your beliefs? And also, who are the colleagues and community members who might challenge you to see different perspectives? In what areas do you most need outside support? And where are your unique skills and talents best offered to create a thriving community? Knowing where to look for mentors and colleagues will set you on a path to success as a rural teacher. However, everyone with whom you interact can be a source of learning. Be prepared to connect with others as you grow and develop as a teacher.

References

Coburn, C. E., Russell, J. L., Kaufman, J. H., & Stein, M. K. (2012). Supporting sustainability: Teachers' advice networks and ambitious instructional reform. *American Journal of Education*, *119*(1), 137–182. doi: https://10.1086/667699

Eckert, L. S., & Alsup, J. (2014). *Literacy teaching and learning in rural communities: Problematizing stereotypes, challenging myths*. Routledge.

Eisner, E. (2002). *What the arts teach and how it shows*. Yale University Press.

International Literacy Association. (2017). *Content area and disciplinary literacy: Strategies and frameworks* [*Literacy leadership brief*]. Newark, DE: International Literacy Association. https://www.literacyworldwide.org/docs/default-source/where-we-stand/ila-content-area-disciplinary-literacy-strategies-frameworks.pdf?sfvrsn=e180a58e_6

Jordon, A. K. (2019). *Early retention in rural schools: Alternate route teachers' perspectives* (Doctoral dissertation). Mississippi State University. https://hdl.handle.net/11668/14531

Kraft, M. A., & Papay, J. P. (2014). Can professional environments in schools promote teacher development? Explaining heterogeneity in returns to teaching experience. *Education Evaluation and Policy Analysis, 36*(4), 476–500. doi: https://10.3102/0162373713519496

10

Policy and the Rural Teacher

Mrs. Williams is teaching fifth-grade science. Her students are using iPads to research information about the ecosystem of a river in their rural community. Mrs. Williams teaches this unit every year because she knows that river ecosystems are part of the mandated science curriculum for her grade level. She's using iPads because the school board recently approved the purchase of the iPads for each fifth-grade classroom in the district after a group of teachers presented research about their potential in the teaching and learning of science.

At the forefront of her mind is the upcoming state standardized test. Her students will likely see questions about river ecosystems. She doesn't know that testing in math, reading, and one other subject is mandated by the federal government in order for her state to access federal funding, and her state has opted to assess science in fifth grade. She is well aware, however, that this particular test is required by her state and will be used to assign a letter grade to her school.

On Friday, she'll collect her paycheck. Her salary reflects the salary scale for educators that has been set by her state. She is an active member of her teacher's union and is optimistic that the union and the state will be able to successfully negotiate a new pay scale next year. However, she worries about reaching an agreement on health care in this round of negotiations. Her state is one of a handful that requires teachers to pay for the cost of their substitutes in the event of extended absences. Her union is working at the state level to get this policy thrown out, but until then, her union will negotiate for a strong health care package.

There are 27 students in her classroom. It is a state law that there can be no more than 28 students in any middle school classroom. Many of her students have water bottles and she has provided bottles for those who don't have one. Last spring, one of her colleagues gave a presentation to the school board about research suggesting that hydration can impact learning. In response, the board approved a new district policy that all students could keep a water bottle with them at all times.

Mrs. Williams recently received a note from her principal reminding her to tell parents about the upcoming state tests. Specifically, the principal wanted parents to be reminded to make sure that their children get a good's night sleep, eat a good breakfast, and have a healthy snack for testing. Some of her students ride the bus for over an hour to and from school. Many catch the bus as early as 6:30 in the morning and don't return until almost 5:00 in the evening. If the students are involved in after school activities such as the upcoming school play, they won't get home to have dinner and start homework until almost 8 pm. Mrs. Williams wondered how it would be possible for parents to follow through on the principal's request in the hours before 6:30 am and after 8 pm. Many parents work multiple jobs or odd hours. With the nearest full-service grocery store located over an hour's drive from the community, it would take an entire evening to travel to and from a store that sells fresh food. Mrs. Williams sends the email as directed but plans to make a trip to the grocery store for breakfast and snacks on testing day after she picks up her own children from the elementary school.

When Mrs. Williams was in her teacher preparation program, she planned to be the kind of teacher who was collegial but worked mostly independently behind a closed door. She didn't see teaching as a political activity, nor herself as a political person. Her involvement with her teacher's union opened her eyes to the extent to which almost everything thing she does in the classroom is an outcome of a policy decision, and how her union affords her the opportunity to make positive change for her students.

Policy Matters

Policy matters. Everything you do in the classroom will be shaped by one or more policies set by different bodies at different levels including building, district, state, and federal. Policy is a slippery concept to define. By policy we mean anything that guides or directs action (Williams, 2002). Policy includes state and federal laws, regulations established by the state or U.S. Department of Education, guidelines set by the local school board, and decisions that administrators make about what can and cannot happen in schools and classrooms. You or your family might have policies about homework or bedtime or whether you eat dinner at the table or in front of the TV. Behind your closed classroom door, engaged in small group discussions of an assigned reading, policy can seem irrelevant and hard to influence. However, policy influences everything you do in the classroom and teachers have an important role to play in understanding and influencing policy.

Your choices as an educator can be constrained or enabled, at least in part, by local, state, and federal policies. The table below provides examples of policies, policy makers, and the types of questions the policies are intended to answer (United States Senate, n.d.).

Action or Outcome/ Subject of the Policy	Policy Maker(s) Who Might Have an Impact	Policy Intention
Required state tests	Federal State	To know what students are learning at school
School accountability	Federal State	To determine if schools are doing a good job?
Student enrollment in your district	State	To establish boundaries of the school district
Furniture in your classroom	State (funding) School board Building administrator	To provide a place for students to learn
Content of the curriculum	State Board of Education School Board Curriculum Committee Curriculum Director	To provide guidance about what students should learn and what teachers should teach
Tardy policies	School board Building administrator Teacher	To decrease interruptions and maximize learning time

For Discussion

Add to the table. Think about any aspect of the school day: the school calendar, the time school starts, the students in the classroom, the dress code, the curriculum, the building, and classroom set up. Brainstorm other characteristics about your school or school community. Each of these characteristics is the result of a decision or a set of decisions. What decision was made (what was the policy?) Who do you think makes those decisions? What might be the intention or intentions that prompted each decision?

In this chapter, we provide a framework for thinking about policy and its influence on teaching and learning. We believe this is important so that you can understand and help to shape the policies that surround your work. When things you are asked to do in your classroom seem like they don't make sense, considering the policy intention behind the decision (e.g. understanding textbook policies or assessment policies) can help you make sense of the policy and decide what to do in your classroom.

It is necessary to recognize that what happens in a classroom is a result of multiple levels of policy making. The most visible of educational policies are decided at three levels: federal, state, and local. Governing bodies at each of these levels have the authority to enact legislation and develop regulations and guidance that influence the implementation of policy. As we discuss federal, state, and local policies, we will use multiple terms to refer to policy.

Terms	Definition of Term
Policy	Policies are anything that guides action and can range from formal public laws to individual guidelines that serve as the basis for decisions and actions.
Legislation	Legislation refers to the laws written and passed by a legislating body such as U.S. Congress or the state legislature. Legislation can also refer to laws passed by local governing bodies such as cities and counties. Large federal legislation may be divided into multiple sections known as titles.
Laws	Legislation creates a set of laws or rules that govern actions and, generally, the consequences for not following the law. A law may also be referred to as an act or a statute.

(Continued)

Terms	Definition of Term
Regulations	Regulations are rules set by an agency or department. In some states, these are called *administrative rules*. Regulations are generally more specific than legislation and define how the law will be enacted or enforced. State and federal regulations are generally enforceable, and there is usually a process of formal rule-making that requires public input before regulations are set. At the federal level, regulations are published in the Federal Register: https://www.archives.gov/federal-register/publications.
Guidelines	State and federal agencies may also issue guidelines for how to interpret or enact a particular law or policy. Guidelines can be issued by a public agency but do not need to follow the rule-making process required for regulations. Guidelines are recommendations for practice and so do not have the same enforcement "teeth" as regulations and laws.

Federal, State, and Local Policy

Federal Policy

Federal laws are written and approved by U.S. Congress and apply to states and other U.S. territories (e.g. Puerto Rico). Federal legislation is usually written and passed in large, comprehensive acts that bundle together multiple provisions with different focus areas and that authorize spending for multiple programs. There are multiple pieces of federal legislation that impact day-to-day work in the classroom. We will highlight a few: the Every Student Succeeds Act [ESSA] (ESSA, 2015), the Individuals with Disabilities Act (IDEA) (U.S. Department of Education, n.d.), Section 504

For Discussion

What federal laws do you know about that influence what happens in the classroom? Have you heard of "ESSA," "IDEA," "Section 504," or "Perkins Career and Technical Education Act"? What do you know about them? Do a Google search if you are unfamiliar. These bills, and many others, establish rules and provide federal funding for education. Why might the federal government make laws to regulate and fund education?

of the Rehabilitation Act of 1973, and the Perkins Career and Technical Education Act (U.S. Department of Education, n.d.).

Every Student Succeeds Act

The federal legislation currently impacting K–12 teaching and learning the most is the Every Student Succeeds Act (ESSA, Public Law 114–95). ESSA is a re-authorization of the Elementary and Secondary Education Act of 1965 (ESEA). The original ESEA was signed into law by President Lyndon Johnson, who was actually a teacher long before he was the president. ESEA was part of the War on Poverty—the intent was to create programs and provide funding to improve educational outcomes for students from impoverished families. ESEA has had multiple iterations that define the federal role in K–12 education.

The current version of this act, ESSA, was passed at the end of 2015 (replacing the No Child Left Behind Act). ESSA is a complex act with many provisions. ESSA authorizes federal spending for K–12 education including federal funding for schools that serve low-income students (Title I), professional development (Title II), grants to states to improve education (Title IV), and many smaller programs such as funding for the education of students who are migrants and experiencing homelessness, and to support bilingual education. ESSA also authorizes multiple competitive grants that states and school districts can apply for. ESSA has "teeth" at the state level because states and schools must follow the laws established in ESSA in order to receive federal funding.

ESSA sets federal requirements for student assessment and school accountability. According to ESSA, states must have rigorous standards for what students should know and be able to do and an accountability system to determine whether schools are adequately helping students achieve those standards. Under ESSA, schools must assess students in reading and mathematics every year in grades 3–8 and once more during high school. Schools must also assess one additional subject (e.g. science or social studies) sometime during the elementary, middle, and secondary grades. States must ensure that at least 95% of students participate in testing and have an accountability system to determine which schools are succeeding and which are "failing" and will receive additional state supports. States have some flexibility in designing the system under which schools are to be judged, but it must include student test scores, student graduation rates and at least one other measure (e.g. student attendance or teacher engagement). Under ESSA, districts must provide families and the community with annual report cards about how schools are doing, and they must provide assessment results that are broken down by categories such as race, disability, and socioeconomic status. The requirement to provide disaggregated results is intended to ensure that schools serve all students well and that average scores do not mask whether schools are not serving a specific subgroup of students well.

ESSA presents some challenges for rural schools. For example, some have questioned whether the Title I funding formula that is meant to support education in schools serving low-income students is fair to rural districts (Alliance for Excellent Education & Rural School and Community Trust, 2016). Accountability measures may be challenging in rural schools, if, for example, states select to use online tests and rural schools have limited broadband access. Similarly, in schools with small populations, only a few low scores can have a big impact on the overall rating of a district (Reeves, 2003). On the other hand, ESSA authorizes a small but important funding program. The Rural Education Advancement Program provides small grants to rural schools that are very small or that serve high percentages of low-income students and it requires states to consult with rural districts in the development of state accountability plans (Brenner, 2016).

Individuals with Disabilities Education Act (IDEA)

The Individuals with Disabilities Education Act of 1990 (Public Law 101–476) is intended to ensure that students with disabilities are provided with education that is free and appropriate for their individual needs. IDEA is a revision of the Education for All Handicapped Children Act that was originally passed in 1975. IDEA requires schools to identify students with disabilities that adversely impact educational performance and to work with families to develop an Individualized Education Plan (IEP) that documents the services and accommodations that are to be provided to each student with a disability. Family members must be involved in developing plans for students with disabilities, and students must be taught in the least restrictive environment possible, meaning that students who are able to learn with their typically developing peers must be allowed to do so. IDEA also authorizes grants to states to support the implementation of special education and early intervention programs in schools and communities.

IDEA is intended to ensure that all students in the US receive an appropriate education.

This is an important law and has led to improvements in education outcomes for students with disabilities. Rural schools, however, may be challenged to comply with all of the provisions of IDEA. Rural schools sometimes struggle to recruit teachers who are trained and certified to teach special education. The funding formula authorized in IDEA is based on the number of students, and rural schools may not receive funding that is sufficient to meet the needs of all students, particularly students with a low-incidence disability. Some rural schools are challenged to provide services to students with IEPs that require costly equipment, transportation, or extensive training.

Section 504 of the Rehabilitation Act of 1973

Section 504 is one section of the larger Rehabilitation Act of 1973. This section is a civil rights mandate. It states that schools cannot discriminate against students who are handicapped (students who have disabilities) if they receive any federal funding. Under Section 504, schools must identify students who have a physical or mental impairment that limits a major life activity (e.g. walking, seeing, hearing, caring for oneself, etc.) and have a plan in place to ensure that the student can get the same or a comparable education. Students may have a 504 plan, even if their disability does not have an adverse impact on their educational attainment. For example, students with asthma or who use a wheelchair must be provided with appropriate accommodations and services so that they can learn in the least restrictive environment (deBettencourt, 2002).

Carl D. Perkins Career and Technical Education Act (Perkins CTE)

Schools have a long history of providing vocational education to students, and federal funding has supported vocational education since 1917 (Dortch, 2012), in part because of the important relationship between technical and vocational education and the economy. The most recent version of Perkins CTE passed in 2018. Now titled the Strengthening Career and Technical Education for the 21st Century Act, the Perkins CTE Act is intended to support and spur improvement in career-focused and technical education in schools. CTE programs in schools help prepare students for jobs in their local and regional communities and may lead to credentials or certificates that allow students to go to work right after high school. Perkins CTE Act states that schools must align CTE programs and pathways with postsecondary and industry opportunities in the region.

Career and technical education play an important role in rural communities. Employment opportunities in many rural communities are changing—traditional and new occupational opportunities increasingly require critical skills that can be learned or prepared for in CTE programs.

However, rural schools may face challenges in implementing effective CTE programs, including offering a variety of choices to students, recruiting and retaining CTE teachers, and funding the equipment and classrooms needed for CTE as local industries change and become more technological (Mezera, 2019).

Other Federal Legislation

The examples above are not the only federal legislation that impacts K–12 education. Education advocates who are interested in policy also pay attention to other federal legislation that impacts K–12 education. For example, the federal school lunch and breakfast programs are funded through the U.S. Department of Agriculture. Health-care legislation impacts the kinds of school nursing programs that can be paid for in rural schools. Immigration and welfare policies impact students and families in rural districts. The Higher Education Act (HEA) authorizes financial aid programs for postsecondary education and scholarships for teachers who are preparing to teach critical shortage subjects such as math. Financial aid programs authorized by HEA sometimes fund dual enrollment courses offered in rural districts and influence rural students' decisions to attend postsecondary education. These and many other federal bills have an impact on rural schools.

The Role of the U.S. Department of Education

The federal agency responsible for implementation of most education legislation is the U.S. Department of Education. You have likely heard of the current Secretary of Education, the official who heads the Department of Education that is appointed by the president (If not, go look them up). The work of the U.S. Department of Education may seem very far removed from the day-to-day work of the classroom. However, the Department of Education, under the leadership of the Secretary of Education, can have a profound impact on what and how you teach. The Department of Education is responsible for the implementation of ESSA and IDEA. The Department has the authority to create regulations and guidelines that determine how states and districts must implement the general provisions of these bills. For example, states must create an accountability plan consistent with the provisions of ESSA, described above. The Department of Education has the authority to review those plans and has provided guidance about how to meet the various parts of ESSA that require states to assess students, identify low performing schools, and design programs to help schools improve. The Department of Education also implements the HEA, which is the federal legislation that provides for financial aid and other programs that impact colleges and universities, including student loan repayment.

State Policy

For Discussion

Maybe you have seen recent articles in the news about teacher salaries, teacher shortages, school funding, reading education, or other education topics. Chances are, these are state-level policy issues that are being discussed in your state. Which state-level education policy decisions have been considered in your state? What are the state advocacy groups sharing information about state policy?

Many educational decisions and policies are set at the state level. The state legislature has the authority to pass any number of laws that influence teachers and schools. States may legislate licensure requirements for teachers and school administrators (e.g. licensure exams, course or GPA requirements, etc.). The number of days students attend in a school year is usually a state mandate (typically somewhere around 180 days). Some state policies require schools to begin after Labor Day. An increasing number of states are allowing schools to select a four-day, rather than a five-day, school week. States also determine specific requirements for student testing, guidelines for participation in athletics, and graduation requirements. Perhaps most significantly, states provide a significant portion of the funding that allow schools to operate.

States set laws, which serve as a general framework, and state Departments and Boards of Education further interpret and expand on those laws through regulation and guidance. For example, Mississippi has laws that new teachers must complete an approved teacher preparation program and have passing scores on specific exams in order to receive a teaching license. The Mississippi State Board of Education has determined the specifics of these requirements, including what counts as an "approved program" and what courses must be included for each degree program, which test is required for which teaching license, and the minimum score needed to pass the test. It can be helpful to know whether requirements that come from the state are requirements that are authorized by legislation that was passed by your state elected officials, or if the policies that impact you are regulations or guidance set by your state Board or Department of Education. FindLaw is a website hosted by Thompson Reuters that summarizes state and national laws (see: https://education.findlaw.com).

Often, particularly in states with large urban areas, state legislators do not understand or address the unique needs of rural schools which can lead to inequities in funding or policies that do not work well in rural places. However, rural educators can work together to make sure that their legislators understand rural contexts and pass laws that help rural schools. For example, rural education advocates in some states, including both Colorado and Missouri, have worked to educate lawmakers about rural education contexts. This has led to more equitable funding formulas in some states and rural-specific legislation in some places such as laws that allow districts to choose to have a four-day school week to help recruit and retain teachers and cut down on transportation costs (Boshart, 2020; Turner et al., 2018).

Local Policy

Public school districts are operated under the authority of a local school board. School board members may be elected or appointed (e.g. appointed by city or county governments) and are responsible for setting a vision and guiding the operation of the district and its schools. School board members are responsible for approving and guiding the day-to-day operation of schools. Typically, school boards approve and monitor the district budget, hire the superintendent, oversee the purchase of curriculum materials, and approve or set policies, such as the school calendar, dress code, and the code of conduct for students. Policies are also set by school district administrators, sometimes with the involvement or approval of the school board. Likewise, building administrators have some independence in setting building-level policy that directly impacts faculty and students.

School boards and administrators work within the framework of legislation and regulations set at the state and federal level. State boards of education, administrators, and teachers interpret laws and regulations and implement them in the classroom. While state and federal laws and regulations create boundaries for what must and must not happen in schools, there is still room for local control in many areas of teaching and learning. As a federal and state example, the federal government now requires that graduation rates be included in state accountability systems. States generally set the requirements that define what it takes to graduate and earn a diploma. School boards, administrators, and teachers make local decisions and set local policies that impact graduation rates—including everything from summer school and remediation programs to discipline codes, attendance policies, and the school climate. At the local level, rural schools and districts implement state and federal policies to the best of their ability as they work to meet the needs of rural students and communities.

For Discussion

Attend a school board meeting for your local school district. Or, if you cannot attend a meeting in person, look online and find a video recording or the agenda and minutes for a board meeting for a school district (e.g. where you went to high school, a district nearby, or where you have field experiences). Observe, watch or read the minutes for the meeting. What happens during the meeting? What appears to be important to them? What decisions do they make? What do you think this means for your work as a teacher?

How Schools Are Funded

One big issue that impacts what happens in your classroom and your work as a rural teacher is school funding. School funding comes from multiple sources including, local, state, and federal funding, and, in some cases, competitive grant funding.

Local Funding

One major source of school funding is the revenue collected through local property taxes. Working within parameters set by state and local governments, schools set a property tax rate, or a "millage." Local millage rates specify the amount that property owners pay in annual taxes based on the value of their property. If school taxes are 14 mills, a person with a home valued at $100,0000 will pay $1,400 each year to support the local school district.

Basing school funding on local property taxes can have a negative impact on rural school districts. The fact that school funding is largely based on local property tax revenues is responsible for large differences in per-pupil funding from state to state and community to community. Taxes on undeveloped land with no homes or industry can be very low, whereas taxes on land with multiple houses, high home prices, and/or thriving industries can result in much higher property tax revenues. Some rural school districts are located in geographic areas where much of the property is publicly owned. No one pays property taxes on public lands, so schools near or inside of national parks, national forests, state game areas, or other public lands collect less revenue from the property within their district boundaries. In locations where land is very valuable, property taxes can provide sufficient resources for rural schools, however, in many rural schools this is not the case, which means that rural schools must heavily rely on state and federal funding in order to operate.

State Funding

States play an important role in school funding and provide about half of the revenue that most schools use to operate. States generally fund local schools on a per-pupil basis, with funding calculated based on average daily attendance or student enrollment. State funding that is based on the number of students enrolled puts small and rural schools at a disadvantage. Even schools with small populations need adequate libraries and facilities for physical education, and access to an engaging curriculum that includes courses such as world languages, arts, and advanced mathematics and science. For small schools, state funding that is based on student enrollment typically does not provide appropriate support to offer courses beyond the basics, particularly in comparison to more wealthy suburban districts that have the option of using property tax to supplement state funding. Additionally, rural schools often have added costs compared to more urban and suburban schools. Transportation, for example, is a significant expenditure for rural districts. To a greater and lesser degree, states also provide funding that is not entirely based on student enrollment, but this funding may not always be sufficient in rural districts.

Federal Funding

Federal funding makes up a small portion of the revenue provided to support the operation of public schools. Federal funds are provided to districts to support the implementation of special education programs, to support school lunch and breakfast programs, Perkins CTE programs, and for teacher professional development. Schools that serve higher percentages of students from low-come families receive what is called Title I funding. Other funding is provided on a per-pupil formula basis to support students who are homeless, whose families are migrant workers, and who speak a language other than English as their first language. As with state funding, rural schools may not receive sufficient funding when money is allocated based on student enrollment. Schools must provide teachers and programs to meet all students' needs but may not have the necessary resources if funding is based on a per pupil allocation and only a handful of students qualify for a particular program (AASA, 2017).

Two federal programs are especially relevant to rural schools. The Rural Education Advancement Program provides a small amount of money to very small rural schools and to rural and low-income schools, recognizing that because of factors such as transportation and low student to teacher ratios, rural schools can be more expensive to operate (Indiana Department of Education, n.d.). In addition, a federal program called Impact Aid provides some revenue to school districts that miss out on property taxes because their district includes federal lands such as national parks or military bases. Although there are many different federal programs, overall, federal revenue makes up less than 10% of most schools' budgets. Local and state funding is by far the largest portion of the funds that schools use to operate.

Competitive Funding

It is important to note that many federal and even state programs provide funding through competitive grants. Schools and districts must apply for competitive grant funding by writing grant applications that are judged based on merit and potential for impact. Many rural schools can and do successfully compete for grant funding, and grants can provide important resources for some rural schools. However, rural schools are often at a disadvantage when funding is based on competition. Unlike larger and more urban districts, it is unusual for rural schools to have a dedicated grant writer on staff. Instead the responsibility for finding and applying for grants falls to an already busy person such as the principal, curriculum director, or even classroom teachers when they can find the time to apply for extra funding. Rural schools may struggle to compete for funding that is distributed in this way.

Inequities in Funding

The way that schools are funded in the U.S. creates disparities. Schools in some states have significantly more resources than others (Kozol, 2012; Schafft, 2016). Sometimes these differences are stark. For example, Utah, Idaho, and Mississippi spend less than $8,000 per pupil enrolled in public school, while Connecticut and New York spend over $18,000 per pupil. Yet children in all five states are held to the same standards of federal accountability (Baker et al., 2018).

Not only are there disparities from state to state, but also within states. Some districts are better funded than others, with districts receiving less than half as much in funding, per student, than districts in another area of the state. For example, districts located in Northern Virginia near Washington D.C., where the population is dense and property values are high, annual per-pupil expenditures are over $19,000. At the other end of the spectrum, per-pupil expenditures in the lowest funded district in Virginia were under $9,000 in the same year (Virginia Department of Education, 2017). These disparities have a profound impact on students' education.

Policy and the Rural Teacher

As you can see, from funding to curriculum to the daily schedule—your work as a rural teacher will be influenced by policy. State and federal policies may or may not take the unique needs and strengths of rural schools into consideration. Even local policies may not work well for all students and have a place-specific impact. For example, a school start time at 7:30 am may work well for students who live close to school but may mean that students with long bus rides are disadvantaged because their school day starts so early.

You may find that there are policies that you feel are unfair or have a negative impact on you and your students. In Chapter 2, we suggested a framework for thinking about social justice and rural schools. Fraser's framework can provide a lens for evaluating policies that impact schools. A focus on economic justice might lead you to think about whether policies, particularly funding, are distributed fairly across rural places. Funding formulas based on enrollment or property taxes may be a barrier to distributive justice. A focus on cultural justice can lead you to examine whether policies value the cultures and traditions of all members of your community. For example, in the rural south many families attend church services on Wednesday nights, and districts often do not hold evening events on Wednesdays to accommodate this cultural practice. Policies can be critiqued for whether they meet the needs of all members of your rural community. A focus on political justice can lead you to ask whether the voices of rural families, teachers, and administrators were consulted in the development of policy, for example, if states implement online testing requirements without first asking whether all schools have adequate access to high-speed internet.

For Discussion

Look up the policies related to teacher licensure in your state. Do you have to complete a degree program? Pass one or more tests? Complete student teaching? Have a certain GPA or certain course? Use the framework of economic, cultural, and political justice to critique those policies. Might those policies impact different people across your state in different ways? Might they pose barriers for rural schools? In what way? How do licensure policies recognize or fail to recognize the values and needs of rural people or communities? Were preservice teachers or educators involved in setting those policies? Are there barriers to justice in your state's licensure policies?

If a policy concerns you on the grounds of distributive, recognition, or representative justice, what can you do then? One of the things to remember is that policy actions do not always have to be grand gestures. While few teachers have the opportunity to propose new legislation, instances of teacher activism and engagement are becoming more common. Recently, we have seen teachers draw attention to low salaries by striking or marching at their state capital and advocating for changes in district procedures to benefit their students. These ways of getting involved can have an impact and we encourage you to participate as you are comfortable. Each teacher needs to find their own path to advocacy that will help them accomplish their purpose as a teacher. Some will be involved from the very beginning and others will grow into the role of advocate over time. Some will join political movements or protests, while others will advocate by showing up at school board meetings or working with the principal to find a solution for the student who never gets to school on time. We believe that all rural teachers are advocates one way or the other. Sometimes, teachers advocate for change. But lack of action is also a way of advocating. By not speaking up, teachers advocate for, or signal acceptance of, the policies that are currently in place. There is no escaping the political reality of teaching.

Often, advocacy actions are smaller than marching on your state's capital. For example, state departments of education often have a public comment period when the public is invited to provide feedback on new regulations. Rural teachers can and should provide feedback about whether or not new policies will work in rural schools or whether there are special considerations that might make proposed changes difficult to implement. Your point of view as a person who is actually working in a classroom every day (or preparing to work in a classroom) can be incredibly powerful.

It can feel daunting to try and keep up with all of the things that are happening in local, state, and federal policy. One way to stay informed is to become a member of professional organizations. Many state and national professional organizations, such as your teacher's union and organizations of teachers of a particular subject or content area (e.g. National Council of Teachers of Mathematics, Council for Exceptional Children, National Rural Education Association, etc.) provide their members with information about pending federal legislation. State chapters and organizations often monitor state legislators and Departments of Education. You may find that these can be helpful sources of information. Some organizations will notify members of an opportunity to provide public commentary on an issue. This is an excellent means of making your voice heard. For example, the Mississippi Department of Education recently asked for public comments about potential changes to state licensure requirements. Many preservice teachers chimed in about how those changes would impact them. Professional organizations also have a variety of resource that can help you understand and advocate for the policies that benefit schools, teachers, and students. Position papers, issue summaries, research reports, and other advocacy tools can help you better understand the issues and articulate your stance to the decision makers that matter.

Carlos has been very concerned about how much time his students are required to spend taking practice tests in advance of standardized testing. He knows the best way to prepare for an assessment is to learn the material, and that there is no evidence that repeated practice tests boost test scores. He has seen news articles about proposed legislation to limit the days spent on testing in the state. However, Carlos knows that decisions about how to prepare for state assessments are typically a local decision. Schools implement practices that they believe will best help students prepare for the test. If Carlos wants to influence how much time students spend practicing test taking, he could focus on finding research or sharing evidence with his school administrator rather than trying to talk with his state legislator.

When you care about a specific issue or outcome, one of the first things to consider is to figure out which is the right venue for any kind of advocacy work. For example, it can be helpful to know whether the issue you care about is a state, federal, or local issue, or if the issue you are concerned about is a law, a regulation, guideline, or an issue of local implementation. Your actions may have the most impact if you advocate with the policy maker that has the most influence over the issue you care about, the way that Carlos did (see call-out box above). When you do decide to advocate, it is important to plan carefully and to be aware of state and local rules around advocacy. Some states have rules that prohibit teachers from certain types of activism, or there may be rules that prohibit you from certain actions during the school day. Knowing the rules about advocacy work can help you decide what to say and when. In the call-out box below, we offer a few suggestions for planning your advocacy work. In addition, there are many online resources that can help you work as an effective advocate for rural students and schools.

Talking with Decision Makers

There are many online resources for helping prepare to talk with decision makers and encourage you to use those resources to prepare for your meeting. See, for example, the resources available at the sites of the National State Teacher of the Year (https://www.nnstoy.org/download/Engaged%20FINAL.pdf) and the Lead with Languages advocacy resources of ACTFL (https://www.leadwithlanguages.org/calling-educators-language-advocacy-toolkit/).

If you are persistent and lucky enough to have the opportunity to talk to a decision maker there are a couple of things to remember:

- *Plan ahead.* You will often have only a short amount of time with a policy maker. Plan ahead so you can be articulate and concise.
- *Be specific.* It can be helpful to make a very specific request so that policy makers know exactly what action you are requesting.
- *Share evidence.* Evidence (research summaries and statistics about the impact of a decision can help justify your request). Policy makers have to make decisions about hundreds of topics and may not have expertise that you have.
- *Use stories and examples.* Concrete examples about the impact of a decision can be powerful and influential (Hollister, 2007).

Remember, there really is strength in numbers. The more voices that speak up about a specific issue, the more decision makers will understand its importance and impact.

In this chapter, we have provided just a brief introduction to education policy. We hope that you have a greater understanding of the many ways that your work as a teacher will be shaped by national, state, and local policy. The work of being a teacher is framed by federal legislation such as ESSA and IDEA. There is a great deal of variation about how states and local districts and schools work within that federal framework that makes it hard to draw generalizations. What is true across all settings is that your work as a rural educator will be influenced by the decisions—by the laws, regulations, and guidelines—set by policy makers outside of your classroom. Those decisions may work well for you and your students, or they may not meet the needs of your students the way you want them to. Policy makers, particularly at the state and national level, do not always understand the unique needs and characteristics of rural contexts. As a rural educator, you can use your expertise to be an advocate for policies that support your students and their families.

References

AASA, The School Superintendents Association. (2017). *Leveling the playing field for rural students.* https://www.aasa.org/uploadedFiles/Equity/AASA_Rural_Equity_Report_FINAL.pdf

Alliance for Excellent Education & Rural School and Community Trust. (2016). *Every Student Succeeds Act primer: Rural schools.* https://mk0all4edorgjxiy8xf9.kinstacdn.com/wp-content/uploads/2016/06/FINAL-ESSA_FactSheet_RuralSchools.pdf

Baker, B. D., Weber, M., Srikanth, A., Kim, R., & Atzbi, M. (2018). *The real shame of the nation: The causes and consequences of interstate inequity in public school investments.* Education Law Center. https:// drive.google.com/file/d/1cm6Jkm6ktUT3SQplzDFjJIy3G3iLWOtJ/view

Brenner, D. (2016). Rural educator policy brief: Rural education and the Every Student Succeeds Act. *The Rural Educator, 37*(2). doi: https://10.35608/ruraled.v37i2.271

Boshart, R. (2020, February 25). Gov. Kim Reynolds signs education funding bill: Money will help with transportation costs and per-pupil spending equity. *The Gazette.* https://www.thegazette.com/subject/news/government/gov-kim-reynolds-signs-education-funding-bill-rural-transportation-20200225

de Bettencourt, L. U. (2002). Understanding the differences between IDEA and Section 504. *Teaching Exceptional Children, 34*(3), 16–23.

Dortch, C. (2012). *Carl D. Perkins Career and Technical Education Act of 2006: Background and performance.* Congressional Research Service. https://fas.org/sgp/crs/misc/R42863.pdf

ESSA. (2015). *Every Student Succeeds Act of 2015, Pub. L. No. 114–95* § 114 Stat. 1177 (2015–2016).

Hollister, D. C. (2007). *A public policy primer: How to get off the sidelines and into the game.* Institute for Educational Leadership.

Indiana Department of Education. (n.d.). *Rural education achievement program.* https://www.doe.in.gov/sites/default/files/rural/rural-education-achievement-program.pdf

Kozol, J. (2012). *Savage inequalities: Children in America's schools.* Broadway Books.

Mezera, D. (2019). *How career technical education can help close the rural/urban education gap* [Web log post]. National Rural Education Association. https://www.nrea.net/Blog_Post?blogid=374011

Reeves, C. (2003). *Implementing the No Child Left Behind act: Implications for rural schools and districts.* North Central Regional Educational Laboratory. http://c3ta.org/kb_files/NCLB_RuralPolicyBrief.pdf

Schafft, K. A. (2016). Rural education as rural development: Understanding the rural school-community well-being linkage in a 21st century policy context. *Peabody Journal of Education, 91*(2), 137–154. doi: https://10.1080/0161956X.2016.1151734

Turner, J., Finch, K., & Uribe-Zarain, X. (2018). The economics of a four-day school week: Community and business leaders' perspectives. *Applied Economics and Finance, 5*(2), 168–174. http://redfame.com/journal/index.php/aef/article/view/2947

United States Senate. (n.d.). *Laws and Regulations.* https://www.senate.gov/reference/reference_index_subjects/Laws_and_Regulations_vrd.htm

U.S. Department of Education. (n.d.). *Carl D. Perkins Career and Technical Education Act of 2006: Reauthorization of Perkins.* https://www2.ed.gov/policy/sectech/leg/perkins/index.html

U.S. Department of Education. (n.d.). *About IDEA.* https://sites.ed.gov/idea/about-idea/

Virginia Department of Education. (2017). *Superintendent's annual report for Virginia.* http://www.doe.virginia.gov/statistics_reports/supts_annual_report/2015_16/table15.pdf

Williams, P. (2002). *Thought about food, a workbook on food security and influencing policy.* Atlantic Health Promotion Research Centre. http://www.foodthoughtful.ca

11

Responding to Trauma

Sharon is a rural teacher in Lake County, California. Her community has experienced wildfires, which are a new trauma layered onto existing generational traumas like poverty and drug use. Here she reflects:

> *We recently had a string of multiple devastation-level fires in our community. It's now a defining factor. People died. People lost their homes and belongings. People lost their jobs. Some of our biggest employers were destroyed. Kids were traumatized. Teachers too. Some families were displaced twice by two separate fires. Also, drugs have an impact here. Many of our students have parents who struggle with drug addiction. We have a high incidence of student learning disabilities because of the fetal impact of drugs. This contributes to lower levels of literacy achievement and achievement gaps. Our skills in the classroom and our abilities to connect with kids are needed in big ways. We want the students to feel like they are seen and heard at school. If one student is struggling with a connection to their teacher, there is another who knows them personally. When tragedy strikes, everyone in the school and community gets involved to help.*

There is an increasing awareness of the negative impact of trauma on students' well-being. It is more or less common knowledge now that trauma impacts students' behavior, sense of safety, and ability to learn at school. In rural schools, especially, where access to school counseling and other supports may be limited, it is necessary for all teachers to understand what trauma is, how it can manifest in young people, and how to help build resiliency as a typical classroom practice and in recovery from traumatic events. In addition, teachers must learn how to maintain their own health and well-being while attending to their students. This chapter is intended to provide you with resources that can help you prepare for and respond to trauma.

What Is Trauma?

Trauma is caused by negative events that overwhelm your ability to respond and adapt. It impacts your emotional, cognitive, physical, spiritual, and social abilities. We can call the deeply distressing experience itself a trauma, but this chapter will generally use trauma as "a term to describe the aftermath or impact of an event, whether real or perceived, that interrupts a person's ability to maintain a sense of psychological and/or physical safety and well-being" (Berardi & Morton, 2019, p. xiii). Trauma can have lasting adverse effects on mental, physical, social, emotional, or spiritual well-being.

Traumatic events take many forms. Trauma may occur in the form of natural disasters, like tornadoes, wildfires, or large-scale flooding, or human violence such as school shootings or domestic abuse. We can encounter traumatic events on a personal level, such as the illness or death of a family member, or homelessness. Trauma can also happen in either a collective or societal context, such as pandemics, natural disasters, or terrorist attacks.

Trauma can be a sudden, powerful event, but trauma can also manifest from systemic patterns or an ongoing series of circumstances that create persistently high levels of unresolved stress. There is some research that shows that children living with toxic levels of stress experience neurological changes in the brain that last a lifetime.

Someone who regularly experiences racism, prejudice, discrimination, or bullying can experience these events as trauma. Microaggressions, for example, are an on ongoing form of trauma. Microaggressions are usually brief but recurring actions, whether intentional or unintentional, that are derogatory or prejudicial insults toward a historically marginalized group. People who experience daily microaggressions over time are more likely to develop trauma as a result.

Adverse Childhood Experiences (ACEs) is a term used to describe potentially traumatic events that take place in childhood (Center for Youth Wellness, 2013). According to the Centers for Disease Control and Prevention, ACEs can be grouped into three categories: abuse, neglect, and household dysfunction. According to the CYW 2013 study in California, 62% of adults have experienced one ACE and 17% have experienced four or more.

Abuse	Neglect	Household Dysfunction
Physical Emotional Sexual	Physical Emotional	Mental illness Incarceration Violence Substance Abuse Divorce

Because ACEs occur in childhood during a time of heightened brain development, ACEs can have profound long-term impacts on students' health and well-being. A high ACE score is associated with increased risk of mental health issues, alcohol abuse, physical illness, disease, and disability, as well as an increase in suicide attempts and partner violence.

You can watch a short video about ACEs by viewing the Center for Disease Control's *Preventing Adverse Experiences Online Training Module* at https://www.youtube.com/watch?v=d-SSwYTe8TY.

Recognize Trauma

Trauma causes emotional, physical, and social responses that you can recognize. Not all children who experience a traumatic event will develop symptoms of traumatic stress. The amount of personal, familial, and community resources that students have to support them can determine the extent to which a child will recover from a traumatic event. Trauma can cause emotional responses that range from sadness, guilt, and fear to anger and shock. There is no normal reaction to trauma and no timeline for recovery. Responding to traumatic events often occurs in stages and varies depending on the scale and longevity of the event.

Trauma can cause behavior challenges. If children do not receive consistent relief from the trauma they experience, their nervous system continues to stay on high alert. In hyperarousal, the heart rate increases and a child will operate from a fight or flight response. Impulsivity or aggression related to the fight or flight response may appear as acts of aggression, defiance, or opposition (McGruder, 2019).

Trauma impacts the brain. The brain is made up of the brain stem (the part which controls automatic responses necessary for survival), the limbic region (including the amygdala and the hippocampus which are responsible for emotion and memory) and the cortex (the prefrontal cortex controls concentration and cognition). In response to trauma, the survival parts of the brain will cause the body to fight, flight, or freeze. If a person is experiencing ongoing trauma, the repeated primitive-type reactions in the brain stem and limbic region can interfere with the thinking part of the brain. The accumulation of disruption to the typical functioning of the parts of the brain can result in unhealthy and harmful outcomes. If stress is relieved quickly and consistently in early childhood, children develop the neural connections to handle stress and trauma in the future (Perry & Szalavitz, 2006). This is why it is critically important for teachers to work with their students to learn how to express their feelings and recognize how their emotions are related to life experiences.

For Discussion

Recall a time you experienced a "fight-or-flight" response. What caused this response? What did it feel like? What helped you recover from the response?

Young people are generally resilient, but children who experience several forms of crises or ongoing painful circumstances will deplete their ability to bounce back more quickly. It is natural to activate your alarm systems during a traumatic event. Post-Traumatic Stress Disorder (PTSD) is the name for what happens when mental and physical response systems stay activated even after a trauma, as a defense against future events. The body stays activated and can behave as though trauma is continuing even after it ends.

Trauma in Rural Communities

We believe that it is important for rural teachers to understand trauma, in part because some forms of trauma are more likely to be present at higher rates in rural communities. There are a number of reasons for this. Rural children are more likely to experience economic hardship than non-rural children and are therefore more likely to experience ACEs that are associated with poverty. According to the U.S. Department of Agriculture, in 2017, 23% of rural children were poor, compared to 18% of urban children. The combination of rurality and poverty can exacerbate trauma. Rural places may have higher rates of illness and disability, lack of access to health care (especially mental health services), lack of public transportation, economic instability, and alcohol abuse when compared to urban and suburban communities. According to the Pew Research Center (Parker et al., 2018), about half of rural residents cite drug addiction as a problem in their community. In one survey by the American Farm Bureau Federation and the National Farmers Union (AFBF & NFU, 2017), 74% of farmers and farm workers indicate they are directly impacted by opioid abuse either by knowing someone, having a family member addicted, having taken an illegal opioid or having dealt with addiction themselves.

Natural disasters are another type of traumatic stress that may impact rural communities. Natural disasters include events such as wildfires, floods, earthquakes, and tornados. Because rural economies are often based in agriculture or tourism or mining, natural disasters can have economic impacts beyond the immediate destruction and loss of life.

Human trafficking, the illegal act of transporting people for the purposes of coerced/forced labor or sexual exploitation, is a growing concern in some rural areas. People who have been trafficked can be hiding in plain sight, working in restaurants, hotels, meat packing plants, factories, and on farms. Young girls, both from the U.S. and other countries, are trafficked for prostitution and are often recruited through social media. Small communities along major interstate highways are common havens for this dehumanizing and traumatizing activity. Intense fear and language limitations can prevent victims from seeking help or escaping their traffickers. In rural communities, geographic isolation and lack of resources can hinder law enforcement in locating victims of human trafficking.

Trauma Response

Teachers make a difference. The teacher–student relationship is key to supporting the well-being of students, particularly those who have experienced trauma. But this work cannot be done solely by a single person. The entire school and community are needed to work together, especially in response to a collective traumatic event. While you play a key role as a teacher, you are not a trained counselor, and when a student exhibits psychological needs that are beyond your skill set, it is your responsibility to seek professional help for the child.

Establishing a supportive classroom environment is some of the most important work you will do as a teacher because trauma can be sudden and unexpected. Your efforts to build and sustain your classroom environment will ensure that your classroom is a soft landing spot for children who need one. Having classroom and school-wide protocols for reacting to unexpected events is also important. Especially if you are new to rural communities, idyllic images of rural places can sometimes prevent us from recognizing traumatic conditions. In order to respond to challenges, it's important to know what the challenges are and whom those challenges impact the most.

The following sections in this chapter will help you think about your role as a teacher in understanding, preparing for, and responding to trauma.

Social and Emotional Learning

The key in providing trauma recovery starts by creating an atmosphere of safety in a classroom based on predictable routines and respectful relationships. Having predictable routines provides students with a sense of stability and safety that supports them in working through their emotions. It is usually very comforting for students to get back to a routine after trauma, so returning to school and their familiar activities can provide a sense of stability.

It can be helpful to infuse social and emotional learning into every part of the school day as good daily practice. The Collaborative for Academic, Social, and Emotional Learning (CASEL) recommends that young people learn five core competencies through their interactions in the classroom, in the school, and in the community. These competencies include self-awareness, self-management, social awareness, relationship skills and responsible decision making. These Social and Emotional Learning (SEL) competencies foster improved behavior and academic achievement and can provide students supportive strategies during times of trauma.

Social and Emotional Learning competencies can be explicitly fostered in the classroom by particular instructional practices:

- Welcoming inclusion activities
- Engaging pedagogy
- Optimistic closure

Welcoming inclusion activities set the tone for the day and provide an opportunity to connect personally with the people around you. (See the website of The Responsive Classroom [https://www.responsiveclassroom.org] for morning meeting ideas.) These activities can help to develop a culture of belonging and respect. Engaging pedagogy activities help students make sense of what they are learning as well as reduce negative behaviors. Optimistic closure gives students an opportunity to reflect on what they've learned and think about what it will mean for them in future lessons or in their life.

For Discussion

Visit the CASEL website (http://casel.org) and learn more about each of the five SEL competencies: self-awareness, self-management, social awareness, relationship skills, and responsible decision making. Identify a time when one of these competencies helped you respond to a trauma or a challenging situation. Discuss why that competency was helpful. Then, explore the resources there for teaching SEL competencies, including the *SEL 3 Signature Practices Playbook*. Identify an instructional practice you would like to try in your classroom.

Respond Appropriately to Student Behaviors

Young people (as well as adults) may respond to traumatic stressors in ways that appear irrational, defiant, or oppositional. When a child is in need of social services and mental health resources due to trauma, punitive measures such as loss of recess, detention, suspension, or expulsion will contribute to the child's trauma response, not improve it. You may need to advocate for children who are acting out in response to acute or chronic trauma. Expelling teenagers from school can be particularly damaging because rural communities have higher rates of young people who are neither enrolled in school nor employed (19%) as compared to suburban or urban communities (11% and 12%) (Lewis, 2019). Disconnection from school is unlikely to help the child and can derail youth on their path to adulthood, result in lower earnings over a lifetime, and negatively impact a community's economic and social vitality.

While it seems clear, perhaps even common sense, that a child should not be punished for their trauma response, how should teachers respond? While keeping in mind that you are not a guidance counselor, therapist, or school psychologist, your students may want or need to discuss tragic events that have caused their distress. While this discussion will look different based on the type of trauma and the age of your students, having a classroom community where students feel safe to express their feelings or ask questions will enable children to share. A good rule of thumb is to use student questions to guide the conversation and offer enough information to help them to feel safe. You might also encourage them to talk with their families, and to help them access additional resources such as a school counselor, if you have one, or trusted agencies in your community. You may ask your colleagues how they have handled similar conversations in the past and see if there are suggested guidelines for your school. Always take care to process your own trauma so that you can assist your students in attending to theirs. (See the self-care section at the end of this chapter.) It is important to allow students (and yourself) to have and to express feelings, including sorrow, grief, anger, and fear. Reassure your students with factual information that will answer their questions and, above all, remind them that all of the adults in the school and community are there to support and care for them.

Secondary Trauma and Self-Care for Teachers

Everything you read previously about trauma and resiliency for your students also applies to you as a teacher. Even if you have not experienced significant trauma yourself, you may experience secondary trauma. Secondary trauma is indirect trauma caused by regular exposure to others who are experiencing trauma. As an empathetic caregiver, you may experience trauma-connected change in your view of the world and your feelings about yourself and your abilities. For that reason, it is important to be proactive about dealing with the stress you experience as a part of your job as a teacher, both your daily stress and the stress associated with traumatic events. Self-care is essential, but professional help may also be necessary to enable healthy processing, particularly in the face of trauma. Secondary traumatic stress can be difficult to identify, particularly in the immediate aftermath of an event.

Trauma can place stresses on the entire school and community system and thus requires a system-wide response. Find out how your school or district systematically attends to the ongoing mental and physical health of its staff. If you find that this has not been a priority, your advocacy may be required. Whatever level of support your school provides, an important part of planning for trauma, and planning for teaching in general, is planning how you will care for yourself. This section will offer a variety of different resources that you can use to make a self-care plan that works for you.

If you have ever been on a plane before, you know that the flight attendant instructs you in case of an emergency to, "place the oxygen mask over your mouth before assisting a child with theirs." You have to take care of yourself first in order to have something to give to others. It is important to be able to recognize when you are experiencing feelings related to your exposure to other people's trauma. When you take care of others, you sometimes don't realize how much of an impact your caregiving has on your body. Something called trauma exposure response occurs when external trauma becomes internally experienced in your body (Lipsky, 2009). Symptoms include feeling helpless and hopeless, exhaustion, physical pain and health issues, an inability to listen or embrace complexity, guilt, fear, anger, and substance use. If you have any suspicion that you are experiencing trauma exposure response, please seek professional help if self-care routines are inadequate.

Those same social and emotional learning competencies you want to foster in your students—self-awareness, self-management, social awareness, relationship skills, and responsible decision making—can help *you* respond to primary and secondary trauma. Developing your social and emotional skills can help you to manage stress in your own life and perhaps better prepare you for just the typical stressors in a rural teaching career. Treat yourself with the same level of kindness and support you give to your students.

Integrate Self-Care into Your School Day

Integrating self-care strategies into your day to day life at school can help you feel as though it's not just one more thing to do. While we are strong advocates for appropriate boundaries between your professional and personal lives, we also think that integrating some self-care into your school day is not only positive for your well-being, but also provides an authentic model of the importance of self-care for your students. Some people find it helpful to start or end the day with a short mindfulness or gratitude activity, or to take a brisk walk outside during lunch. Sometimes, walking and talking with your students can foster relationships with students.

Perhaps none of these suggestions are quite right for you. Wilson (1997) asks us to consider how "nourishing habitats" could be cultivated at school. Talk with your students about how you might work together to cultivate nourishing habits that can enhance well-being and resiliency for the entire community.

Journaling and Reflection: Paying Attention to Self

The journaling recommended in Chapter 18 about teacher inquiry can also be an important self-care tool. In that chapter, we encourage you to write about your classroom and your students on a regular basis. Your entries can also work as "data" to help you identify potential trauma exposure and reflect on ways to create more resilient practices in your teaching and in your life. Here are some ideas that may help to get you started:

- Why am I a teacher?
- What do I love about this school and its community?
- What makes me feel hopeful?
- What is one worry that I have right now?

- How do I want my students to remember me?
- What did I learn from my students today?
- What was something hard that I've experienced recently?
- What went well today?
- Think of your most challenging student. What do you think their family loves the most about them?

What are some other prompts you could use? If you are doing a field placement this semester, maybe you would like to try to journal regularly and see if you find the practice helpful. Use prompts like these to remind yourself of what is important to you in this profession and why you were called to teaching. If daily journaling isn't for you, you might consider writing short purpose statements, affirmations, or professional goals and posting them where you can see them frequently as a way of helping you to stay present in your purpose. Devon, one of the authors of this book, keeps every thank-you letter and email expression of praise taped to the wall above her computer to remind herself that she is competent and doing just fine during hard times.

If you suspect that you are not only having trauma exposure with your students, but you are also dealing with some personal trauma you have experienced throughout your own lifetime, self-care and sharing your feelings with friends, family, and trusted colleagues is important, but might not be sufficient to meet your needs. In this case, please consult with a mental health professional. Remember that you have to put on your own oxygen mask before you can help someone else with theirs.

Personal Practices: Exercise and Meditation

You may be a person that is naturally athletic and have a personal exercise routine that you are dedicated to. Stress is a physical response. If you raise your heart rate and break a sweat almost every day you can physically metabolize the stress that you are taking into your body. Exercise releases endorphins that energize your mood, boost your self-esteem, and trigger an overall sense of well-being. We encourage you to find a way to integrate some form of activity into your routine—either formally or informally, indoors or outdoors. While we suggested earlier that you might make space in your lunch period for a brief walk, that may not be enough. YouTube offers hundreds of free fitness classes. If you have physical or mobility limitations, consult with a physical therapist about some appropriate exercises for you that promote cardiovascular health, strength, and flexibility.

There are many adaptive aids and workout routines that can meet a variety of needs.

In addition to physical movement, meditation may help you respond to stress by helping you focus your concentration. Taking a few moments out of every day to focus just on breathing or clearing the mind of stressful thoughts can be an important investment. There are several websites and free apps to help teachers to engage in mindfulness or meditation.

Commuting and Self-Care

It is not unusual for rural teachers (and especially student teachers) to commute to their schools. If you commute, plan to use your time intentionally. Of course, your primary focus should be on safe driving, but there are ways you can also use commuting time to support your well-being. If you drive alone, you may use that time to reflect on your day. On the way home, give yourself a few pats on the back for small (or big) victories. Some teachers use voice-to-text to record their observations or journal about the day. You might want to try listening to an audio book or podcast. There are numerous podcasts about personal or professional support. One popular podcast about everything teaching is *Cult of Pedagogy*. It can be downloaded at: https://www.cultofpedagogy.com/pod/.

If you commute with colleagues, you might use that drive home to debrief the day and support one another. To prevent this time from devolving into an energy-sapping gripe session, you might make an agreement to intentionally structure your time together. Each day of the week you have a different topic such as:

- Monday: What superpower did you use today?
- Tuesday: What was the brightest spot of your day?
- Wednesday: No talking about school! Someone is the DJ.
- Thursday: What is a favorite memory from your own K–12 schooling?
- Friday: What makes you feel hopeful about next week?

For Discussion

Sometimes, self-care strategies are dismissed as unimportant. Especially during times of trauma, it can be easy to put off self-care for things that seem more important. Why might it be important to make the time for self-care on a day-to-day basis and in times of trauma?

Final Thoughts

Unfortunately, teaching can be a stressful profession and trauma is a reality. Individual or collective, immediate or ongoing, traumatic events are likely to impact your students and your school. As we have seen with COVID-19, crises can turn our worlds around in a very short space of time. While traumatic experiences can happen anywhere, they can be particularly challenging for rural communities and their teachers. We hope these strategies help you as you develop a repertoire of teaching practices that are informed by your understanding of trauma and the importance of self-care and mental health. We encourage you to learn more about trauma so that you can care for yourself and others in your rural classroom.

Additional Resources

- **National Child and Traumatic Stress Network** provides a large variety of resources about various types of trauma, including documents available in Spanish: https://www.nctsn.org/
- **Trauma Aware Schools** is sponsored by the Substance Abuse and Mental Health Services Administration and provides many different resources to identify and respond to different types of trauma in schools with a section specifically on secondary traumatic stress in teachers: https://traumaawareschools.org/
- **Collaborative for Academic, Social, and Emotional Learning** provides curricular materials to support SEL. It also is a great resource for research and information about how to influence policy: https://casel.org/
- **National Center on Safe and Supportive Learning Environments** provides print and video resources about all types of issues, with a large collection designated to human trafficking: https://safesupportivelearning.ed.gov/human-trafficking-americas-schools
- **Ready Kids** is sponsored by the U.S. government and provides disaster readiness information geared specifically for children and those who work with youth: https://www.ready.gov/kids

References

American Farm Bureau Federation & National Farmers Union [AFBF & NFU]. (2017, December 8). *Survey shows massive opioid impact in farm country; Farm groups call for dialogue, action.* [Press release]. https://blog. apastyle.org/apastyle/2010/09/how-to-cite-a-press-release-in-apa-style. html

Berardi, A., & Morton, B. (2019). *Trauma-informed school practices: Building expertise to transform schools.* George Fox University. https:// digitalcomm ons.georgefox.edu/pennington_epress/4

Center for Youth Wellness. (2013, June). *A hidden crisis: Findings on adverse childhood experiences.* https://centerforyouthwellness.org/wp-content/ themes/cyw/build/img/building-a-movement/hidden- crisis.pdf

Lewis, K. (2019). *Making the connection: Transportation and youth disconnection.* Measure of America, Social Science Research Council. https://mea sureofamerica.org/youth-disconnection-2019/

Lipsky, L. V. N. (2009). *Trauma stewardship: An everyday guide to caring for self while caring for others.* Berrett-Koehler.

McGruder, K. (2019). Children learn what they live: Addressing early childhood trauma resulting in toxic stress in schools. *Mid-Western Educational Researcher, 31*(1) 117–137.

Parker, K., Horowitz, J., Brown, A, Fry, R., Cohn, D., & Igielnik, R. (2018, May 22). *What unites and divides urban, suburban and rural communities.* Pew Research Center. https://www.pewsocialtrends.org/2018/05/22/ what-unites-and-divides-urban-suburban-and-rural-communities/

Perry, B. D., & Szalavitz, M. D. (2006). *The boy who was raised as a dog.* Basic Books.

Wilson, R. (1997). A sense of place. *Early Childhood Education Journal, 24*(3), 191–194.

12

Multi-Grade Teaching

It is the end of September in a small rural school. Ms. Dewberry is starting the day with open writing time. The eight third graders and seven fourth graders in her classroom all open their writing folders and begin the day adding more to the letters to the editor they are working on in a combined social studies and literacy project. The fourth graders are familiar with this writing routine. They were all students in Ms. Dewberry's class last year during third grade. The chairs are arranged so that third graders alternate with fourth graders, and if a younger student has a question about what to do if they need a sharper pencil or ideas for revising their writing, they can ask the more experienced fourth grader sitting next to them. After 20 minutes of free writing time, Ms. Dewberry transitions to centers and mathematics. The third graders rotate to one of three open centers while the fourth graders meet with Ms. Dewberry on the carpet to talk about division. After the whole-group lesson, fourth graders return to their tables to work on math while Ms. Dewberry circulates among both grades, offering words of encouragement or solving problems. After 20 minutes, students swap roles. The third graders meet on the carpet for the day's math lesson while the fourth graders rotate through the centers.

Halfway through the morning, the students all clean up and sit at their desks. Ms. Dewberry leaves the classroom for 45 minutes while the itinerant music teacher visits for her twice-weekly lesson. Ms. Cameron visits each classroom in the school two times a week. She brings her cart with rhythm sticks and the students work on practicing rhythms for a while. Then she plugs in her keyboard and amplifier and helps the students practice singing a song they'll share at the school assembly later in the month. After the lesson is over, Ms. Cameron stows her equipment back on the cart and moves on to the next classroom. The third and fourth graders move on to independent reading time, reading in comfortable locations around the room, while Ms. Dewberry works on spelling patterns and comprehension skills with small groups of students at the table at the front of the room.

Rural Ways of Organizing Classrooms

In the U.S., the "typical" elementary and middle schools are organized by grades. Students move through school with other children who are approximately their same age and attend classrooms with teachers that teach a single grade at a time. This is not the only structure for the elementary school, however. There are other ways of organizing classrooms that you might encounter, particularly in rural schools. In this chapter, we want to think about multi-grade classrooms, a common way of organizing instruction in smaller rural schools, as well as looping and itinerant teaching. Each of these are strategies that schools sometimes use when overall enrollment is small or when enrollments are changing, as is common in rural schools.

A multi-grade classroom is one where an individual teacher instructs students who are enrolled in two or more grade levels. Sometimes these classrooms are called split classrooms (such as "a 4/5 split class") or combination classrooms (such as "a 3/4 combo class"). Not every classroom that has students from more than one grade level is a multi-grade classroom. In high schools and even most middle schools, it is common to have students who are in multiple grades learning the same content together. Many specialized classes—athletics, band, music, creative writing electives, even science and math classes—are made up of students who are in different grades but are grouped together to learn the same thing. Multi-grade classrooms are different because teachers are teaching different content to multiple groups of students in the same physical space.

For Discussion

What do you think of when you hear the term "multi-grade classroom"? Have you or anyone you know been a student in a multi-grade classroom? What was it like? What do you imagine might be the pros and cons of teaching in a multi-grade classroom—for the teacher and for the students?

It's also important to understand that a "multi-grade classroom" is not necessarily the same thing as a "multi-age classroom." A multi-*grade* classroom is composed of students from two or more grades who retain their grade level designation, while a multi-*age* classroom is comprised of students of mixed ages and traditional grade designations are not used. The focus in a multi-age classroom is on grouping students of similar ability irrespective of age and grade for the purpose of helping each student make continuous learning progress (Mulryan-Kyne, 2007).

Multi-grade classrooms (where students from two or more grades are taught together) are more common than you might expect. Many countries such as Australia, Canada, and the U.S., as well as countries across the continents of Europe, South America, Africa, and Asia, offer multi-grade classrooms to meet students' learning needs (Little, 2006; Mulryan-Kyne, 2005). As we will discuss below, multi-grade classrooms are particularly common in rural settings in the U.S. and you may be asked to teach more than one grade at a time.

Looping often goes hand-in-hand with multi-grade teaching. Students "loop" when they stay with the same teacher for more than one year. Sometimes, two or more teachers take turns looping, such as when a third- and a fourth-grade teacher use looping to teach the same class of students for two years in a row. Each year, one teacher follows her third graders into fourth grade, and the other teacher starts with a new set of third graders. Looping lets teachers build longer term relationships with students. In the second year of looping, students already know the classroom rules and procedures and can start learning content right away. Most multi-grade configurations also include looping—some students stay with the same teacher from year to year while some move on to the next grade after two or three years in a multi-grade classroom. For example, Devon's daughter attended a K–1–2 multi-grade classroom in elementary school. Each year only one-third of students in the classroom were new, but most of the students were in their second and third year with the same teacher. By second grade, her daughter had formed a lasting relationship with the teacher and knew all the classroom routines.

What Do Multi-Grade Classrooms Look Like?

Typically, students in multi-grade classrooms learn their own grade-level curriculum using grade-level materials. Students spend part of the school day learning together and part of the school day working on their grade-level curriculum. But that's where the commonality ends. There are many other ways that multi-grade classrooms are different from place to place. Multi-grade classrooms can vary by:

- The number of grade levels in the classroom—some classrooms have just two grades in one classroom, but in others, such a one-room school that serves all elementary students in a remote community, can serve all nine grades from Kindergarten through eighth grade.
- The size of the class—some multi-grade classrooms have as few as four students, others could have as many as 30.
- The range of students—in a K–8 school the students could range in age from 5 to 14 years.
- The size of the school—multi-grade classrooms can be located in schools ranging in size from a one-room school with a handful of students to a large school with several hundred students.
- The location of the school—multi-grade classrooms can be found in urban, suburban, town, rural, and remote settings.
- The resources and support available to the school and the classroom—some multi-grade classrooms are very well resourced and others deal with serious levels of underfunding.

Why Do Multi-Grade Classrooms Exist?

Many schools implement multi-grade classrooms out of a desire to meet students' developmental needs. There is evidence that multi-grade classrooms allow for the development of academic and social skills as the teacher encourages cross-age interactions through tutoring and shared discovery (Vincent & Ley, 1999). Students have opportunities to learn at their own pace and revisit curriculum when they loop in a multi-grade classroom. Multi-grade classrooms allow for flexible grouping of students and offer opportunities for students to work cooperatively. Multi-grade classrooms can promote a family and community atmosphere, where students have time to build deep relationships with their teacher and their classrooms, particularly when students loop from one grade to the next. Multi-grade classrooms also provide an appropriate environment to facilitate cross-age peer learning. Students in lower grades can enrich their learning by listening to the material presented to the higher grades. Students in higher grades can benefit from opportunities to tutor and interact with younger students.

There are a couple of reasons that multi-grade classrooms might be found in rural schools, including student enrollment and school finances. Rural schools tend to be smaller and there may not be enough students for a full set of single-grade classrooms. This is particularly true when a school or district is located in a remote area where there are only a handful of students at each grade level. This is why there are over 60 one- and two-room schools in Montana that serve students in grades K–8. Even larger schools may not have enough students to fill an entire classroom or they may have an imbalance in student numbers—too many students for one grade-level class but not enough for two grade-level classes. For example, in a school with 35 third and 36 fourth graders, the formation of a multi-grade classroom might make sense. A school might end up arranging the students into three class groupings: A single-grade classroom for third grade and fourth grade and a multi-grade classroom for both grades.

Multi-grade classrooms may be the result of financial constraints. When resources are tight, there might not be enough funding to support multiple low-enrolled single-grade classrooms. Forming multi-grade classes can be an option that allows a school to continue to operate. Multi-grade classrooms also may be the best way to meet students' needs when the only other option is closing a school. Given that long bus rides before and after the school day can be physically, cognitively, and emotionally taxing for young students, a multi-grade classroom can provide primary education close to home and increase students' well-being and connection to local community.

What Are the Outcomes of Multi-Grade Classrooms?

This question has been studied by a number of different researchers. Some studies report positive effects of multi-grade classrooms (e.g. Guo et al., 2014), while others point to null (e.g. Veenman, 1995) or negative outcomes for students (e.g. Ansari, 2016; Bell et al., 2013; Mason & Burns, 1996; Moller et al., 2008; Thomas, 2012). Part of the difficulty in forming a definitive answer for this question is due to that fact that studies have found varying outcomes for different ages of children. For example, early childhood research suggests that five-year olds in a multi-grade pre-K and Kindergarten class did not do as well as children the same age kindergarten-only classrooms (Ansari, 2016). However, studies which examine students in first grade and beyond have reported more positive results. For example, a study from Sweden found that rural students in multi-grade classrooms did as well or better than their peers in single-grade classrooms on standardized tests and also had better attitudes toward school (Aberg-Bengtsson, 2009). In fact, research suggests that in most cases students do at least as well or better academically in multi-grade classrooms, and that multi-grade classrooms also lead to better social outcomes, with students having a more positive self-concept and perceptions of other students (Vincent & Ley, 1999; Veenman, 1995).

What Are the Key Skills and Strategies for Success in a Multi-Grade Classroom?

In order to facilitate positive outcomes for rural students, multi-grade teachers have a complex task: They are expected to teach the curriculum for two (or more) grades, and they need to accomplish this in the same amount of time that is available to the single-grade teacher. While this arrangement can create some unique challenges for the rural multi-grade teacher, it can also provide opportunities for creative and innovative approaches to engaging students in the learning process.

Research has identified several teaching practices that appear to be associated with positive learning outcomes for students in multi-grade classrooms (e.g. Thomas and Shaw, 1992; Vincent & Ley, 1999). Three key aspects of teacher practice that are essential for effective multi-grade instruction are curriculum planning, classroom organization and management, and grouping of students for delivery of instruction.

Curriculum Planning

Out of all the recommendations for how to best support student learning in multi-grade classrooms, one of the most important elements will be your approach to planning your curriculum sequence. One expert in the field of rural multi-grade teaching is Allison Nys who taught in a fifth/sixth multi-grade classroom in rural Montana for 12 years. We talked to her about what she learned throughout her experience and she offered several insights to help new multi-grade rural teachers get a running start.

Her first tip for new multi-grade rural teachers is to start your planning by looking at the state standards for each grade and mapping out the areas where the standards connect and where students might be expected to learn the same or similar content. She said, "Just because you're teaching two grades doesn't mean you have to teach two separate curriculums. It's better to look at the standards overall and find where those standards overlap."

Once you have created a map of the connections between the grade standards, then you can use the areas of overlap to integrate grade levels and content in subjects such as English language arts, science, and social studies. By making connections, you can blend and shape two grades' worth of content into a realistic set of goals for a single school year. It can be helpful to focus on the standards and curriculum for the oldest student or highest grade you are teaching to make sure they get what they need. The younger students/lower grades will have more time in subsequent years if there are any gaps.

Curriculum guides can be helpful at this point, but as you are planning for a multi-grade classroom it is also important to understand that you do not have to use a textbook from front to back. It is more effective to focus your planning based on the standards and then use your textbooks and other curriculum as resources. As you plan to meet the needs of all your students, you can do the majority of your planning at the unit level rather than at the lesson level. This is where you will have the most capacity to blend subject content and standards and meet your learning goals for all the students in your class. As an example, you can plan a science unit about the prairie ecosystem and engage students in reading and writing about the plants, animals, weather, and systems in the prairie that would be of interest to both the fourth and fifth graders in your class. From there, you can pick specific texts, writing assignments, and areas of focus that are specific to each grade—having one group of students focus on the food web and the other focus on the water cycle, for example, as is consistent with their grade level.

Allison told us that in her experience, "Math is the exception to this rule." Typically, the content in the math class is more sequential, and students have to understand the content that is to be taught in one grade level to understand what comes next. In this case, classroom organization and management will play an important role so that you can work with both groups of students on grade-appropriate content.

Classroom Organization and Management

Every classroom, whether single grade or multi-grade, urban or rural, will be a more effective learning environment when there is clear organization and management. As a multi-grade rural teacher, you will want to think carefully about how you arrange the physical space in your room as well as how you organize your instructional resources to best facilitate learning for all your students.

In a multi-grade classroom, it can be especially important to develop and implement classroom guidelines and routines that provide clear, predictable expectations for student behavior, particularly around patterns that enhance students' independence, interdependence, and responsibility for their own learning. From Allison's perspective, "the most important component of classroom management in a multi-grade classroom is respect, period. You will never have good classroom management until you have respect of your students and their parents." Chapters 6 and 7 provide suggestions for understanding the community and building relationships with families that can help you build respectful relationships with your rural students.

It is also important in a multi-grade setting for the teacher to make behavioral expectations clear for all students when they are working with the teacher and when they are working independently or in groups away from the teacher. Organization and management are essential in a multi-grade classroom because the teacher will need to work with some students on grade level content while other students are engaged in learning experiences away from the teacher. For example, students will need to know what to do if they need materials, if they run into problems, or if their work is completed early, and they'll need to solve all these problems, without asking for help from the teacher who will be busy with other students.

Students also need clearly communicated (and consistently enforced) consequences for off-task behaviors. Allison described how she worked hard to foster students' sense of personal responsibility for their behaviors by communicating clear expectations and consequences for her students. By reminding students of the consequences for off-task behavior, Allison knew that they understood the rules and were ready to follow them.

Allison looped with her students, so that fifth graders became sixth graders in the next year. She had the advantage of having half her class familiar with routines and procedures at the start of every new school year. The experienced students could help the newer, younger students learn the ropes at the beginning of the year, giving them a sense of confidence and maturity. If you loop with students in your multi-grade classroom, your second-year experts can play an important role in helping you establish routines, organization, and management.

Grouping of Students for Delivery of Instruction

The final component of teacher practice that is essential for effective multi-grade instruction is the selection of instructional strategies and routines that leverage the strengths of a multi-grade classroom environment by organizing learning activities across and within grade levels. The use of different grouping strategies is key to providing maximum learning opportunities. Depending on the goals and the assignment, students might be grouped by their interests, allowed to choose to work with friends, or grouped by their achievement or academic needs (the stronger writers together in one group, the students who need more help in another). Other times, you might group students specifically to mix up ability and grades for cooperative learning. When carefully structured, using a variety of grouping strategies can help to develop students' interdependence and cooperation. Some teachers form groups with different labels so that they can quickly assign students to group work—where your "red" group might be other students in the same grade with the same achievement level, your "blue" group might be a mixed-grade group, and your "green" partner is your reading buddy and your "turn and talk" partner is yet another classmate that sits nearby. When groups and partners are prearranged the teacher can simply tell students to get into their red, blue, or green groups depending on the current activity assigned.

Peer tutoring is a grouping strategy where older students have the opportunity to read with or instruct younger students. Peer tutoring can have positive outcomes for both sets of students. Older students gain a sense of confidence and civic responsibility while younger students get help learning content and enjoy interacting with their peers. Peer tutoring will take specific planning and structure. Students may need to be taught how to help without taking over and how to solve problems and work independently for example. Peer tutoring can be an important component of a multi-grade classroom.

Differentiating Instruction

In a multi-grade classroom it is especially obvious that you will have students with different skill levels and abilities. When teachers use different strategies for different students in order to help individual students succeed, this is known as differentiation. Teachers differentiate instruction for each student in all classrooms because even students in the same grade and of the same age need different supports to be successful. For example, let's say you are asking students to complete a writing assignment and some students have more experience writing than others. You might begin by teaching the whole class to write a paragraph about a topic. That topic can vary depending on the levels or interests of the students. You might request more advanced students to write longer paragraphs, use particular types of vocabulary, or reference particular readings. Younger or less experienced students might write shorter paragraphs with fewer details or that focus on different texts. The idea is that all the students have a shared or similar assignment but where they "enter" varies by grade or skill level.

Sharon is a multi-grade teacher in a small community in the mountains. She has several different spelling levels in her classroom. In order to work with small groups individually, she records herself, often in entertaining costumes, giving the spelling list for one group of students. She even asks the students questions or instructs them to do things. Then, she plays that video for a small group of students while she's working with another group in the back of the room. Video recording is even something you might have older students do, especially if you can align the task with educational technology standards or oral speaking standards for your grade levels. There are more examples of technology use in Chapter 14. In a multi-grade classroom, technology can be a useful tool to engage and support learning for one group of students while the teacher is working with another group of students.

Bring in Volunteers and Helpers

Having your students' family members volunteer in the classroom can be helpful when you are managing more than one grade. Another adult can work with students who need extra help or when the teacher is busy with a small group. Another adult can also supervise independent learning time or read with groups of students. However, do this cautiously. Sometimes it can be more work to have someone you need to teach or monitor, in addition to the students. Setting some parameters can be a good idea before inviting adult volunteers. First, be selective about who you invite. You may even have a volunteer training period to go over some basic information they will need to know. You might teach them about your classroom, district guidelines about discipline, how to act in a classroom full of children, and why they must protect students' information and privacy. In a small town, sometimes the family dynamics can cause additional situations you might want to avoid. It can be helpful to know your students and their families before scheduling volunteers.

If you do decide to invite volunteers into your classroom, determine what types of activities will be best for a non-teacher to lead. Plan lessons for the types of volunteers you have, just as you have planned them for the students, so that you create an opportunity for everyone to have a successful experience. Putting forth some effort ahead of time can save you some time and frustration later.

Daily Schedule in a Multi-grade Classroom

Here is an example of a typical day schedule from a multi-grade classroom in rural Montana. You can see how the teacher has set up the day to address content areas for each grade level, and where the students engage in teacher-led learning, peer learning, and self-directed learning.

For Discussion

Take a close look at the daily schedule. What do you notice about how the different time periods allow for each grade level (each block) to participate in both whole-group and grade-level instruction? What do you notice about the combination of independent, peer, and whole-group instruction? Can you imagine teaching a schedule like this? Why or why not? How do you think this schedule and way of teaching could be a benefit for students?

Time	Topic	Grade Level A	Grade Level B
8:30–9:00	**Morning Agenda** Jobs (put up flag, set up supplies in classroom, run attendance) Homework support—students who need support from nightly work can use time to work with peers and/or teacher Teacher/student grade conferencing (standards met, standards that need support—student-led with teacher support) Class meeting—set expectations for the day and schedule of events	All grade levels participate	

(Continued)

Time	Topic	Grade Level A	Grade Level B
9:00–10:15	**Math** Two 10–12 minute blocks and 1 large block Block 1: 9:00–9:10 Block 2: 9:10–9:20 Block 3: Remaining time (approx. 9:20–10:15)	**Block 1: Collaboration / Peer review** Review (prepared standard-specific review created by teacher) Collaboration: students take review and peer edit/correct/reteach	**Block 1: Teacher-Led review** Teacher and student correct homework from day before (if any) If no homework—it is a teacher-led review
		Block 2: Teacher-Led review Teacher and student correct homework from day before (if any) If no homework—it is a teacher-led review	**Block 2: Collaboration/Peer review** Review (prepared standard-specific review created by teacher) Collaboration: students take review and peer edit/correct/reteach
		Block 3: Instruction 9:20–9:40 instruction for lower grade level on new topics, while upper grade level previews lesson, discusses best strategies to go about problem solving, lessons, and/or includes test prep (higher-level thinking questions). 9:40–10:00 instruction for the higher grade level on new topics, while lower grade level works on completion of assignment/task given and/or includes test prep (higher-level thinking questions). 10:00–10:15 all students working on completion of activities included during instruction.	

(Continued)

Time	Topic	Grade Level A	Grade Level B
10:15–10:30	Break (Snack/Recess)	All grade levels participate	
10:30–11:45	ELA Block 1 45 minutes: Reading: Novels/stories that are aligned to grade-appropriate standards that overlap the Social Studies or Science curriculum for inter-disciplinary units. Include comprehension and fluency lessons into this block. 30 minutes: Writing: Incorporate writing standards into the novel/story being read by class. Include opinion pieces, compare/contrast characters, plots, etc. into this writing block.	Novel studies, language usage, writing can all be on the same topics and split out by standard for each grade level taught.	
11:45–12:15	Lunch Break	All grade levels participate	
12:15–12:45	ELA Block 2 Language Usage/Vocabulary—incorporate your writing from the morning and do peer editing, revising, language usage (nouns, pronouns, etc.) into this time.	All grade levels participate	

(Continued)

Time	Topic	Grade Level A	Grade Level B
12:45–2:00	Science or Social Studies Due to lack of time in a day, alternate your units. Spend a week or two on Science, then a week or two on Social Studies (or alternate days of the week; however, doing to big units at once can be overbearing on students) Align standards in Science and Social Studies for grade levels taught and create units of study for the entire class. You will find that in these two subject areas, many of the standards overlap and by teaching to the higher standard you can reach all students appropriately.	All grade levels participate	
2:00–3:00	Specialty Time i.e. Art, Computer Tech, PE, Music	All grade levels participate	
3:00–3:30	Class Closure Jobs (10 minutes—clean room, reorganize materials, be ready for tomorrow) Teacher-led review of day (5 minutes) How did we do today? What did we do great? What should we work on better tomorrow? Make a plan for a great day	All grade levels participate	

(Continued)

Time	Topic	Grade Level A	Grade Level B
	Preview tomorrow (10 minutes—schedule, changes, due dates, important forms, questions from students, etc.) Exit ticket (5 minutes—class/school closure—asking students to write what they will personally do better tomorrow—or what they found interesting today—or what they need help with tomorrow.		

Multi-Grade Teaching Is Worth It

While the challenges are not trivial, the rewards of being a multi-grade teacher in a rural school are considerable. Teachers in multi-grade classrooms can help students develop self-directed learning skills such as self-monitoring and personal responsibility for learning. These skills enable students to function with a fairly high level of independence and efficiency in learning and will allow you to offer activities to a group of students with independent learning while you provide instruction for another group.

As a multi-grade teacher you will have the opportunity to build significant meaningful relationships with students, their families, and the community, particularly if you teach the same students for more than one year. As Allison Nys described it, "You are part of a family." Those close relationships with students, their family, and the community make teaching a joy.

Itinerant Teaching

Before this chapter concludes, we want to touch just briefly on the role of the itinerant teacher. For many of the same reasons that schools implement multi-grade classrooms, schools in rural places also often rely on itinerant teachers to provide specialized instruction. Itinerant teachers are teachers who travel from site to site to teach their content. Itinerant teachers may be located within a single school, and travel up and down the hallways to "push in" to other teachers' classrooms to teach special subjects like music and art. Itinerant teachers also often travel from school to school, spending part of each day or different days each week in different schools in a district. Special education and gifted resource teachers who provide specialized services to students in more than one school are an example of itinerant teachers. Schools sometimes share teachers, particularly teachers of specialized subjects like foreign languages and advanced mathematics and science. Sharing the services of an itinerant teacher can allow schools to offer subjects and meet the needs of students even when there are not enough students to employ a full-time teacher, avoiding the need to consolidate or close schools in order to make sure students have access to a rich curriculum.

There can be many positives to being an itinerant teacher. Often times, teachers who travel from classroom to classroom feel a greater sense of independence. Itinerant teachers often enjoy the short breaks they get as they travel from classroom to classroom or school to school. This kind of teaching also offers a great deal of variety and flexibility and provides opportunities to collaborate with your colleagues. On the other hand, itinerant teaching comes with some challenges. It can be difficult not to have a classroom or even a desk to call your own, particularly if you usually teach in other teachers' classrooms. The work can be complex or even complicated. You will be working with numerous students and teachers in a variety of settings, and you may have more than one administrator with different goals and expectations. Itinerant teachers need to be flexible, organized, and positive in order to be successful. Communication and ability to work well with others and adapt to the unexpected is especially important to your success as an itinerant teacher, particularly if you are moving from school to school. As you travel, you have to be prepared for times when students are absent or on a field trip, when road construction or wildlife hampers your travel, when the room you are supposed to teach in is being used for testing, and other unexpected events.

If you are a teacher in a rural school your role may change from year to year. You may teach a single grade for a while, you may loop with students for a year because the third-grade cohort is the biggest in the school, you may teach a multi-grade class for a while as enrollment in your district grows, or you may travel about as an itinerant teacher. Whatever the role, careful planning, organization, management, and resourcefulness will help you thrive as a rural teacher.

References

Aberg-Bengtsson, L. (2009). The smaller the better? A review of research on small rural schools in Sweden. *International Journal of Educational Research, 48,* 100–108. doi: https://10.1016/j.ijer.2009.02.007

Ansari, A. (2016). Multigrade kindergarten classrooms and children's academic achievement, executive function, and socioemotional development. *Infant and Child Development, 26,* 1–19.

Bell, E. R., Greenfield, D. B., & Bulotsky-Shearer, R. J. (2013). Classroom age composition and rates of change in school readiness for children enrolled in Head Start. *Early Child Research Quarterly, 28,* 1–10. doi: https://10.1002/icd.2036

Guo, Y., Tompkins, V., Justice, L., & Petscher, Y. (2014). Classroom age composition and vocabulary development among at-risk preschoolers. *Early Education and Development, 25,* 1016–1034. doi: https://10.1080/10409289.2014.893759

Little, A. (Ed.) (2006). *Education for all and multi-grade teaching: Challenges and opportunities.* Springer.

Mason, D., & Burns, R. (1996). "Simply no worse and simply no better" may simply be wrong: A critique of Veenman's conclusion about multigrade classes. *Review of Educational Research, 66,* 307–322. doi: https://10.2307/1170525

Moller, A., Forbes-Jones, E., & Hightower, A. (2008). Classroom age composition and developmental change in 70 urban preschool classrooms. *Journal of Educational Psychology, 100,* 741–753. doi: https://10.1037/a0013099

Mulryan-Kyne, C. (2005). The grouping practices of teachers in small two-teacher primary schools in the Republic of Ireland. *Journal of Research in Rural Education, 20*(17) 1–14.

Mulryan-Kyne, C. (2007). The preparation of teachers for multigrade teaching. *Teaching and Teacher Education, 23,* 501–514. doi: https://10.1016/j.tate.2006.12.003

Thomas, J. (2012). Combination classes and educational achievement. *Economics of Education Review, 31,* 1058–1066. doi: https://10.1016/j.econedurev.2012.07.013

Thomas, C., & Shaw, C. (1992). *Issues in the development of multigrade schools.* World Bank Technical Paper no. 172. The World Bank.

Veenman, S. (1995). Cognitive and noncognitive effects of multigrade and multi-age classes: A best-evidence synthesis. *Review of Educational Research, 65,* 319–381. doi: https://10.3102/00346543065004319

Vincent, S. & Ley, J. (1999). *The multigrade classroom: A resource handbook for small rural schools: Book 1: Review of the research on multigrade instruction.* Northwest Regional Educational Laboratory. https://educationnorth west.org/sites/default/files/multigrade-classroom-books1-7.pdf

Part Four
Thriving in Rural Classrooms

13

Place-Conscious Instruction

I moved to Hillsville, Virginia, in Carroll County some 25 years ago from sunny Florida. They were worlds apart. To be perfectly honest I had my own set of prejudices about almost everything in the first few years we lived here. There were only three radio stations that I could get on my car radio and only one at the house. I was used to a radio station at every click in Florida. At a 45-minute drive, Walmart was the closest chain store. In Florida anything that I wanted to shop for was just outside my door. And don't even get me started on the Appalachian dialect. Sometimes it sounded like I was in a foreign country listening to broken English with words that were alien to me. But in time I grew to appreciate the quiet of the evenings on the porch, the kindness and wisdom of our neighbors, and the pure, honest charm of the beautiful Appalachian landforms. So when I had the chance to teach a place-based curriculum to the very students that I had grown to value and respect, I jumped at it.

While using a place-based curriculum to teach, some of the things that the students did not know surprised me and even made me a little sad that they may not cherish their Appalachian heritage. They knew very little about traditional oral storytelling but quickly grew fond of it as if it were a part of them hidden in a secret place of their being. They would ask me every day if I would tell them a story. They caught on quickly to the folklore that had morals and would often predict what it would be and how it applied to their lives. They especially liked the retelling of the fairytales, such as Ashpet (Cinderella) and Little Red Cap (Little Red Riding Hood), because it related to their culture here in the mountains of Virginia.

Through the curriculum we learned to look for events and places around us that we could use to relate the instruction such as our annual flea market that takes up the entire town and our local Fiddler's

Convention that highlights traditional music and musicians. We talked about the importance of everyday life and work here in the Appalachians that affected communities well beyond our mountain range. Together we found many contributions to be proud of that are made here daily. We even overcame some of our own prejudices about other cultures.

Being able to relate instruction to children is critical to their learning. Taking them from the unknown to the known needs a vehicle that is familiar to them so it sticks to their brains. They are inundated with huge amounts of stimuli and the world fights for their attention and brain space. As teachers we have an obligation to take our curriculum and creatively relate it to their lives and their situations so that they move from the surface to a deeper application of the learning ... that is just what a place-based curriculum will do.

Shanda Warren, Gifted Specialist, Carroll County, Virginia

Shanda has been involved in a project for the last several years implementing a language arts curriculum for high-achieving rural elementary students. The language arts units make use of local contexts as a key component in reading and writing instruction. Place-based education has been around for some time and many scholars point to John Dewey, who advocated for connecting curricula to students' lives, as the originator of the theory. Place-based education makes use of the community to nurture place identities or, conversely, capitalizes on place identities by using local contexts to foster greater interest in the standardized curriculum. David Sobel (2004) defined place-based education as the "process of using the local community and environment as a starting point to teach concepts in language arts, mathematics, social studies, science, and other subjects across the curriculum" (p. 4). Sobel argues that this pedagogical approach can increase achievement, foster stronger ties with community, and ultimately develop more engaged citizens. Throughout the project, Shanda found this to be true—that students were more engaged as they had opportunities to connect the curriculum to their everyday lives outside the classroom.

In Chapter 4, we provided a theoretical discussion about the importance of a critical pedagogy of place. A critical pedagogy of place prioritizes learning connections between the local, regional, national, and global contexts, *while also* considering power and privilege. In this chapter, we think more about how you might plan instruction with place in the curriculum and how that instruction can be critical in nature.

Critical theorists (e.g. Freire & Macedo, 1987) have argued that developing a critical understanding of the world is a necessary act of learning and that a critical literacy campaign is a necessary part of democracy. Freire offered a concept of "reading the word and the world" as a way to think about literacy (and learning in general) as a form of cultural politics. But, what does this look like in practice? In the curriculum Shanda used, students had the opportunity to connect learning to local contexts while also reflecting on cultural norms in their community, regional dialects, and stereotypes. In this chapter, we provide ways for thinking about and designing critical, place-based—or what we prefer to call place-conscious—instruction. The difference marks a nuance in that we are not necessarily *basing* instruction in place but rather being conscious of how place might influence the ways we interact with and come to know our world. Using place in the curriculum is one step in enacting a critical pedagogy of place but there are important and necessary ways to deepen and extend that work. As one of this book's authors, Karen, argues elsewhere (Eppley, 2016), we see rural schools inextricably tied to rural people and places; therefore, *honoring, valuing, and embracing local contexts* in the curriculum can allow rural students to see themselves in their own learning which can be an empowering *or emancipatory* aspect of a democratic education.

Designing Place-Conscious Instruction

To get started, we need to understand why place-conscious teaching is important, how you might plan for place-conscious instruction, and the possible challenges and benefits of this work.

Place-conscious education has its roots in environmental and ecological studies with an emphasis on connecting schools and communities (Sobel, 2004); however, place can be integrated across a variety of disciplines—as seen, for example, in *Rural Voices: Place-Conscious Education and the Teaching of Writing* (Brooke, 2003), an edited volume celebrating place-conscious writing instruction from the Nebraska Writing Project. Placed projects often focus on equipping students with skills for thinking about what it means to "live well" (i.e. ecologically, politically, economically, and spiritually) in a particular place (Haas & Nachtigal, 1998). In *Teaching the Commons*, Paul Theobald (1997) argued that attention to place could provide renewal for rural communities and provide context for rural learners.

One of the most well-known examples for this type of work is the Foxfire project. Originating in Rabun Gap, Georgia, a novice teacher (new to teaching and the area) struggled to engage his students with the English curriculum. In an effort to make the content more relevant, students learned literacy skills by interviewing family and community members, resulting in a project about Appalachian traditions that has endured for more than 50 years. Foxfire is an illustrative example of engaging students with their local community. (See the Foxfire website at https://www.foxfire.org/ for more information.) Similarly, the Teton Science Schools (https://www.tetonscience.org/) is a model of using place at the center of its educational programming.

These examples align with important questions about using local learning for instructional planning (Demarest, 2015), such as:

- How can I better relate school to my students' life experiences?
- How can I help students better understand how this big idea works in the real world?
- How can I help students better understand this place?
- How can I help students better understand themselves and their possible futures?

These questions are situated within four aspects of place-conscious instruction designed for authentic local learning. Given the above questions, consider using place in a variety of ways. For one, it can be used to connect learning to students' lived experiences. Consider how using place might make the curriculum more meaningful and relevant for rural learners. Students often ask, "Why do we have to learn this?" Using place and connecting learning to local contexts can provide an important response to that question. Using place in a demanding content area, like geometry for example, might make the objectives easier for students to grasp if they are solving local challenges (food planning and design, fencing, quilting, recreational activities, etc.).

Second, place can be used as a scaffold to bring more local relevance to big ideas and concepts that might seem remote for students. For example, in learning about the importance of waterways to ancient civilizations, students might first consider waterways or other means for transporting goods and services in their local communities. How does the land provide for the community? What challenges does it impose? Who profits from those opportunities and barriers?

Finally, place-conscious instruction can be used to answer the final two questions. How can an understanding of place empower students and their possible futures? Look back at Chapter 4, and consider how a critical examination of place might bring awareness for rural students to answer those questions. Consider again the Foxfire project. Having students interview local residents and research community traditions make use of place-conscious practices.

For Discussion

Why is having a sense of one's history and culture important? Whose stories are told or untold in the recounting of that history and its traditions?

A writing exercise based on a popular poem, "Where I'm From" by George Ella Lyon, gives another format for exploring what it means to be in or of or from a place. (You can find several "Where I'm From" templates readily available online.)

Content, Context, and Criticality

How do content and context influence one another? How might a local (rural) context influence the ways students understand and value content? How can content be influenced by a particular context? This *transactional* process, as Louise Rosenblatt (1978) once explained, describes a reciprocal relationship where learners make meaning of content and, thus, shape its understanding. For example, a book like *To Kill a Mockingbird* by Harper Lee can mean different things to different readers. Symbols work in the same way. As Freire explained, we are always reading the word (content) within a particular world (context).

For Discussion

Brainstorm with a partner some books, content, or symbols that might have different meanings in different places. For each example, discuss how the "context" makes meaning of the "content."

So much of what we teach students in school is focused on the learning of measurable content. Across all grade levels, there is content to "cover," standards to meet, and assessments to give. And in this era of the Common Core State Standards, it is easy to forget that content and the ways we come to learn, use, and grow from that content can be deeply contextualized. Context can be a powerful mediator in the ways young people come to grasp meaning in various disciplines.

A simple place to begin might be to examine whether the curricular materials you have access to represent rural places at all. Many commercial curriculum products feature mostly urban examples. Take a look at the images and examples in textbooks and other resources you are provided with and examine whether rural communities are represented. If not, you might search for additional resources to bring in. For example, English Language Arts teachers might consider award winning books highlighting the complexity of rural living, like the young adult literature featured in the Whippoorwill Award List (see https://whippoorwillaward.weebly.com/).

Here's an activity to help you begin planning for place-conscious instruction for all content areas and grade levels.

Step 1: Evaluate the curriculum. Look at the curriculum and standards you are expected to teach. What are the major topics and objectives that you should accomplish? On a piece of paper, make a table with three columns. On the left, write "Content," and jot down several key concepts.

Step 2: Take stock of the local context. Think about the local context where you are or will be teaching. What's the geography, economy, industry? What are the local legends and folklore? Where do people go? What are the important landmarks? In Chapter 6, we suggested you conduct a Rural Community Walk to learn more about the assets, resources, and unique attributes of your community. Use those as you start planning.

Step 3: Identify opportunities for meaningful connections. Identify connections between the curriculum (the content) and your local context. What opportunities are there to make connections with the features you brainstormed in the first step? Return to your list, and in the middle column, write "Local Context," and see if you can match up community places or features to the curricular topics, standards, or objectives in the left column.

Step 4: Brainstorm critical questions. Choose one of the connections from your list and brainstorm how you might incorporate a critical understanding of the topic. Look back to the table in Chapter 4 and think about how you can deepen and extend understanding. In the final column, write "Critical Pedagogy of Place," and record a few ideas for deepening place-conscious learning.

Here's an example: An Earth Science teacher is expected to teach content focusing on Earth's composition, structure, processes, and history. Specific standards might include teaching the rock cycle, geologic processes, freshwater resources, development of karst topography, and evolution. Amy grew up between two Appalachian mountain ranges, providing a depth of resources to apply to these concepts. Additionally, the Luray Caverns, in the town where she grew up, are some of the most famous caves in the world. Students in the area are familiar with the caverns. Teachers reference the caverns as a relevant way to discuss the chemical weathering of limestone and that limestone forms from the eroding of seashells. That means that Luray was once under the ocean! Millions of shell animals died, weathered, compacted, then slowly eroded, creating the caverns that make up the local landmark. Teachers could then extend these lessons for even more critical understandings about tourist economies in rural places. They could look at the history of the privatization and commercialization of the caverns or policies that impact the community. Students might think about the relationship between the Earth's features and policies that serve to protect or diminish natural features, such as the caverns. Who gets to decide what is valued about a natural landmark, and who profits or suffers as a result? What are the economic pros and cons of rural communities dependent on tourism as a major industry?

Thinking about Community

Place-conscious instruction may also lead to or make room for place-focused engagement with the community. At the very least, embracing place-conscious instruction might promote civic engagement or allow students to think more about issues close to home. For example, Amy and a colleague, Sean Ruday, did a research project using place to teach students about argumentative writing (Ruday & Azano, 2019). Not only did students learn about persuasion and rhetoric, students chose local issues that affected them and their community. One student wrote about commercial fast food franchises replacing Mom and Pop stands at the local fair. Not only was this a concern of local interest but it was critical in nature as the student considered the impact of globalization on the local economy. Another student wrote about the economic considerations for a proposed bypass that would take travelers around (rather than through) their small, rural community. Not only were the objectives met for the language arts standards, but students also had an opportunity to develop critical understandings of the relationship between community decisions and their local economy. Importantly, students were not given a list of topics to choose from. Rather, they identified a place-conscious topic of importance to them.

Title	Question
When the Whippoorwill Calls (Ransom & Bulcken Root, 1995)	How did the establishment of the Shenandoah National Park affect the people who previously lived within its boundaries?
Letting Swift River Go (Yolen, 1992)	How are communities affected when natural resources in rural areas are used (extracted, exploited) for urban/suburban areas or for the "greater good"?
Grandpa's Tractor (Garland, 2011)	How has suburban sprawl changed the lives of family farmers?
Home (Baker, 2004).	How does human development affect the natural environment?
Window (Baker, 1991)	How can humans revitalize urban spaces?
The Little House (Burton, 1978)	How do rural communities become urbanized?

Scaffolding and Building Bridges

In developing a critical pedagogy of place, consider how your instruction and the curriculum can serve as scaffolds to content that seems more remote. For example, many high school English students read world literature texts, such as *Things Fall Apart* by Chinua Achebe. The novel is about colonization in Nigeria which might, initially, make students question its relevance to a small rural town in the United States. However, the first part of the novel explores the life of an Igbo man and the importance of family and customs in their community. These are universal themes and an exploration into considering why we value certain traditions in our community might allow students to extend that understanding to people who seem "different" or for traditions that might seem unusual.

Considering Your Sense of Place

It is important to consider the meaning you have made from places in your life if you want to employ place-conscious practices. This requires reflecting about place and, inevitably, sharing your experiences, feelings, and points of view. Your position as a teacher is powerful and there is always a risk that *your* understandings of place becoming the default for others in your classroom. Likewise, you'll have students who have experienced place differently, such as transient students or those for whom this place is not where they feel safe. You might even have students who feel no real sense of place even if they haven't moved around. *That's okay.* This is deeply personal work, and not everyone has strong place attachments.

The Critical Nature of this Work

The practice of building place-conscious curricula can reposition rural from the "periphery" to the "core," upending the core–periphery dynamic. The idea of the core–periphery model is a term used in sociology and economics to explain how influence or power is distributed between a core system and dependent or peripheral systems. In education, many decisions are made in a state's urban center and then the influence of those decisions proliferates into rural regions. The same is true for learning objectives and standardized curricula. By using local contexts, you create a more immediate context for learning. Students won't be learning concepts limited to textbooks and faraway places but, instead about the everyday things that make up their lives. This does not mean, of course, that global understandings and learning about distant people or places aren't important. Place-conscious learning *is not at the expense of learning about other places.* It is not a mutually exclusive concept! Place is simply a lens through which we can view the world. More importantly, when this work is critical in nature, it prioritizes learning connections between the local, regional, national, and global contexts, while calling into question power and privilege.

There has been some debate about using place in rural classrooms—and for good reason. Using place can do many things for the rural learner, such as increase engagement, which has been shown to correlate with achievement. However, place-conscious learning and critical place teaching should not be done in ways that are exclusionary. By exclusionary we mean that you don't want the learning of place to come at the expense of teaching students more global concepts or in ways that might engender provincial or close-minded thinking. It is important to leverage place as a way to make connections between local, national, and global contexts.

Praise and Appraisal

Place-conscious learning is not simply a means to praise and value everything wonderful about a place. Like people, places are fraught with complications and contradictions. Places are complex and so, too, should our learning of them be. Consider the social justice themes you read about in Chapter 2. As you plan for place-conscious instruction, consider ways to engage students with a critical look at economic, political, and cultural justice. Moving from a place of praise to a place of praise *and* appraisal allows us to be critical in our understanding of any given place.

Affirming a student's sense of place does not have to be limited by "positive" experiences alone. Considering the histories of a particular place or how places have been dispossessed or communities displaced provide an opportunity for young people to think critically about the complex meanings of place. Below you can find a list of picture books that engage readers with questions about place.

Value and Evaluate

When we move to appraisal in safe and challenging ways, students can learn to both value and evaluate their place. This allows us to critique with care. Many of us grew up in places with complex and painful histories. Place is not one dimensional. Therefore, our relationships with place shouldn't be one dimensional either. In doing this work, consider circling back to critical questions about rural places that have been discussed in other chapters that invite students to *remember* what is strong about rural communities, *restore* that which benefits rural people and places, *conserve* qualities about rural communities that should be protected, *change* that which oppresses or divides us, and *create* new, innovative ways to help rural communities thrive (Greenwood, 2013). Place conscious instruction can help you and your students engage in this work.

References

Baker, J. (2004). *Home*. Greenwillow Books.

Baker, J. (1991). *Window*. Greenwillow Books.

Brooke, R. (Ed.) (2003). *Rural voices: Place-conscious education and the teaching of writing*. Teachers College Press and the National Writing Project.

Burton, V. (1978). *The little house*. Houghton Mifflin.

Demarest, A. B. (2015). *Place-based curriculum design: Exceeding standards through local investigations*. Routledge.

Eppley, K., (2016). Forum: Rural science education as social justice. *Cultural studies in science education*, 12(1), 45–52. doi: https://10.1007/s11422-016-9751-7

Freire, P., & Macedo, D. (1987). *Literacy: Reading the word and the world*. Bergin & Garvey Publishers.

Garland, M. (2011). *Grandpa's tractor*. New York: Boyd's Mill Press.

Greenwood, D. A. (2013). A critical theory of place-conscious education. In R. B. Stevenson, M. Brody, J. Dillon, & A. E. J. Wals (Eds.), *International handbook of research on environmental education* (pp. 93–100). Routledge.

Haas, T., & Nachtigal, P. (1998). *Place value: An educator's guide to good literature on rural lifeways, environments, and purposes of education*. ERIC Clearinghouse on Rural Education and Small Schools.

Ransom, C., & Bulcken Root, K. (1995). *When the whippoorwill calls*. Harper Collins.

Rosenblatt, L. M. (1978). *The reader, the text, the poem: The transactional theory of the literary work*. Southern Illinois University Press.

Ruday, S., & Azano, A. P. (2019). Arguments that matter: A place based approach to teaching argument writing to rural students. *Journal of teaching Writing*, 34(1), 1–29.

Sobel, D. (2004). *Place-based education: connecting classrooms and communities*. Orion Society.

Theobald, P. (1997). *Teaching the commons: Place, pride, and the renewal of community*. Westview.

Yolen, J. (1992). *Letting Swift River go*. Little, Brown and Company.

14

Technology for Learning in the Rural Classroom

Instructional technology refers to various tools used in and out of the classroom to stimulate students' interest and engagement, support their comprehension and learning, and augment curricular offerings. While there are many aspects of instructional technology used daily in rural classrooms in the United States, there are some practical challenges to implementing various types of resources and accessing equipment and broadband internet service. This chapter explores some of the ways you can use instructional technology to best support student learning.

What Do We Mean by the Term Technology?

When you ask an engineer to define technology, they will tend to describe technology as *a man-made tool or process to manipulate the environment*. And they might also go on to provide you with a detailed narrative about the history of the word (technology comes from the Greek word *techne* originally meaning craft, craftsmanship, or art) accompanied by an explanation of how the various forms of technology have constantly changed and evolved over the years to provide our world with the precision tools and instruments we need to support our lives and livelihoods. But depending on who you talk with today, you may hear a lot of different descriptions of the various forms of technology in our world. For example, if you talk to people who work in construction, or mining, or farming, each will be able to describe the various machines, tools, software, and hardware in use today and explain how all of these have developed and changed over the years.

What comes to mind when you consider the ways that technology is used in the field of education? When we think about the various kinds of technology in schools and classrooms across the country today, most of us picture various types of electronic or computer-related devices such as phones, tablets, computers, cameras, robots, and 3D printers rather than the original Greek idea of arts or craftsmanship. Some rural schools are very well-equipped with electronic devices. For example, Jordan Bear is a rural K–8 teacher in the Neoga School District, in Central Illinois. He describes some of the different types of devices used across his district:

> We have classroom sets of Chromebooks all the way down to second grade, as well as three computer labs with new desktop computers and Promethean Boards in every classroom. We have three 3D printers and students as young as third grade are using Computer Aided Design (CAD) to create and print 3D models. Students build and code Lego Robots to complete challenges. We have a drone and a GoPro that we use for photo and video editing. Elementary students do a newscast that we put on YouTube (NES News) and we use green screen technology, a camcorder and audio and video editing to put together a small newscast for the school. With some of my junior high students we have built an arcade using a Raspberry Pi; we are working with the Neoga Agriculture Department to build a case for the arcade using their CNC machine. Junior high students are also coding using Arduino microcontrollers that were purchased for our classroom by the Neoga PTO. Larger schools may have some or even all of these resources to some capacity, but the difference at a rural school with smaller classes is that every student will have these classes in the elementary and junior high and have exposure and experience with these technologies. It is not an elective, it is part of the curriculum.
>
> Read more about Jordan's story at http://iamaruralteacher.org

Purpose of Technology in the Rural Classroom

When we think about using technology in the classroom, it's important to think not only about the equipment and instruments, but also about the ways in which technology can be used to assist people and increase access to information and understanding. In this way, technology in the classroom is much more than a device; it's also a critical process of providing access, assistance, and support that come together to increase student learning. And so it's really important to think about both the products and the processes involved in student learning—the hardware (phones, tablets, computers, cameras, robots, 3D printers, etc.), the various software programs

g on those devices, the connections to the internet, as well as the
ied access and assistance that students need to process and learn
important ideas and information. In this light, the purpose of technology in
the rural classroom is to facilitate student learning.

For Discussion

What technology (hardware and software) have you used in the last 24
hours? How did that technology help you? What purpose did it serve or
what did you use it for (communication? learning? entertainment? to
create? etc.)? How did that technology help you learn?

Rural teachers who approach technology with student learning in mind
do not treat hardware, software, and internet access as a replacement for
good teaching. Rather, when used in pedagogically appropriate and intentional ways, technology can be integrated into teaching as an important tool
to foster student curiosity, inquiry, and ultimately learning. Effective use of
technology starts by identifying student learning needs and goals and then
selecting the best available tools to meet those goals. This requires that
teachers adopt a skeptical and thoughtful approach to technology integration where screen time is not "bell-to-bell" but is deliberately managed in
service of student learning.

Here is an example from a rural teacher in Montana who carefully
integrated technology to support student learning: While on a trip to Wisconsin, Chateau Van Voast (who teaches fourth, seventh, and eighth grade),
collected some different types of cheese to bring back and share with her
students. In order to taste the cheese, the students had to work together to
complete a Digital Breakout activity (an online escape room) about the state
of Wisconsin using clues from articles, word puzzles, pictures, and Google
maps such as number codes, direction codes, word codes, and color pattern
codes. This social studies lesson created an authentic sense of engagement
and inquiry and also fostered the development of students' collaboration,
problem solving, and communication skills. Read more from other rural
teachers at https://mfbf.org/Article/Ag-in-MY-Classroom-WinWin-for-Tea
chers-and-Agriculture.

Affordances of Technology to Support Student Learning

As Chateau's example shows, technology can provide useful tools for teachers as they seek to improve learning outcomes for students. Over the

years, educators have recognized that no matter the age, ability, or content area, all students will experience barriers to learning at different times. Typically, these barriers occur when information is presented in only one way, and while the approach may be a good fit for some students, it is not a good fit for others. Thus, when technology is carefully integrated in the classroom, it can serve to reduce the different barriers to learning that students experience.

How can teachers most effectively use technological tools to support learning? A group of researchers (www.cast.org) have been working to develop a set of principles that can help teachers proactively recognize and address the learning needs of all students. This set of principles is called the Universal Design for Learning (UDL) framework. The UDL framework is an important way of thinking about teaching because it provides teachers with guidance and ideas for multiple ways to: 1) engage students in the learning process; 2) increase student understanding of content; and 3) enable students to demonstrate what they are understanding and where they still need to grow. The UDL framework also helps teachers to select and use technological tools that will increase student engagement, representation, and expression. Further information about the UDL framework can be found on the National Center on Universal Design for Learning website http://www.udlcenter.org/aboutudl/udlguidelines.

When technological tools are integrated carefully and with intention, they can help to optimize learning for all students and provide avenues for each student to grow and succeed. These types of tools can be leveraged to meet students' learning needs by providing a variety of ways to stimulate student interest, increase access to the content, and allow students to demonstrate what they have learned. Also, various forms of Assistive Technology can also make a significant difference for students with disabilities. Overall, engaging with technology in the classroom gives all students opportunities to build the knowledge and skills they will need to be engaged members of our society.

Stimulating Student Interest and Engagement

When properly and skillfully integrated in learning experiences, technological tools can serve as ways to increase student interest and engagement. These types of tools can help to motivate students to begin the learning process and then once underway, help them to actively focus on the learning goals and increase their attention to the work of learning. As students use technology tools to be more focused and less distracted, they will be able to spend more time-on-task, and this can lead to increased comprehension. Furthermore, when technology (such as a well-designed game or application) provides a way for students to engage in authentic learning by thinking for themselves, making decisions, and creating meaningful products, well-designed games and other apps enable students to become active and successful learners.

Increasing Student Access to Information

Technology can provide students with access to information and opportunities that go well beyond the walls of the classroom. With internet connectivity, information from around the world can be accessible to your rural classroom. You can introduce your students to an amazing array of resources through virtual field trips of museums, historical landmarks, and geological sites to help your students learn about the world beyond their local community. You can also introduce your class to student-friendly online research tools and databases such as the Digital Public Library of America, Gooru, or online encyclopedias and reference tools. Countless primary sources have been digitized and made available by the Library of Congress and other archives.

Of course, it is important to teach students to develop and use strong media literacy skills. You will need to teach them specific developmentally appropriate skills about how to locate, evaluate, and use the information they find online. They need to know how to identify different types of media, and critique these sources to identify biased or false information. Student also need to be taught how to stay safe when they are working online. Organizations such as Common Sense (https://www.commonsense.org/education/) can provide you with resources you need to help your students become savvy digital citizens.

Expanding Student Creativity, Collaboration, and Communication

Technology tools can be used to foster student creativity and collaboration in the classroom. Students in your classroom could work in pairs or groups to conduct research on a topic and then collaborate to design and create a presentation, a document, or a project to share their learning. One powerful example of this affordance is the use of digital story telling where students have the opportunity to create multimedia presentations that combine different types of pictures, graphics, or videos along with text to communicate their learning in powerful ways. Some digital story telling tools include: Google Tourbuilder (https://tourbuilder.withgoogle.com), ArcGIS Story-Maps (https://storymaps.arcgis.com), or Storybird (https://storybird.com).

Your students' collaboration and communication skills can also be enhanced via technologically facilitated connections with students and adults at other schools. You could arrange to have experiences such as digital pen pals, emails to experts in the field, or video interviews with authors to further your students' understanding. You could set up e-pals or Zoom buddies to help your students practice their language skills. However, in all these cases, best practice requires that students be taught internet safety and privacy skills and any type of online collaboration or interaction with people outside of school must always be aligned with your district's technology use policies.

Assistive Technology to Support Student Learning

A particularly powerful use of technology is to provide Assistive Technology to students with disabilities. Assistive Technology is the term used to describe products, technological tools, or other systems that help students with disabilities with daily functioning and learning (Israel et al., 2014). Assistive Technology includes a variety of types of hardware, software, specialized curriculum and communication aids, as well as devices such as wheelchairs, walkers, braces, or supports that meet the needs of students. Assistive Technology can be used to help students with daily living and learning tasks. For example, text-to-speech tools "read" text out loud and can help to increase students' access to content. A speech-to-text application can transform a student's spoken words into text and increase students' ability to demonstrate their understanding. Braille readers, screen readers and magnifiers help students with vision impairment. Laser pointers attached to head gear can help students with mobility issues to point at objects or navigate a computer screen. Communication devices allow students to point, tap, or click if they are unable to speak. Some teachers wear portable microphones for students who need amplification (https://www.atia.org/home/at-resources/what-is-at/).

While some rural schools may have limited access to Assistive Technology for their students, organizations across the country are developing innovative ways to address this need. For example, an increasing number of Assistive Technology supports are being developed for phones and tablets. Smart phones can magnify text or convert speech to text. There is even an app (Be My Eyes) that people who are blind or have low vision can use that connects them via video chat with volunteer readers to read the labels, directions, or any text for which the need assistance. In some rural places, mobile classrooms equipped with assistive technologies are made accessible to the school via car, converted van, bus, or RV that can travel to rural communities.

Preparing for the Workforce of the Future

When you carefully integrate technology in your classroom, you are also helping to prepare your students for careers in new and emerging fields. Many rural communities are finding that changing technologies are creating new opportunities for economic development. There is an increasing demand for employees who know how to write code, design virtual reality programs, develop apps for phones, and pilot drones. As internet connectivity continues to improve, it will become increasingly possible to live in rural places and work just about anywhere in the world. For example, a radiologist who lives in Michigan reads X-rays and CT scans for hospitals in Arizona and Tennessee. More and more, students' fluency with various technological tools and the development of skills such as computational thinking will help them to be prepared to contribute as knowledgeable and productive employees, employers, and rural community members.

For Discussion

What technology (hardware, software, etc.) have you seen that you would like to integrate in your teaching? What websites or tools seem particularly useful? How would they increase students' attention and focus, deepen their learning, help them create and synthesize knowledge, or develop twenty-first-century skills such as collaboration and communication?

Addressing Technology Challenges in Rural Schools and Homes

As we saw in the story at the beginning of this chapter, the rural teacher from the Neoga School District in Illinois described access to outstanding technology resources in terms of hardware, software, and internet access. However, this is not the case for all rural communities. While technology offers many affordances to support student learning, rural schools and communities face several challenges as they seek to integrate technology for student learning in classrooms, schools, and homes.

Funding for Technology

Across the country, communities are struggling to find ways to fully fund their schools. This means that there are many rural schools that do not have the financial capacity to purchase cutting-edge tools for robotics or virtual reality, let alone to provide laptops or tablets for every student or classroom. In those schools, principals and superintendents stretch their resources the best they can and teachers use their creativity and innovative skills to engage students with the technology that is available.

As a rural teacher, you may have the opportunity to write grant proposals seeking funding from a government agency, foundation, or a local business partner to support a technology-related program or a project in your school. You can also search for possible grant funding on websites such as https://www.grants4teachers.com or https://www.getedfunding.com. Grant proposals can range anywhere from a few hundred dollars to thousands of dollars depending on the needs of the school and the parameters of the funding organization. If you locate a grant opportunity, you will need to be sure to follow your school board's policies and requirements for submitting the proposal. And as you prepare to write your grant, here are the questions you will need to be able answer for the funding source in a clear and compelling manner:

- What is the problem you are trying to solve?
- What will be achieved through the funding?
- How will the goals be achieved?
- How long it will take?
- How will you know if you were successful?
- Who will be involved?
- How much will it cost?

Disparities in Broadband Internet Connectivity

Broadband internet connectivity is also a serious concern in many rural areas. While some rural areas have excellent internet connectivity, there are also many towns and counties where the connectivity is very poor and broadband internet speeds do not meet minimum federal standards. In fact, according to the Federal Communications Commission (FCC, 2019), over 26% of people in rural areas and 32% of people in Tribal lands lack adequate broadband coverage, while only 1.7% of people in urban areas lack adequate access. Rural scholars have clearly shown how direct access to high quality broadband is critical for the well-being of every aspect of a community's life including, "consumer welfare, civic participation, public safety, community development, health care delivery, education, private sector investment, entrepreneurial activity and economic growth" (Eppley & Shannon, 2015, p. 64).

Rural leaders have called for broadband connectivity to be treated as a basic utility; this would mean that all communities in the country would receive broadband access in the same way that utilities such as water, electricity, and telephone are provided for residents even when the community has a small population or is located in a very remote location. In this light, adequate broadband access becomes a critical issue of social justice that needs to be addressed to provide rural students with the connectivity needed to fully engage with their place and their world. In 2020, the Federal Communications Commission (FCC) established the Rural Digital Opportunity Fund of $20.4 billion over 10 years for the purpose of providing high-speed broadband internet for rural areas across the U.S. (www.fcc.gov/document/fcc-launches-20-billion-rural-digital-opportunity-fund-0). The federal government is also working to improve the broadband internet infrastructure in unserved and underserved rural communities through efforts such as the American Broadband Initiative (ABI) (www.ntia.doc.gov/category/american-broadband-initiative) and provisions contained in proposed legislation such as the HR2 Moving Forward Act (https://transportation.house.gov/imo/media/doc/Fact%20sheet%20HR%202%20Moving%20Forward%20Act%20FINAL.pdf).

However, until connectivity is universal, it is important for rural teachers to remember that even though their students may have access to devices and internet connectivity at school, they may not have computers and/or internet access when they get home. Sometimes this situation has been referred to as the homework gap. Rural students report struggling to complete homework assignments for various computer-related reasons: they may have to share a computer with parents and siblings; their devices are too old to run current programs; their internet is slow, intermittent, unstable, or non-existent. Some students may need to access the internet through connections at their community library. And while some rural families may be able to use their phones for access to the internet, it important to remember that just because a student may have a smartphone, this does not mean they will have cell service where they live. There are still many rural areas that do not have adequate cell service. Furthermore, students who rely solely on their smartphones for homework completion perform as poorly as those who have no internet access at all. So as you think about at-home assignments for your students, it will be good to consider whether or not your students have a computer and internet access at home, if their daily living situation requires them to split their time between multiple homes with different types of access, or if there are adults available at home to provide support for digital tasks.

In an effort to close the homework gap, some districts have installed Wi-Fi hotspots on school buses to give students access to the internet. In some districts, these are available or for students during their morning and afternoon bus rides. These hotspots work by connecting to a 3G or 4G cellular network and then sharing that connection via Wi-Fi to nearby devices; however, this solution only works in rural areas that have a 3G or 4G cell network. Some districts use the hotspots to stream math or science video content for students to watch on their hour-long rides to and from school. Others hope students will use the Wi-Fi hotspots to support homework completion. Anecdotal evidence suggests that some students are taking advantage of this opportunity, and some schools report improvements in student grades, confidence, and homework completion. However, other reports indicate that students are using the available Wi-Fi to engage with social media and entertainment sites rather than finish their homework. This is not surprising, given how difficult it can be to concentrate on schoolwork on a noisy bus on dusty, bumpy roads in all sorts of weather, not to mention the risk of motion sickness. Other districts are parking the buses with Wi-Fi hotspots in rural areas so students can park nearby and do homework in the car. Neither of these bus options is perfect, and neither ensures student learning or equal access to opportunities to learn, but they are steps rural districts are taking to try and increase broadband access for students.

Teaching with Technology in the Rural Classroom

Technology can be an important tool in your work as a rural teacher, both for enhancing your students' learning and for supporting your own instructional planning, teaching, and assessment. A web-based learning management system can help you manage student assignments and grading. Digital tools can help you assess your students' learning, identify where knowledge gaps still exist, and provide data to help you with ongoing instructional decision making. In these ways, technology can empower both you and your students in the teaching–learning process.

You may have access to various types of equipment, tools, and devices similar to what Mr. Bear described at the beginning of this chapter. You may also have a great deal of support in your school and district as you begin to integrate technology in your classroom. Your district may have a dedicated tech support person who can help you set up your hardware and manage your software, as well as technology coaches who can help you identify resources and tools to meet your goals, or experts in robotics and virtual reality and coding and 3D printing who can help you share new technologies with your students.

However, some rural schools may have fewer resources to help you as you plan to integrate technology in your classroom. In those cases, you may need to locate some professional development opportunities (either online or in person) to help you get started. There are numerous professional organizations, both for specific content areas and those focusing on technology, such as the International Society for Technology in Education (ITSE), that can give you advice and share trusted resources for your discipline (See Chapter 9). And of course, there are numerous online sources including how-to videos, tutorials, and resources that can help you achieve your goals with technology. In Chapter 9, we discussed the importance of building a professional learning network using social media (e.g. Twitter) to build connections with other teachers to share expertise and ideas. As you work to learn about technology it may be helpful to build a learning network focused around the technology tools you would like to use in your classroom. For example, there are online professional communities where you can learn about tools such as Merge Cubes (a programmable, multi-sensory virtual reality tool), Nearpod (an interactive presentation tool), or pursue training to become a Google Certified Educator.

For Discussion

Visit the website of ISTE (http://www.iste.org). Explore the ISTE standards and the learning resources they have there. Which ones provide useful information that can help you plan learning experiences for technology in your classroom? Then, search Twitter or another platform. Can you find other educators who are posting about technology tools you have heard of or that you would like to learn more about?

Remote Teaching and Learning in Rural Places

Finally, we want to discuss the challenges created in rural contexts when there is a need for remote learning as we experienced during the coronavirus global pandemic of 2020. As we were writing this textbook, we found our world turned upside down as we all grappled with the impact of the COVID-19 disease, the need for social distancing, stay-at-home orders, and nation-wide school and university closures. Throughout these difficult days educators everywhere did their best to continue teaching and supporting student learning, while also caring for themselves and their loved ones.

Technology provided useful tools for teachers and students during this difficult time. But the crisis also revealed serious disparities in access to technology and broadband connectivity as educators turned to various video platforms to meet synchronously with their students and share recorded lectures. Some teachers made curriculum accessible via Google Classroom. Schools which were able loaned Chromebooks to students who didn't have a computer at home. Districts created tech hotlines to provide support for families and put Wi-Fi hotspots on their school buses and parked them in places where students could access the signal. Even some service providers were reducing their fees or providing additional free Wi-Fi to help support students.

See the two-page guide from the Regional Educational Laboratory Central called *Strategies to Support Learning Along a Continuum of Internet Access* for more information about how to support remote learning. The guide can be accessed at https://ies.ed.gov/ncee/edlabs/regions/central/pdf/RELCentral_Remote-Learning-QC-Handout.pdf.

Teachers were very aware of the digital inequalities in their students' lives. They understood that for some of their students, it could take 90 minutes to upload a two-minute video, and that was only after driving many miles to connect to a local Wi-Fi hotspot. And so many teachers also had to find ways to connect with students who had limited devices and internet access. For students with limited internet access, rural teachers used some lower-technology-intensive approaches. For example, they had students record themselves reading for submission later. They had students save their work to a thumb drive that could be dropped off at the school once a week. They created materials that could be downloaded online at a local hotspot and used off-line at home. Others created a learning schedule for the week whereby students could watch educational television content from various providers and complete carefully aligned projects to strengthen student learning.

In the situations where students had no digital technology, teachers worked tirelessly to share resources by developing and delivering or mailing paper packets to students and connecting with them via landline phones where cell service didn't exist. They created family read-aloud activities, games, and flash cards that students could keep, as well as tubs with materials and library book exchanges that could be loaned out to families and then disinfected upon return. In all these cases, the focus was on supporting student learning and whether through high tech, low tech, or no tech, students' well-being and best interests remained front and center.

References

Eppley, K., & Shannon, P. (2015). Literacy education for the lumps and divots of smart cities and rural places. In S. Grimes, & A. Grooms (Eds.). *Educational opportunity in rural contexts: The politics of place.* (p. 59–73). Information Age Publishing.

Federal Communications Commission [FCC]. (2019). *Broadband deployment report: Inquiry concerning deployment of advanced telecommunications capability to all Americans in a reasonable and timely fashion.* https://docs.fcc.gov/public/attachments/FCC-19-44A1.pdf

Israel, M., Ribuffo, C., & Smith, S. (2014). *Universal design for learning: Recommendations for teacher preparation and professional development (Document No. IC-7).* University of Florida, Collaboration for Effective Educator, Development, Accountability, and Reform Center. http://ceedar.education.ufl.edu/tools/innovation-configurations/

15

Diversity in the Rural Classroom

Amy, one of the authors of this book, writes:

Estela Knott, the daughter of a Mexican mother and a Scots-Irish father, is a childhood friend of mine. We went to school together in Virginia's She-nandoah Valley, attended the same church, and our parents have been life-long friends. While Estela was raised on homemade tortillas and other authentic Mexican cuisine at home, we both grew up on Southern country-fried food, traditional folk songs, and clogging. And, like most kids in our small town, we eagerly awaited the Page County Industrial and Agri-cultural Fair—the annual event with its tractor pull and demolition derby signaling the end of summer. Having grown up in Luray, our identities were shaped by those experiences, and a sense of place continues to play prominently in both our lives—for me, as a rural education scholar, doing the sort of work represented in this book, and for Estela, as a cultural organizer, teacher, and musician committed to telling the untold stories of immigrants in the Shenandoah Valley and sharing a musical tradition that humanizes a marginalized population. Estela's group, Lua, is an original music ensemble that blends elements of Latin and Appalachian song tradi-tions. She explains, "Mexilachian music is the soundtrack of my life."

Estela's mother, Guadalupe, was born in Juarez Chihuahua, Mexico, just across the border from El Paso, Texas. They moved to El Paso when she was nine years old. As a young adult, she met Estela's father, Roger, when he was stationed in the Army at Fort Bliss. Upon his release from the Army, they married and moved back to Luray, at a time when interracial marriages were still illegal in some states and not accepted in most. There was no one from Latin America living in Luray so the language was a challenge as no one spoke Spanish in the community. Estela has a distinct memory of being a young girl (maybe seven or eight) and shopping with her mother in a local store. As her mother said "hello" to a woman with whom she was familiar, Estela remembers the woman looking embarrassed that "Lupe" was speaking to her in public. When she asked her mother about the woman's odd behavior, her mother explained that people are afraid of what they don't understand. Estela took that simple lesson to heart and—in addition to her extensive community work (e.g., establishing cultural arts programs and events)—she and her husband also work in regional schools on programs that celebrate not just Mexican and Latinx cultures but also "Mexilachian" culture—a celebration of Mexican heritage expressed through language, food, dress, dance, and song—that is also contextualized by life in Appalachia. She wants young people of color coming into rural communities to know that they don't have to assimilate in a way that totally abandons their own cultural identity or cultural heritage. She explains that it's so important for kids to see themselves and their culture in their broader community. However, her work also addresses what her wise mother shared with her as a young girl—that people are fearful of what they don't understand. She says, "It's so important for us to educate them and share with them the rich cultural life that we bring to the community." She hopes their cultural work also celebrates diversity in ways that highlight how that diversity contributes to and constructs local culture.

In this chapter, we take up the issue of diversity in rural classrooms. In its simplest explanation, diversity is what makes us different from one another. We can be different from one another in many ways. Your students will have different personalities, abilities, interests, and values. These differences make your classroom a more interesting and vibrant place. You will want to make sure that every student feels welcome and celebrated in your classroom. We invite you to consider and celebrate the unique attributes of each student. We want you to think about diversity in rural schools in complex ways.

Why Diversity Matters

Traditional ways of thinking about diversity typically focus on race, ethnicity, religion, sexual orientation, gender expression, and neurodiversity (among others)—and we often speak of "others" as "being diverse" because they are *different* from majority White and Western notions of *typical*. But throughout the world, this is not the case and in fact in many places in the United States and in some rural places there are "majority minority" populations where an idea of diversity as different majority would not fit. Additionally, there are many ways iɪ identities intersect with other ways of being. For example, Estela is American *and* Appalachian. In this chapter we consider those intersecting identities and the ways rural teachers should be prepared to meet the needs of all students in the classroom.

We aim to challenge some of the traditional ways of thinking about diversity. One reason for this stance is that the teachers in the United States tend to have a lot in common culturally. While the number of White students enrolled in U.S. schools has decreased to 48% (and is projected to continue decreasing), 79% of the nation's teachers are White, and the majority (76%) of them are women (Hussar et al., 2020). In addition, several studies have indicated that a significant number of preservice teachers have grown up with limited personal relationships with people who come from backgrounds different from their own.

In her research, Ann, one of the authors of this book, investigated this increasing cultural mismatch between teachers and their students. As a White, working-class, Christian, cisgender, English-speaking woman, Ann shares a similar background with her preservice teachers. Her research explores questions about how she can prepare the future teachers in her classes to build relationships with all students, especially those with backgrounds different from hers and most of her students. A strongly shared culture among teachers and students can make it difficult to challenge our thinking and perspectives, especially when it comes to talking about topics like racism, classism, and heteronormativity. This can also present a challenge for students in a class whose identity is different from the instructor and most others in the group. This person can sometimes be expected to be a "spokesperson" and represent everyone or be the expert about the identity under discussion.

Not all educators are White women, and it is important for all educators to think in complex ways about issues of diversity. Jamon Flowers studies how race is related to privilege and power in rural schools. Dr. Flowers explains that race informs meaning making in the professional lives (e.g., behaviors and attitudes), leadership practices (e.g., leadership approaches and work ethics), and self-views of African American rural principals (Flowers, 2020). In other words, a person's identity permeates their work in schools.

In Chapter 6, we invited you to reflect on your assumptions about rural places and challenge your preconceived notions by getting to know your community. In the same way, we hope this chapter will offer several new ways to think about how our perceptions of our students are shaped by our backgrounds and experiences, and how interrogating the assumptions we make as a result of those perceptions can lead us to see difference as a strength. But this work, for all people, begins with a look at our own conceptions about difference.

Deficit Thinking

The concept of deficit thinking is critical to understanding why diversity matters. Although as a preservice teacher you value diversity, you may still have implicit, and sometimes explicit, preexisting ideas about others. Often, those implicit assumptions represent deficit thinking. Deficit thinking is when the assumption that differences—differences in values, behaviors, beliefs, socioeconomic status—are signs of something lacking or "wrong" about another person or group. Negative or stereotypical images in popular culture and the media about people and communities that have been historically marginalized and oppressed (see Chapter 2 for more on the history of rural places) can also lead to deficit thinking.

Teachers' deficit thinking about students and their families is not uncommon (Purcell-Gates, 2002). For example, Estela's mom, in the opening vignette of this chapter, was made to feel unwelcome when she first came to Luray, Virginia, because people had deficit assumptions about her, including assumptions about her immigration status. Many assumed she was in the United States illegally and had married Estela's father to become a citizen when she was, in fact, already a citizen. Another deficit assumption was that she came from a lower-class family when, in reality, she came from an economically secure business-class family who gave up that security when they moved to the U.S. in order to seek medical care and an education for a family member.

Deficit ways of thinking can take many forms and can be hard to recognize, since our default assumptions tend to be based on dominant White upper-middle-class ideals and values. For example, our ideas about what counts as "proper" or "correct" language use is one area where deficit assumptions are common. In particular, the power of standardized language norms reinforces beliefs that some ways of speaking are objectively more "correct" than others. It is no coincidence that these ways of speaking tend to be the language variety of our dominant cultural and linguistic group (Lippi-Green, 2012). In the United States, "correct" language, no matter the situation, is incorrectly understood as an unmarked, "unaccented" variety of English spoken by a monolingual speaker. Nonstandard language varieties (like African American English or Appalachian English) and heritage languages (like Spanish and Tagalog) represent a deficit in the classroom. Often in classrooms, language varieties are something to be eradicated. An essential step towards combatting these deficit views of home language varieties is learning about language diversity. In realizing the varied ways that students might express themselves—at home and at school—educators can begin to acknowledge that all students' ways of speaking have value and demonstrate rich and complex communication. We want you to think about how to invite students to *add* language varieties, including language varieties used in official situations and formal settings, rather than replace students' language usage.

Understanding Less Obvious Difference

Diversity also matters in ways that can be less obvious. Now that you've had the chance to learn about deficit thinking, you can use what you've learned to consider in complex ways about how diversity is not readily apparent in classrooms. In what at first glance might seem like a culturally homogenous rural community, the ways in which a classroom is diverse is not always obvious. For example, Kara, a second-grade teacher in Western Michigan, might see her students as mostly similar. The box next to "White" is ticked on their demographic information form. The school building itself is located out in the country, too far from any neighborhoods for students to walk to school, so all her students ride the bus. Her students are the same age and have similar interests. They enjoy when she reads aloud, smile when she praises how hard they work, and wish that recess lasted just a little longer.

But as Kara got to know her students and their families, she could see there are important ways they are unique and different from one another. More than half of the families attend a Protestant church on the weekend, but many families do not attend church, and one student's family members are Jehovah's Witnesses. There is some neurodiversity within the class; six of the students have been identified for special education services for learning disabilities in reading or math, and one student with autism. Many of the students' families have lived in the area for three or more generations, but a handful of Kara's students are relative newcomers and a few of them are emergent bilingual. They moved to the area only a few years ago for work in the hydraulic fracking industry. The longstanding but now defunct garment factory, just two miles from the elementary school, had once employed many of the adults in the community. Some families are still struggling to recover financially from its closure. Because of this and other economic struggles in the community, approximately two-thirds of Kara's students qualify for free lunch. Some of the families have a mom and a dad and one family has two moms. Other students have a single parent or live with grandparents. One student was recently adopted out of foster care. Kara's students have interesting differences in background, experience, and values that bring richness and variety into the classroom.

For Discussion

Talk with a partner. What are some things the two of you have in common? What are ways that you are different from each other? Which of these similarities and differences is a typical category that comes to mind when we think about "diversity"? Which of these are obvious to outsiders? Which are less obvious?

Sometimes, teachers who grew up in the same community in which they teach already feel as though they know a lot about students simply by knowing where they live or who their siblings are. Or a teacher may be new to the community but bring with them several preconceptions. In either case, you bring a point of view with you to the classroom. What you think you know as a result of your experience being from the community or a newcomer is filtered through that lens and may obscure your ability to see your classroom as a diverse space.

Stereotype Threat

Another reason diversity matters is because deficit ideologies can influence teaching and learning. Stereotype threat is a construct used to explain how deficit thinking and negative stereotypes can affect learners. Stereotype threat has been described as the sensation of living under a cloud (Steele, 2010). These clouds are made up of others' assumptions about you and can be found everywhere in society, including in rural communities. Stereotype threat is defined as "being at risk of conforming, as self-characteristic, a negative stereotype about one's group" (Steele & Aronson, 1995, p. 797). In other words, students internalize negative stereotypes which can affect outcomes in academic settings when they rely on those stereotypes as accurate descriptions of the groups they belong to.

There are many factors contributing to students' susceptibility of stereotype threat, including situations with an especially difficult task, being aware of the stigma related to the group, and identifying strongly with the stereotyped group (Pennington et al., 2016). Therefore, it can be helpful to consider stereotype threat as it relates to rural students, in particular. It is not uncommon for people to have negative stereotypes about rural people and places that perpetuate deficit assumptions. Outsiders who do not know rural communities well may assume that rural students are not interested in the arts or classical music, might assume that rural teenagers are not interested in advanced sciences or going to college, or might assume that farmers and miners are yokels who do not understand the larger economy or the way the world works. None of these assumptions is accurate. Because there are so many negative stereotypes about rural people this idea of stereotypes as a "threat" to academic engagement and performance is an important one to consider. For rural students with strong connections to place, this threat may be even greater.

For Discussion

Think about images of rural people in the media. Make a list of who or what comes to mind. Evaluate if the images are positive. Or, do they perpetuate a deficit stereotype? Have you experienced stereotype threat related to your rural upbringing or other aspects of your background?

Challenging Deficit Thinking

There are ways to disrupt deficit thinking and to reduce stereotype threat for students. Teaching for diversity means that you become self-aware about your conceptions of difference and consider different frames of reference as you learn about your students in all of their diversity. Critical reflection and learning about your students as individuals are places to start. There are a number of important theories, frameworks, and approaches about diversity that will be helpful in your career as an educator. We hope you will have an opportunity to delve deeper into those ideas in other classes or during professional development opportunities. In this book, we want to challenge you to specifically think about how diversity is represented and celebrated in rural spaces. Chapters 5 and 7 also help you identify and challenge deficit ways of thinking about rural families and communities. The intention in this chapter is to encourage your sense of self-awareness.

Become Self-Aware

It is normal to find affinity with others who are most like you and to see the world through the lenses of your own experience and background.

Whether we are "from here" or "from away," our perceptions of others may be inaccurate. Our identities can sometimes serve as a type of blinder that might lead to us to make assumptions. For example, if you are in a heteronormative relationship, you might casually share details about your partner, or ask someone about their partner in ways that will demonstrate your assumption that they, too, are heterosexual. If you regularly attend religious services, you might ask about what church someone belongs to, without recognizing how your question implies that they *ought* to be attending Sunday church services. While you would never intend to make someone uncomfortable, your comments could communicate your bias and prejudice. To become more self-aware is to consider your frames of reference and stay attuned to how they shape your perceptions, your judgements, and your assumptions about your students and their families.

Teaching all students well means you work explicitly to reflect on personal beliefs and assumptions, examine biases, and learn about and understand your students. Every one of us, no matter where we are from, has a built-in perspective about ourselves and others. Our identities, our sense of ourselves, and how we understand, are learned as we interact with those around us. Sometimes, identities and life experiences create a frame of reference that may seem in conflict with other perspectives in your rural community. When these issues arise, rather than "agreeing to disagree," you have an opportunity to honor your differences and create compassion in your classroom. To become self-aware, you must engage in critical reflection with a sense of cultural humility (see Chapter 6), that is, with an understanding that your way of acting and seeing the world are different from, but not necessarily better than others. Critical reflection is important because simply naming and being aware of difference may reinforce stereotypes if that awareness does not come with knowledge and reflection.

Assume Funds of Knowledge

You can become more self-aware and disrupt deficit thinking if you work to learn about and invite students' funds of knowledge (González et al., 2005; Moll et al., 1992) into the classroom. In a previous chapter, we shared Paulo Freire's critique of what he called the "banking model" of education. In that critique, he explained that traditional instruction treats students as passive learners waiting for the "deposits" of knowledge given by all-knowing teachers. "Funds" of knowledge capitalize on students' wealth of information and experiences. Students are not empty vessels waiting for deposits of information. They have knowledge learned at home, from their families and communities, and these funds of knowledge represent skills and expertise, and should be recognized as worthwhile. However, students' informal, out-of-school funds of knowledge may not always be recognized or appreciated in formal school settings or by individuals who are not familiar with the community. Rural students, for example, may know how to hunt, or fish, or ride horses. They might know when the wild raspberries growing on the side of the road are ripe and how to pick them without getting scratched by the thorns. Rural students may also know how to solve engineering puzzles, play video games, how to can beans, or how to make sure you get the right change when you stop at the Dollar General for a bag of hot chips. These funds of knowledge demonstrate students' experiences, values, and creativity. They can serve as the foundation for future learning when teachers refuse to take a deficit stance.

Build Knowledge about Students

As a teacher, you can challenge your own assumptions by working to build knowledge about your students, including their funds of knowledge. The goal of this approach to teaching is to validate your students in whatever way you can and support them to express themselves authentically (Bartolome, 1994). This may be even more important when you have students in your classroom who represent a type of identity that might be considered outside the norm in community.

One way to do this is by taking an interest in the things your students are interested in. You might design assignments that allow students to bring in artifacts or objects from home and demonstrate their skill or knowledge or allow students to write or talk about the traditions, music, or activities they do at home. Chapters 6 and 7, which focus on understanding the community and working with families, will give you concrete ideas for this.

Connecting with students from any background is about meeting them where they are at. This applies to all types of identities and backgrounds. The extent to which you are able to get to know your students as people will significantly impact your ability to know them as learners. Each aspect of their identity is part of what shapes their perspectives.

It is also important to make sure you have, or build, knowledge about your community and your students' and families' role in the community. As we discuss in Chapters 2 and 3, the United States, and rural places in particular, have a long history of practices that have led to inequal access to education and resources. The more you know about historic and present-day barriers to economic, social, and political justice in your community, the more you can teach in ways that explicitly address and work to dismantle these barriers. If you, or your students, belong to one or more groups which have been a victim of racism, classism, ableism, or other forces, these are and will always be present in your diverse classroom and are likely to be important aspects of your students' experience.

Rethink Labels

As you may already suspect, labels may contribute to creating economic, social, and political injustice. Every student has a label of some kind, but some are more impactful than others. Labels, such as "low-achieving," "smart," "struggling reader," and "at-risk" tend to be used to permanently categorize students as what they are and what they're not. These types of labels are very difficult to shed. The issue of labels in schools is an especially difficult issue. Labeling often results in a distinctly negative outcome. For example, schools often use a child's test scores (below basic, basic, proficient, advanced) as labels. A student with a test score of "below basic" in middle school may not have access to particular classes. On the other hand, necessary special education services require a diagnosis that results in a label. In this case, the label is key to accessing services. Understandably, some parents refuse testing for special education services because they want to avoid the negative effects of an official diagnosis and label. As a result, some children do not get needed services.

In schools, labels are often used to identify students' demographic backgrounds, and often these categories are imposed by outsiders. However, they may mask important differences. Different international and ethnic groups have different preferences about identifiers. For example, students are often described as Hispanic on school records. Technically Hispanic is a term related to language derivation and relates to anyone from a Spanish speaking country. But students may also identify as Latino/a/x, which means they or their families are from Latin America (the "x" is used when people prefer a single gender-neutral term). Instead of using generalized terms such as Hispanic, when you are able, find out and use an individual's preferred term. Ideally you would learn if your students identify as, for example, as Mexican American, Guatemalan, or Puerto Rican. Additionally, just because someone identifies as Latinx does not mean they are an immigrant. They may have been in the U.S. for several generations, may or may not speak Spanish, and may have never traveled outside their rural community—once again, avoiding bias and building knowledge about your students can help you be respectful.

History has also seen many different names for Indigenous people. In some areas of the country the term Native American or American Indian is typical, while in other areas the term Indigenous is more common. It is always better to use the correct tribal association when you know it, if that is your student's preference. If for any reason you would need to refer to a child as Native American, with their permission, you would honor them by using their tribal name, such as, "Browning shared a story about his Potawatomi culture and traditions."

It has become more common to have transgender, nonbinary, or gender fluid students in our classrooms. Gender labels, stereotypes, and bullying can be incredibly painful, especially for young people who may not feel accepted in their homes or community. Our compulsion for labeling, especially in binary terms, can make this even more difficult for students. Navigating this terrain with families can be difficult, for example, if the family and student disagree about name and pronoun use (e.g., a preference for they/them instead of she/her). The best rule of thumb is to choose the path that is most *validating* for your student—that is whatever helps them to be their most authentic self. A classroom is the place where students should feel the least afraid. That's why a teacher should always respect students' gender identity.

Finally, names are one of the most powerful labels and one of the most basic ways we identify ourselves. It is important to get that right for your students. Some Ann(e)s feel very strongly about having the "e" at the end of their name. Some students in your class may have names that are previously unknown to you, and it may take you and the other students some practice to pronounce their names correctly. Sometimes people have conceded to, or have chosen to, Anglicize their name, or perhaps they go by a nickname to avoid the continual mispronunciation. What is important is that you do your best to honor that person's humanity by calling them what they wish. When you first meet your classes, rather than calling roll aloud, invite students to introduce themselves to you and their classmates. This avoids mispronouncing or calling a student by a name that is not their preferred one.

For more information about the importance of learning and pronouncing students' names, see the article "Names Do Matter" at the Teaching Tolerance website: https://www.tolerance.org/magazine/names-do-matter.

Words matter. Thinking about the relationship between labels and diversity is important work. In rural communities, labels can serve as a powerful *text*, particularly if a student feels they are alone in an otherwise close-knit community. Taking the time to understand who students are means you are in an authentic relationship with them. Every effective teacher will tell you that having a good relationship with each of your students is critical for learning.

Your Work as a Rural Teacher

The suggestions above—to be self-aware, build knowledge, embrace funds of knowledge, and to rethink labels—are all important steps you can take. These are not the only actions. You can work to ensure that your curriculum materials represent a diversity of people, cultures, histories, and voices—including those that are rural. This work will help all students in your classroom feel welcome. It will also help to prepare students for the world outside the walls of your classroom.

Finally, it is important to take action in order to enact your beliefs. You do this when you give your students an opportunity to be an ally for those who need one and to identify and dismantle barriers to justice in your classroom and community. You can start by having students think about the people closest to them that may need someone to stand up for them. Maybe it's a younger sibling, or a grandparent, or a neighbor. Then use the information you learned about others outside of your immediate experience to develop strategies that provide opportunities for more voices to be heard. You also do this work when you draw attention to larger patterns of inequity and teach students how to resist or change those patterns. Is the girls' locker room smaller and dingier than the boys? Do all students feel welcome at school dances? Are some holidays celebrated and not others? Students can work together to propose strategies to change these situations.

When Estela's mother came to the Shenandoah Valley in the 1960s, she was the only Mexican in their community. In addition to being discriminated against, there were language barriers that made preserving important parts of her culture even more difficult. There were no ingredients locally to make traditional Mexican food—no pinto beans or masa for corn tortillas. No chiles and none of the fruits and vegetables she was used to eating and using in recipes. Estela's father made tools, like a sawed-off metal pipe, for her mother to use to roll the tortillas on the occasions when she could buy ingredients found in nearby cities. Cultural identities and personal histories matter. A generation later, Estela encounters racism just as her mother did. More diversity does not always mean more acceptance. In Estela's work as a cultural organizer and musician, she enacts a critical pedagogy of place that questions the experiences of immigrants and people of color as they are contextualized regionally.

The work of teaching for diversity is constant, and it matters. Your work as a teacher who embraces diversity and advances economic, social, and political justice benefits your students and your rural communities.

References

Bartolome, L. (1994). Beyond the methods fetish: Toward a humanizing pedagogy. *Harvard Educational Review, 64*, 173–194.

Flowers, J. (2020). *What about us? The lived experiences of African American rural principals leading predominantly White rural schools* (Unpublished doctoral dissertation). William & Mary.

González, N., Moll, L., & Amanti, C. (Eds.). (2005). *Funds of knowledge: Theorizing practices in households, communities and classrooms.* Erlbaum.

Hussar, B., Zhang, J., Hein, S., Wang, K., Roberts, A., Cui, J., Smith, M., Bullock Mann, F., Barmer, A., & Dilig, R. (2020). The condition of education 2020 (NCES 2020-144). U.S. Department of Education, National Center for Education Statistics. https:// nces.ed.gov/pubsearch/pubsinfo.asp?pubid=2020144

Lippi-Green, R. (2012). *English with an accent: Language, Ideology and Discrimination in the United States.* 2nd ed. Routledge.

Moll, L. C., Amanti, C., Neff, D., & Gonzalez, N. (1992). Funds of knowledge for teaching: Using a qualitative approach to connect homes and classrooms. *Theory Into Practice, 31*(2), 132–141.

Pennington, C. R., Heim, D., Levy, A. R., & Larkin, D. T. (2016). Twenty years of stereotype threat research: A review of psychological mediators. *PLoS ONE, 11*(1), 1–25. doi: https://10.1371/journal.pone.0146487

Purcell-Gates, V. (2002). "… As soon as she opened her mouth!": Issues of language, literacy, and power. In L. Delpit (Ed.), *The skin that we speak: Thoughts on language and culture in the classroom* (pp. 121–141). The New Press.

Steele, C. (2010). *Whistling Vivaldi: How stereotypes affect us and what we can do.* W.W. Norton.

Steele, C. M., & Aronson, J. (1995). Stereotype threat and the intellectual test performance of African Americans. *Journal of Personality & Social Psychology, 69*(5), 797. doi: https://10.1037/0022-3514.69.5.797

16

Teaching Exceptional Learners in Rural Classrooms

I always knew I wanted to be a teacher but had no intentions of pursuing special education—not until I took a course on special education law during my teacher education program. It awoke a purpose, and I often say that special education chose me! I was so excited to begin applying all the new strategies and techniques I was learning about to meet the needs of students in special education. However, when I entered the profession with my first teaching placement in a rural school a decade ago, I was disheartened and frustrated that everything I knew to be "best practices" were non-existent. I was met with an overwhelming challenge to not only meet the needs of my individual students but to do so without resources (materials, support, guidance). No one seemed to understand my sense of urgency, or they simply responded: That's just the way we've always done things.

I worked with wonderful, hardworking teachers, but I knew there was more we could be doing for our students. I started serving on the Special Education Advisory Committee for my school district, volunteered as the gifted education chairperson for my school, and began attending any professional development my district would allow. Not only did these activities help me grow as a teacher, more importantly they gave me a connection to others outside my rural community. I was determined to bring similar programs, initiatives, and ideas to my school community. We didn't have a lot of resources and people were initially reluctant to change, but I quickly learned that what our district lacked in resources, programs, and supports due to our rural location could be offset by a strength in personal relationships and connections. Once I realized this, amazing things began to happen in my community!

A multifaceted approach of advocacy, awareness, and education with colleagues, families, and the community led to increased buy-in and support with community groups that partnered with us on several fronts. We formed a non-profit group, "A Voice for Our Children," and hosted a Disability Awareness Walk which raised money for a wheelchair swing at my school and buddy benches for all four of our elementary schools. We even sponsored and hosted a community resource fair helping local agencies connect families with resources available to them.

I provided professional development sessions on classroom strategies with general and special education teachers (and paraprofessionals) which resulted in flexible seating and other accommodations. With time, planning, and trust, our school division has moved toward inclusion, supporting students in general education classrooms that were previously in self-contained settings, with all students reaping the benefits of having disabled and non-disabled peers learning and growing together. It's easy to get overwhelmed by what schools don't have but positive change is possible—even in the most remote rural communities.

Kim Hess, Principal, Buchanan County Public Schools, Virginia

Kim's story is a powerful one because it invites us to find opportunity even in the greatest of challenges. In Chapter 6, we talk about community assets and strengths. Kim's efforts exemplify a way of looking at assets and opportunities within one's self, school, and community as a way of advocating for students. In the chapter that follows this one, we talk about evaluating what counts as evidence in rural schools when "best practices" seem unattainable. Kim looked at how practice could be modified to meet the unique needs of her students within a particular place, relying on family and community partnerships to make it happen.

In this chapter, we look at exceptionalities as they relate to special education and gifted education and how rural schools and communities contextualize the experiences for exceptional rural learners. In the previous chapter, you were asked to think about diverse learners in rural schools. Some of the topics in the previous chapter—stereotype threat, labels, and deficit ideologies—apply in this chapter as well. Here, though, we want to apply those topics as they relate to our perceptions of exceptional learners. The ways we think about and value difference play a critical role in how we serve students with exceptionalities. Despite "differences," all people want to feel accepted and valued, to feel capable and empowered, to love and have friends. A person with a severe or profound disability is not exempt from having those same feelings. All children deserve the opportunity to learn and experience growth every year in school, including gifted students. Thinking through any biases you may have about special and gifted education are key to meeting the needs of all students in the classroom.

For Discussion

Think for a moment about the quality of your life and answer the following questions:

- What contributes to the quality of my life?
- Who do I spend time with, and what do we do together?
- What choices do I have that allow me to enjoy my life?
- Where do I go and how do I get there?
- How do I contribute to society?

Most people want the same kinds of things: To have friends, to be loved, to make decisions about their own life, to travel in and outside of their communities, to be able to take care of themselves, and to make a contribution to society. Ann and Rud Turnbull (2013), who have a son with a disability, shared a vision advocating that all students—including those with disabilities—have "an enviable life"—enviable meaning a life you would want for yourself (You can view a recording of Ann Turnbull speaking at the 2013 OSEP Project Director's Conference at https://www.youtube.com/watch?v=yTIaHW1IyTo). This vision includes:

- Having high expectations for all students
- Recognizing that all students can make positive contributions
- Abandoning the "fix-it" approach and, instead, focus on students' strengths
- Fostering self-determination by helping all students develop their abilities
- Facilitating the development of students' relationships
- Supporting students' full citizenship by building capacities so they can exercise their Rights and responsibilities.

In thinking about exceptionalities, we begin and end the chapter with this vision—asking: What makes this vision possible in rural schools?

Disability or Differently-Abled

As we discuss in the previous chapter, deficit ideologies can influence our conception of difference as something that is "less than" or inadequate when compared to "typical." When it comes to disabilities, this is especially true. Research has medicalized disability in such a way that it casts disability in need of *curing* (Connor, 2008). Within the medical model of disability, difference is a medical abnormality or deficit within an individual. By comparison, the social model looks at a "disability" as a cultural construct—one that is created by society, not difference itself. You might hear people say "differently-abled" to suggest that disability is not an inherent deficiency but, rather, an ability to do or see or think or understand in a different way. In other words, the social model of disability is "a way of thinking about bodies, rather than as something that is wrong with bodies" (Ware, 2009, p. 400). It considers disability as a cultural construct that does not need to be fixed or cured.

The social model of disability changes the ways teachers approach, discuss, and think about disability. In order to adopt this view, teachers can reflect on how they understand disabilities and how their understandings and past experiences connect to their work in the classroom. Students with and without disabilities should be invited to explore their own ideas about disabilities and challenge the medical model when it exists.

Not all scholars, researchers, and practitioners agree on the appropriateness of these different models for understanding disability (Cochran-Smith & Dudley-Marling, 2012). The medical model focuses on identification and improving conditions caused by the disability. By comparison, the sociocultural view embraces the notion of a widespread distribution of human capacity, considering how a student's success can be determined by societal factors more so than inherent deficits (Biviano, 2019). In either case, teachers need tools for critiquing stereotypes. That is why more progressive views about exceptionality help to push against commonly found tropes. For an example of a more progressive view, see the 2020 Netflix documentary, *Crip Camp: A Disability Revolution*, a film about a group of campers turned activists who shaped the future of the disability-rights movement and created accessibility legislation for everyone.

As we discussed in Chapter 3, our ways of thinking about rural are influenced by a variety of factors. There are countless TV shows and pop culture references to rural people and communities as deficient. The same is true for thinking about disabilities. We internalize these messages, and they can influence everything we do in the classroom. This can even be the case with something that is well-intended. For example, you may want to portray positive images of people with disabilities by displaying "inspirational" posters in your classroom. However, many disability advocates explain that doing so may unintentionally portray "people of disabilities as one-dimensional saints who only exist to warm the hearts and open the minds of able-bodied people" (Wanshel, 2017). As disability rights advocate, Stella Young (2014), stated, "No amount of smiling at a flight of stairs has made it into a ramp!" Her point is that a having a positive attitude about being in a wheelchair does not make the world more accessible. A person's "disability" is not the use of a wheelchair for mobility. The physical disability only becomes disabling when a person's access is limited due to inaccessible structures in public places. The lack of a ramp is the disability, not the person in the wheelchair.

We also convey our ableist beliefs about disability in speaking with families when we express sympathy for a disability, asking, for example, "Oh no, is your son deaf?" in a sympathetic voice, assuming that the child's disability is a limitation or, by definition, is in some sense tragic. By comparison, asking something like, "Tell me about your child! I can't wait to learn more about how we'll communicate and learn together" would communicate openness and acceptance.

This deficit idea of disability as tragic is also reinforced in literature commonly read in high schools. For example, students might encounter Charles Dickens' portrayal of a pathetic Tiny Tim in *A Christmas Carol*, the angry wooden-legged Captain Ahab in Herman Melville's *Moby-Dick*, or the mysterious Boo Radley in Harper Lee's *To Kill a Mockingbird*. These stereotypes reinforce deficit ideologies for those with and without disabilities.

For Discussion

Consider images of people with disabilities. Critique those images. Are the characters portrayed as stereotypes or are they portrayed as whole and complex individuals with full participation in the world? How does a sociocultural perspective help you reflect on what you see?

People and Identity-First Language

In the previous chapter about diversity, we address the idea of rethinking labels. In the field of special education, person-first language is the norm. Person-first language emphasizes the person first and the condition second, because this condition is only one aspect of the person. For example, instead of saying a "learning-disabled student," you would say a "student with a learning disability." When you say the "child who uses a wheel-chair," you acknowledge that the wheelchair has just one purpose in that child's life, and it's related to mobility. However, there is also space for identity-first language. If a person with autism identifies as autistic then that label can also be appropriate. What's important in terms of labels and diversity is to understand and honor preferences of the individual. It may be uncomfortable for you, but sometimes asking is the only way to know. Person- and identity-driven language allows us to *see* the person for their way of being in the world. What was "handicapped parking" is now referred to as "accessible parking," signaling a shift to asset-based language and labels. An English Language Learner is also an Emerging Bilingual. In Deaf Culture, for example, it is offensive to describe a child who is deaf or hard of hearing as "hearing impaired" (National Association of the Deaf, https://www.nad.org/).

What is important is to realize that words and labels matter and can shift over time. Your care with language sends an important message to other teachers, students, and families about how you value and see your students. To build an inclusive space for all students, you want to act with empathy and earnestness, inviting families and students to educate you and help you grow as their ally and advocate. Don't be afraid to ask about which terms are most respectful.

Rural Special Education

In Chapter 10, we reviewed the policies related to special education, namely the Individuals with Disabilities Education Act (IDEA) and Section 504. These laws provide regulations and guidance around ensuring that students with disabilities cannot be discriminated against in instruction, assessments, and accessibility. While there are laws in place to ensure that students can access a quality, accessible, and equitable education, the realities of rural schools influence how these laws are implemented and experienced. For example, from the opening story of Kim's experience, she found that what students needed as "best practice" was missing from her rural school. Rural schools have struggled to recruit teachers for a century, and the need for special education teachers is a persistent theme in the field of rural teacher education. So, while there are laws designed to ensure equity, the reality is that a rural special education teacher may have a large caseload or might be an itinerant teacher serving a larger geographic area. Sometimes, students do not have access to teachers who have training and education relevant to their needs.

For students utilizing special education resources in rural schools, it is important to remember that students and their families may not have access to those resources outside of school. Rural schools tend to be a home base for families when they have a concern for a child, directing them to resources where the child might be evaluated. Families in rural areas may lack geographic access to social- and health-related services (Kiani et al., 2013). As a result, a student with autism, for example, may be older when they are evaluated for autism (Mandell et al., 2005). A later evaluation has implications for early intervention and other evidence-based treatment. This issue is further complicated by the fact that rural areas tend to experience difficulties staffing and retaining special education teachers and specialists, which can in turn limit available resources (Pennington et al., 2009). In a rural region that is medically underserved and has higher than average poverty levels and uneven access to health insurance (Behringer & Friedell, 2006; Haverson et al., 2004), families face further constraints to find or advocate for resources. Further, due to deficit thinking, community members can hold intolerant perceptions about students who are *different* (Azano & Tackett, 2017), and families may be reluctant to access services.

Takeaways for the Rural Classroom

What does this mean for general education teachers in the rural classroom? It can be difficult to know how to serve the needs of students if you do not feel readily prepared, especially if they have significant learning challenges, limited communication, or behavioral needs. Because rural areas may have other challenges related to healthcare, rural schools experience heightened positions of responsibility with the rural community (Azano & Tackett, 2017).

When Kim first started working at her school, she was persistent in finding resources. She became actively involved in several organizations within and outside of her school. She sought ways to make improvements for her school district. With her leadership, her school district worked with state universities to secure grants to work with students with autism, providing extensive training for staff and parents. Another university grant supported gifted education identification processes for the district. A collaboration with several charities led to funding for the Sensory Room Project. The district now has a sensory room (a therapeutic space designed for sensory stimulation for students with special needs) at all four elementary schools—rooms that are available for *all children to use as needed.*

Yes, these types of initiatives take time—*extra* time—and you may find that your rural school is well resourced to meet the needs of students receiving special education services. At the very least, regardless of your teaching certification or the resources available at your school, you might consider joining the American Council on Rural Special Education (ACRES) so you can continue to learn how best to serve all students. Here are some of other suggestions:

- *Talk with families:* Learn more about your students and the ways they excel outside of school. You might learn some helpful strategies that you can apply to the classroom.
- *Access resources:* Learn about resources within your school and rural community. Talk to community members, school personnel, and local healthcare providers to learn more about community resources.
- *Get involved:* Think of the ways you can serve as an advocate for students. Learn about grant funding, assistive technology (see Chapter 14), and other ways you can serve as an ally.
- *Practice inclusivity:* As you plan instruction, field trips, activities, be sure to think about access, sensory challenges, and ways to overcome other barriers that might interfere with full participation.

One other thing to note. Some rural districts partner together to provide special education services for students. In Michigan, for example, each county has several smaller local school districts. The county-wide Intermediate School District provides a central location where some special education services are provided. Students who need greater support may ride the bus to the county seat for some or all of the school day. Teachers may need to play a special role in helping these students feel connected to their peers as they transition to and from the classroom.

Rural Gifted Education

For Discussion

What comes to mind when you hear the word "gifted"? What are the common images of giftedness in the media? Who is missing from those images? Do rural students readily fit into those images? Why or why not?

Gifted education is a topic not always discussed in conversations about rural education, but it is an important one to consider. Unlike special education, gifted education programming is not protected by federal mandates and, therefore, varies from state to state and school to school. This means funding depends on school board priorities or school leaders' beliefs about the value of gifted education. In rural schools that may already be struggling financially (see Chapter 10 for policy and funding information), gifted education may seem like a nonessential budget item. Sometimes, the belief that gifted students will thrive without instruction or programming is used as the rationale for inadequate or non-existent programming, despite evidence suggesting otherwise. Additionally, because many affluent school districts are willing and able to prioritize gifted education, pervasive opportunity gaps persist for gifted children across schools based on the economic strength of a district, but also the beliefs of decision makers about the value of gifted services.

When there are limited resources for gifted education, the identification of students will often depend on a referral process as opposed to a universal screening process. Universal screeners allow for each child at a certain grade level (for example, all second graders) to be evaluated for gifted education services. By comparison, a referral process depends on teachers or parents to refer the child for an evaluation. This can be problematic because enduring images of Einstein, Sheldon Cooper, and Rory Gilmore limit our capacity to recognize gifts, including those gifts that may be expressed in unique ways in rural learners. This is one reason why rural students are often underrepresented in gifted education.

This underrepresentation means it is often the general education teacher who is asked to meet the needs of students identified as gifted. Because rural students are underrepresented in conversations about gifted education, many people default to myths about gifted students. For example, one myth is that they will be "okay" without instruction or programming. Other myths, such as academic acceleration is harmful or that gifted students are well-served in the general education classroom (National Association for Gifted Children, https://www.nagc.org/myths-about-gifted-students), further impede access to appropriate learning opportunities for gifted students. Also, stereotype threat, as you learned about in the previous chapter, can also affect gifted students. The combination of stereotypes about being rural and gifted can add power to the effects of stereotype threat on student performance.

Opportunity and achievement gaps can be more pronounced for rural students due to financially constrained programming and limited access to out-of-school resources (Callahan & Azano, 2019). Additionally, as noted above, rural schools have struggled to recruit and retain teachers. When there is a gifted resource teacher in a rural school, they often experience professional isolation (Azano et al., 2014), working as the "lone wolf," as is typical for itinerant teachers (see Chapter 12).

Understanding structural barriers such as staffing and funding helps not only to identify the challenges but also to find solutions. For example, many rural schools are working to use multiple types of tests (e.g., teaching ratings, portfolio assessments, cognitive or standardized tests) that allow for identification and advanced instruction for high-achieving students. However, these measures, along with a universal screening process, will not in and of themselves lead to more equitable opportunities for under-represented populations. Of equal importance is how scores and assessments are interpreted, how decisions are made about identification, and the quality of the programming that follows. Lohman (2013), for example, recommends using local norms so that students are compared with others who have similar opportunities to learn.

Takeaways for the Rural Classroom

What does this mean for you in the rural classroom? It could mean that the services you provide are the only ones available to your gifted student. If that's the case, here are some helpful tips for meeting the needs of gifted students (or students who you suspect may be gifted) in the general education classroom:

- *Gather information on the current performance levels of gifted students.* Use data from prior achievement tests, from pre-tests available in teachers' guides, or open-ended curriculum based assessments you construct about the content and skill of the next unit of instruction—oral or written. For example, you can ask students: "Tell me everything you know about the settling of the colonies," "Write down all the words you associate with the word pollution," or "Give examples of a metaphor and an analogy."
- *Compact the curriculum.* For all areas in which students already know the content or skills you are going to teach, compact their curriculum. Instead of repeating or extending instruction (or assigning homework), create higher level learning that deepens their thinking beyond the grade-level standards.
- *Avoid using the gifted student as a tutor.* While it is tempting to think of your high-achieving student as a helper or tutor, it limits the potential for the gifted student. When pairing students, pair high-achieving students together to work on more advanced, challenging learning activities so they can support each other's academic growth.

- *Go deeper (not longer or more).* Rather than assigning more, consider assigning projects that are more complex and or require deeper understanding of a topic. Avoid doubling down on assignments that will feel only like busy work for the gifted student. Instead, assign projects that require deeper understanding of the content, greater leaps in understanding and expression of understanding, sophisticated transformation and application of the content and skill used, more connections across disciplines, and the big ideas from those disciplines.
- *Accelerate students in specific content areas as warranted.* Collaborate with other teachers and administrators to provide opportunities for the study of advanced content through acceleration (e.g., moving students who already know and understand the third-grade math content to a fourth- or fifth-grade classroom for math instruction).

Great Expectations for All Students

While there may be barriers that seem insurmountable there *are* ways you can effect change in your classroom each and every day. At the beginning of this chapter, we considered a vision for *all* children. The Turnbulls had a vision for their son. Kim Hess, the teacher featured in the opening of this chapter, had a vision for her students. Kim says if you had told her in 2011 when she first started teaching that her elementary school would have a sensory room, she would not have believed you. She and other rural special education teachers faced challenges related to the local norms of the school and community about how differently abled people are valued, limited resources at the school and community level, and the level of awareness and education across community and teachers members. In 2016, Kim became the principal of her school and continues to focus her efforts on continually improving educational practices for all students. For novice teachers she says that your first teaching placement will be met with challenges and situations where you might feel you can't make a difference. It may seem, especially in rural areas, that the challenges are impossible to overcome, especially if they are due to funding structures that seem beyond your reach. Kim says it takes determination, resolve, and a commitment to working with families—earning their trust and learning from them in return.

Kim's determination also required that she focus on equity rather than equality when advocating for exceptional rural students. Sometimes doing what's fair does not mean ensuring that all students receive the "same." Believing that all students deserve equitable opportunities to grow means we must differentiate for all students. All students deserve the opportunity to fully capitalize on their talents. A social studies or math test with discussion questions may disadvantage students with a reading or other learning disability. Telling a child to "sit still" because they're being distracting to other students can shame a child who needs sensory stimulation to focus. Asking a student to look at you while you're speaking may be difficult for some when eye contact is difficult. Enabling students to move through the world in their way of being in your classroom is not only inclusive but humanizing. While some resources are certainly limited in rural schools, believing in the strengths of all children and creating an inclusive environment where all students can thrive are not.

References

Azano, A. P., Callahan, C. M., Missett, T. C., & Brunner, M. (2014). Understanding the experiences of gifted education teachers and fidelity of implementation in rural schools. *Journal of Advanced Academics*, 25(2), 87–99. doi: https://10.1177/1932202X14524405

Azano, A. P., & Tackett, M. E. (2017). Perceptions of teachers and parents on the educational experiences of students with autism in a remote rural community. *Rural Educator*, 38(3), 39–54. doi: https://10.35608/ruraled.v38i3.219

Behringer, B., & Friedell, G. H. (2006). Appalachia: where place matters in health. *Preventing Chronic Diseases*, 3(4). www.ncbi.nlm.nih.gov/pmc/articles/PMC1779277/

Biviano, A. C. (2019). *A case study of one teacher's experience using a sociocultural view of disability in the English classroom.* (Unpublished doctoral dissertation). Virginia Tech.

Callahan, C. M., & Azano, A. P. (2019). Place-based gifted education in rural schools. In S. Smith (Ed.), *Handbook of giftedness and talent development in the Asia-Pacific* (pp. 1–2). https://link.springer.com/referenceworkentry/10.1007%2F978-981-13-3021-6_25-1

Cochran-Smith, M., & Dudley-Marling, C. (2012). Diversity in teacher education and special education: The issues that divide. *Journal of Teacher Education*, 63(4), 237–244. doi: https://10.1177/0022487112446512

Connor, D. J. (2008). Not so strange bedfellows: The promise of disability studies and critical race theory. In S. Gabel, & S. Danforth (Eds.),

Disability & the politics of education: An international reader, (p. 451–476). Peter Lang.

Haverson, J., Ma, L., & Harner, E. J. (2004). *An analysis of disparities in health status and access to care in the Appalachian region.* Appalachian Regional Commission. www.arc.gov/assets/research_reports/AnalysisofHealth DisparitiesIntroductionExecutiveSummary.pdf

Kiani, R., Tyrer, F., Hodgson, A., Berkin, N., & Bhaumik, S. (2013). Urban-rural differences in the nature and prevalence of mental ill-health in adults with intellectual disabilities. *Journal of Intellectual Disability Research, 57(2)*, 119–127.

Lohman, D. F. (2013). Identifying gifted students: Nontraditional uses of traditional measures. In C. M. Callahan & H. L. Hertberg-Davis (Eds.), *Fundamentals of gifted education: Considering multiple perspectives* (pp. 112–127). Routledge.

Mandell, D. S., Novak, M. M., & Zubritsky, C. D. (2005). Factors associated with age of diagnosis among children with autism spectrum disorders. *Pediatrics, 116(6)*, 1480–1486.

Pennington, R., Horn, C., & Berrong, A. (2009). An evaluation of the differences between big city and small town special education services for students with low incidence disabilities in Kentucky. *Rural Special Education Quarterly, 28(4)*, 3–9.

Turnbull, A. [University of Kansas School of Education]. (2013, October 3). *Enviable Lives: A lifespan perspective on family and community partnerships* [Video file]. https://www.youtube.com/watch?v=yTIaHW1IyTo

Wanshel, E. (2017, January 16). "Speechless" Just schooled everyone on disability "inspiration porn. *Huffington Post.* http://www.huffingtonp ost.com/entry/speechless-disability-porn_us_5877ddf6e4b0e58057fdc342

Ware, L. (2009). Many possible futures, many different directions: Merging critical special education and disability studies. Writing, identity, and the other: Dare we do disability studies? *Journal of Teacher Education, 52(2)*, 107–123.

Young, S. (2014). *Inspiration porn and the objectification of disability: Stella Young.* https://tedxsydney.com/talk/inspiration-porn-and-the-objectification-of-disability-stella-young/

17

Evidence in the Rural Classroom

I moved to rural Mississippi after going to college in Washington, D.C. I had been mentally preparing myself for an isolating environment. Instead, I was pleasantly surprised to learn that there was a strong and diverse community of young educators and artists in the Mississippi Delta. Over time, I felt more a part of a community in rural Mississippi than I ever had in Washington, D.C. When I began teaching, I was also surprised to find that the Title I school where I started as a second-grade teacher had a multitude of physical resources—computers, curricula, a school library, and a literacy room. But I got very little guidance on which curriculum I should use, and I quickly realized that I would need to adapt most of the resources to be more engaging and straightforward.

At first, I felt disheartened by the lack of support when it came to lesson planning. Over time, I learned to seek out support through other sources. I read teaching books and sought advice from veteran teachers. I've grown to love the freedom that comes with teaching in a rural school, and I spend each Sunday creating the next week's units of study. I love that my classroom is a place to experiment with new ideas for activities, writing prompts, class discussions, and creative projects.

Margot Besnard, First Grade Teacher, Cleveland, MS

Importance of Effective Practice

Think of your experience as a student in K–12 schools and college. You have likely been in some classrooms where you learned a lot, where the assignments were interesting and engaging and your understanding of the content, or your understanding of the world, changed. There were probably some classrooms where you felt engaged while you were there, where you did projects that were interesting, or you had opportunities to talk to your classmates about engaging topics. Hopefully, you have been in classrooms where you recognized that you knew more about mathematics or history at the end of the year than you did at the beginning. You had great teachers in those classrooms—teachers who may have had different styles but who had one thing in common—they planned instruction that helped students learn.

We assume that you want to be a great teacher, too. You want students to learn in your class and know that what they're learning is important. Often, educators use the term "effective practice" to describe the kind of teaching where students are engaged and learning—where students are building their knowledge and skills and abilities. When students have effective teachers, students not only perform well on standardized assessments they have to take, but they also build a rich understanding of the world and grow in their ability to solve problems. In effective classrooms, students learn what they need to be ready for whatever comes next—the next grade level, the next opportunity—and, by the end of their K–12 education, what they need to be ready for work or postsecondary education, civic responsibility, and all the things that come after high school.

Part of being an effective teacher is deciding what and how to teach. You have probably heard the term "evidence-based practice" to describe effective classroom teaching. In most cases, knowing about and applying the research evidence can help you make choices so that you can be an effective teacher. In this chapter, we will examine evidence-based practice and the importance of being able to be a smart, critical consumer of evidence. We will also consider why evidence-based practice might be a special concern for rural classrooms and how *practice-based evidence,* that is, evaluating whether your teaching practices are effective for your students and your goals in your context, can help you be a more effective teacher.

Planning Effective Teaching Practice

In order to be an effective teacher, you need to select effective teaching practices. By teaching practices, we refer to the planning and delivery of the activities and lessons that are intended to help students learn. Effective teachers select and plan teaching practices that are most likely to positively impact student learning. That is, they select and implement teaching practices that will help students get from where they are now to where you want them to go. Some teaching practices are discipline specific—using letter tiles to help students learn phonics in reading, for example, or conducting experiments and keeping lab notes in science. Some teaching practices are utilized across disciplines—writing summaries after reading and small group discussions, for example.

Assessment, the process of finding out what students already know and are ready to learn next, should be the basis of effective instructional planning. Student assessment can take many forms—from summative, high-stakes standardized testing to highly useful formative assessment data in the form of student work samples or classroom observations. Assessments will help you to determine what students already know and what they are already able to do, where they may have gaps in their understanding, and what they are ready to learn next. There is not sufficient room in this book to thoroughly address the affordances and limitations of the many different assessments that you might use in the classroom (including concerns that standardized assessments often place rural students at a distinct disadvantage). For our purposes here, it is enough to say that we believe that assessment is an essential component of effective teaching practice.

State standards are another factor to consider as you plan for effective teaching in your classroom. By definition, standards are descriptions of the knowledge, skills, and abilities that students are expected to master at different stages of their education. If assessments describe where students are now, standards define where students should go, and help you establish your goals and plans for teaching.

There is no shortage of resources to help you plan for and implement effective teaching practice. Some resources will be provided by your school or your district. The district where you teach will likely recommend or, more likely, *require* curriculum materials. The provided curricular materials, along with district-sponsored professional development, school norms, and the influence of your school and district instructional leaders, are factors that, in combination, will suggest or require you to teach in particular ways. Standards are typically accompanied by teaching guides or other resources that are intended to help you create instruction that meets the defined goals and objectives. For example, teachers in states that have adopted the Common Core State Standards are often required to use teaching materials aligned to the Common Core State Standards. For English Language Arts and Literacy, commercial publishers are required to design teaching materials according to the "Publishers' Criteria for the Common Core State Standards in English Language Arts and Literacy, Grades 3–12" (Coleman & Pimentel, 2012). The publishers' criteria describe its role as "underscoring what matters most in the standards" (p. 1) and assisting publishers in the production of aligned products for classroom use. This means that if you teach in a Common Core state, you will very likely be required to use particular commercial materials for classroom instruction. You can see the National Governors Association/CCSSO Publisher's Criteria at the following link: www.corestandards.org/assets/Math_Publishers_Criteria_K-8_Summer%202012_FINAL.pdf (2012).

Within the parameters set by the state standards and your school and district, you will have some discretion to select practices and materials as you plan your instruction. Depending on where you teach, you may have more or less autonomy, but you will almost always be able to make decisions about how to group students, classroom management strategies, and how to spend instructional time outside of required curriculum and you will come to your first teaching position with your own ideas about effective teaching and learning. You will learn (or have already learned) about teaching practices in the methods courses that you take as part of your teacher preparation program. You also have a repertoire of teaching practices you remember from when you were a student yourself. Some of those you will seek to replicate. Others you will seek to purposefully avoid. Other ideas may come from more informal sources such as friends and colleagues and internet sites where teachers share ideas. Wherever your teaching ideas come from, you will want to consider the evidence base for practices as you are considering which practices and programs to adopt and which to reject.

Evidence-Based Practice

Effective teachers stay up to date with and implement practices that have a strong evidence base in order to plan for teaching and learning. Education researchers generate evidence about whether or not a practice or program "works" for a particular goal or outcome. For example, research shows that copying dictionary definitions or memorizing lists of words is not the most effective way to teach vocabulary. Students learn vocabulary when they have multiple, meaningful encounters with words in context (for example, when they read a lot) and benefit from explicit instruction of carefully chosen words, word families, and meaningful chunks of words = such as root words, prefixes, and suffixes (Foorman et al., 2016; Lehr et al., 2004). Likewise, there is ample evidence that writing is a means to foster reading comprehension. When learners write in response to their reading, they remember more and have deeper understanding than if they just talk about their reading or answer multiple choice questions (Foorman et al, 2016; Graham & Hebert, 2010). These are just two examples of practices that have been shown to be effective in the classroom.

Increasingly, the phrase "evidence-based practice" is being used to describe the kinds of teaching practices that have been shown to work in studies that evaluate whether students learn more in classrooms using one practice compared to another. However, as we discuss below, "evidence" can have a variety of meanings. Just as there are teaching practices that have a strong evidence base, there are a lot of teaching ideas, and a lot of teaching materials for sale, that are based on weak or biased evidence. Many programs and commercial materials claim that the products they are selling are based on evidence even though the research base is flimsy or all of the "studies" have been paid for by the company hoping to make a profit from your purchase.

Sometimes a teaching idea or practice has been researched and does have a strong evidence base, but that research does not necessarily suggest that the practice or program will work in your rural context, with your rural students. As you seek out and examine the evidence for a particular practice, you will need to keep a critical mindset and evaluate the evidence, keeping your context with your rural students front and center in your decision making. The following questions are useful to guide your decision making.

What Evidence Is There?

The first question you might ask about any particular teaching practice is "What evidence is there?" When you are analyzing the evidence base for a particular practice, you will want to consider the depth and the quality of the evidence. You can think about whether there is a great deal of evidence for a practice or program, or whether the idea is something just one person is recommending. You can look at whether there is research to support a practice or if the publications are mostly stories and anecdotes. If there is research, are there multiple studies conducted in multiple settings and published in a variety of sources or is there just one publication? Is the practice summarized in a review of research or a report that synthesizes evidence from a number of research studies? Sometimes there is a note on the study disclosing who funded the research. When there are multiple studies by different authors, and different types of studies, conducted in a variety of settings over time that all point to the same conclusion, this can give you more confidence that the practice is something that has been shown to work fairly consistently.

In addition to thinking about the number of studies, another way to think about the evidence is to consider what evidence is being used to determine that something "works." A wide variety of information data can be used to make claims about the effectiveness of a practice. The studies can be large studies of many students that return statistical data or smaller studies that are more descriptive in nature. In either case, a study should tell you about the data the researchers used to draw their conclusions. Look for the "outcome measures" or assessments used to determine the impact of a practice or program.

Large experimental studies that compare the performance of one randomly selected group that receives a particular intervention to another group that does not (Randomized Controlled Trials, or RCTs) can provide information about the practice being studied. The federal Every Student Succeeds Act (ESSA) requires schools and districts to evaluate select practices that have a strong evidence base when federal funds are being spent. In ESSA, "evidence" mostly refers to experiments known as RCTs with treatment and control groups (comparisons of students who do and do not take part in the program or intervention being studied) using large numbers of participants. Other research evidence might include quasi-experimental studies that compare one class or school to another, before and after studies that look at the outcome of a practice with a single group of students, or even correlational studies that look at relationships between two or more things.

Many studies, especially RCTs, use quantitative data like test scores to determine impact, but there are many other kinds of evidence that can provide you with helpful information about the effectiveness of a practice. Evidence might include student work samples and assignments, classroom observations, interviews with students, surveys, attendance or classroom behavior data, and so on. As you consider the evidence for any practice, you can reflect on whether the evidence is valid, reliable, and consistent with the suggestions that researchers are making about the product or practice (Stanovich & Stanovich, 2003). You will also want to examine the population being studied. The students in the research you are reading might not share many of the characteristics of your students, which might mean the practice will not work as well for your students. The next chapter in this text will guide you in how to ask these types of questions in your own classroom.

Formal research is not the only evidence to consider. Stories and anecdotes can also be valuable. If your colleague or friend has tried something and it seemed to work for them, it might be worth trying in your classroom. Even when the "evidence" is a story from your peer's classroom, you

Professional Organization	Stated Mission	Journals
National Council of Teachers of English https://ncte.org	The Council promotes the development of literacy and the use of language to construct personal and public worlds and to achieve full participation in society through the learning and teaching of English and the related arts and sciences of language.	*Language Arts* *Voices from the Middle* *English Journal* *Research in the Teaching of English*
National Council of Teachers of Mathematics www.nctm.org	The National Council of Teachers of Mathematics advocates for high-quality mathematics teaching and learning for each and every student.	*Mathematics Teacher: Learning and Teaching PK-12* *Journal of Research in Mathematics Education*
National Science Teachers Association www.nsta.org	NSTA is the largest organization in the world committed to promoting excellence and innovation in science teaching and learning for all.	*Science and Children* *Science Scope* *The Science Teacher*
National Council for the Social Studies www.socialstudies.org	The mission of the National Council for the Social Studies is to advocate and build capacity for high-quality social studies by providing leadership, services, and support to educators.	*Social Studies and the Young Learner* *Middle Level Learning* *Social Education* *Theory & Research in Social Education* *Social Studies & Exceptional learners*

(Continued)

Professional Organization	Stated Mission	Journals
International Literacy Association www.literacyworldwide.org	Our mission is to empower educators, inspire students, and encourage leaders with the resources they need to make literacy accessible for all.	*The Reading Teacher* *Journal of Adolescent & Adult Literacy* *Reading Research Quarterly*
American Council on the Teaching of Foreign Languages www.actfl.org	Providing vision, leadership, and support for quality teaching and learning of languages.	*The Language Educator* *Foreign Language Annals*
The Council for Exceptional Children www.cec.sped.org	The Council for Exceptional Children is a professional association of educators dedicated to advancing the success of children with exceptionalities.	*Teaching Exceptional Children* *Exceptional Children*
National Rural Education Association www.nrea.net	The National Rural Education Association (NREA) is the voice of all rural schools and rural communities across the United States.	*The Rural Educator*

can still ask about the "evidence" by finding out how your friend knows that the idea they are recommending had a positive impact. However, if a practice involves a big investment of time, resources, or money (or if there could be any downside for students), it may be best to consider whether the evidence base is rich and deep enough to justify that investment.

For Discussion

Think of something you've seen that "works" in a classroom. Describe that practice. How do you know it works? Can you find evidence that the practice has positive outcomes for students? What kind of data makes up the evidence?

Is the Evidence from a Trustworthy Source?

In order to draw conclusions about the evidence base for a particular practice or program, you have to find evidence. A quick internet search will probably yield a number of results for just about any practice or program or product you might be considering.

Not all sources of research and evidence are equally trustworthy. Critical thinking about the source of information can help you evaluate whether the source might be biased and whether there is reason to be skeptical about the recommendations. One place to start is to think about whether the source of information stands to make money and whether profits might influence the evidence being shared. As a general rule, a website selling a program or materials is not a good place to read about all of the research on the product because the website will only show studies with positive results. If there is research to support a particular program or product, for example, you should examine whether those studies were conducted by the companies that will profit from your purchase or by independent researchers and evaluate accordingly. Not all vendors will give you biased information, but a critical frame of mind can help you make wise choices.

Even if there is no profit to be made, you might still consider the perspectives of the source you are evaluating and whether the authors have a bias that would influence their recommendations. Sometimes, you can determine that the evidence is being promoted by a particular organization that takes a stance about education that might influence their recommendation and the quality of the evidence. Careful analysis of the source of information can help you decide which practices are worth trying in your classroom.

Professional Journals

One trustworthy source for evidence about instructional practices is professional organizations. Professional organizations provide a number of resources for their members (often free online). The websites for professional organizations provide research summaries and practice recommendations as well as lesson plans and other resources that can help you select and implement instructional practices in your classroom. Some have listservs that you may find useful as well. While the professional organization membership fees can be expensive, we feel professional organizations to be a useful and trustworthy source of ideas about effective teaching practice. Many make teaching resources available for free.

The journals published by professional organizations often include both peer-reviewed research and articles written by teachers about how they are implementing research-based practices in their classrooms. For example, the opening vignette in Chapter 7 described the outcomes of an after-school family and school partnership. A research article describing that after-school program and documenting its impact of family partnerships was published in *Language Arts*, the journal of the National Council of Teachers of English (Brenner et al., 2003).

For Discussion

Visit a few of the organizations in the chart on page 229–230 (or the many others that are listed in Chapter 9). Each organization has national, regional, and state conferences that you may be able to attend. In addition to conferences, what resources do they offer that could be helpful to you now as a preservice teacher and, later, as an in-service teacher? Specifically, what ideas seem to be important to the organization?

You can also use Google Scholar or other databases to search for information on a topic or a particular program. Google Scholar differs from a general Google search in that Google Scholar (https://scholar.google.com) narrows your search to studies that have been published in scholarly journals. Another important source is ERIC, the Education Resources Information Center (www.eric.ed.gov). Here, you will find free access to a wide variety of research articles on a dizzying array of topics. The studies range from large quantitative studies that report on how interventions led to changes in standardized test scores to small situated studies. Three rural-focused research journals include *The Journal of Research in Rural Education, The Rural Educator,* and *Rural Special Education Quarterly.* These journals publish research that is intended to address questions of practice relevant to rural educators.

Another place you can turn to for reviews of research and summaries of evidence is the federal What Works Clearinghouse (WCC) (see call-out box). The WWC works to synthesize and evaluate the evidence for particular practices and programs; they particularly review whether there are RCTs and try to evaluate the depth of the evidence base for practices.

What Works Clearing House (https://ies.ed.gov/ncee/wwc/)
The U.S. Department of Education's WWC is a source for information about educational programs, interventions, and policies. The WWC has practice guides, intervention reports, and reviews of individual studies:

- Practice guides summarize findings from a large number of studies to make specific recommendations that can guide practice. Practice guides focus on a number of topics—effective writing instruction, dropout prevention, teaching reading, addressing student behavior, and more.
- Intervention reports summarize the research about the effectiveness of a particular program. An intervention report will tell you how many studies there are about a specific program and what those studies found.
- Reviews of individual studies evaluate the quality of evidence in a single study.

The WWC resources can provide a starting point for evaluating programs in the district where you work.

For Discussion

Think of a curriculum program that you have seen used in classrooms during your field experiences. Visit the WWC and look to see if they have published reports or research reviews about that program. Or, think of an education issue that is of concern in your area (e.g. early reading, dropout prevention, career and technical education, absenteeism, etc.). Visit the WWC and see if there are intervention reports or practice guides about that issue. See what kind of evidence they use to draw conclusions about effective practice.

Will This Practice Work in My Rural Classroom?

Not all practices work equally well in all places and with all students. As you consider the evidence for a particular practice, you should consider not just if the practice works, but also for *which* students and *where* the practice has been shown to be effective. This question is vital in the process of evaluating whether a practice is likely to achieve your desired outcomes.

In comparison to the number of research studies that include urban or suburban children, there is limited research done in rural schools. Most education research takes place in areas where there are larger populations. It is often easier to do a study that compares outcomes between groups of students when there are more students and schools in close proximity. Also, for a variety of reasons as discussed in earlier chapters, there has not been as much focus on rural education research compared to suburban or urban. Research in rural schools is limited. As a rural teacher, this provides good opportunities for you to take the initiative to systematically study your own practice (see Chapter 18).

Many research-supported practices, such as reading to promote vocabulary learning and writing to promote reading comprehension, do work with all students regardless of context. But more often, place does matter. Your students, for example, often will have rural context-specific knowledge that differs from the context-specific knowledge in urban or suburban communities. A city subway system, for example, may be an unfamiliar concept to a primary age rural child.

For Discussion

Research suggests a program for middle school readers is effective at fostering the reading comprehension of young urban adolescents. One of the writing prompts in the program asks students to write about how immigration has changed their neighborhood. Consider how a rural student, whose nearest neighbor is half a mile away, might respond to this prompt. As a teacher required to use this curriculum, how might you respond to this scenario? Although this program is indeed evidence-based, how might your students be disadvantaged by its urban focus?

The fact is that not all programs or teaching ideas will work in your rural setting (Eppley et al., 2018). As a rural teacher, an important part of your job will be to consider whether the materials, curriculum, resources, and research will work as expected in your context, if you need to adapt, or look for another idea. At times, you may be mandated to use materials or methods that you suspect are ineffective. In this case, we suggest systematically studying the materials or methods (see Chapter 18) so you can have an informed opinion. You will also need to use additional resources, scaffold unfamiliar concepts, and/or work as a liaison between the content and your learners in order to help them connect unfamiliar content to what they already know.

Will This Practice Help Me Achieve My Purpose?

An important step in thinking whether or not a practice is likely to be an effective practice is to think about your ultimate goals for instruction. In Chapter 19, you will be invited to write about your purpose as a rural teacher. We will ask you to describe what you believe to be one or two of the most essential qualities of an educated person in a democracy and, in turn, what you want to happen in your classroom in order for students to achieve those qualities. Are you most interested in fostering critical thinkers who can solve problems independently? Is your main focus on creating independent learners who know how to use resources and collaborate so that they can foster their own learning? Are you trying to help students value and understand the place where they live or gain more understanding of global issues and places? Or a combination of these? Your purpose for teaching can and should inform your day-to-day goals. As you consider adopting practices for your classroom, you should evaluate whether a recommended practice is likely to help you fulfill your purpose.

This question "Will this practice help me achieve my purpose?" can be especially important when you are thinking about other people's research or considering materials being recommended by vendors. You are likely to encounter a variety of promotional materials that recommend that you purchase a particular curriculum program or software in your classroom. Often, the sales pitches will make the claim that they are "evidence-based" and that there is evidence that the program "works." For example, some studies of reading instruction claim to have a positive impact on students' reading because after using the program, students are better at sounding out nonsense words like "bub" and "dif." Other research on reading instruction focuses on whether students can understand the text and provide a verbal or written summary after they read. Your goals for reading instruction will help you figure out if the product being pitched is likely to work for your students based on what they can already do and what they need to learn and how the study's authors defined "worked."

The same question—"Will this practice help me achieve my purpose?"—can be asked about any idea about teaching ranging from recommendations from your friends to online teacher sites to district-provided professional development. For example, you will encounter a lot of ideas about how to manage your classroom. Many teachers in schools are encouraged to use a clip or stoplight system that publicly shows which kids are meeting behavior expectations and which kids are in the warning zone. These systems might seem to "work" in the moment, encouraging students to calm down or correct their behavior, but a close look at the research behind this practice suggests that the practice may result in students who are not intrinsically motivated to behave, and leads to worsening behavior over time (Deci, Koestner, & Ryan, 2001). Wherever you encounter ideas about teaching, you should carefully examine what it is that the recommenders are claiming the practice will do and whether that matches with your purpose and goals.

These four questions, then, are important to think about as you are considering practices and planning for effective instruction. These questions are just meant to get you started. There are other important considerations. For example, it might be important to think about the cost of a practice compared to the potential benefit. An expensive program might help a few students with mathematics but leave few resources for the teaching of science and social studies. The time it would take to cut out and laminate all the pieces of a game board your friend recommends might be better spent getting home to eat dinner with your family. We hope these questions provide you with a framework to think about and select practices that might be effective for your students in your rural classroom. Planning your instruction, that is, how you will enact your purpose and teach your content, is such an important part of teaching. The final question in our framework asks you to consider the evidence for your success while you are teaching and implementing the practices you have chosen so carefully.

Questions to ask about the evidence as you are considering practices and planning effective instruction:

- What evidence is there?
- Is the evidence from a trustworthy source?
- Will this practice work in my rural place?
- Will this practice help me achieve my purpose?

And one question to think about during and after teaching:

- is there practice-based evidence that this works in my rural classroom with my students?

Practice-Based Evidence: Finding What Works for Your Classroom?

Effective teachers make thoughtful, important choices about their practices that are informed by assessments, standards and goals for teaching, and the evidence about whether their teaching is likely to have an impact. They also reflect on and evaluate the impact of their teaching decisions. Effective teachers ask, "Did it work in my classroom with my students? Did it work for all my students, and if not, why not?" The process of collecting data and reflecting on your own teaching allows you to adjust your teaching on a day-to-day basis and make informed decisions going forward. Assessment will help you understand the extent to which your instruction worked the way you hoped that it would, and to figure out why it might not be working—even if it did not work for just a small number of your students. Effective teachers collect data and use that to evaluate and improve their teaching—from tests and formal assessments to classroom observations to parent surveys to records about student behavior. All of the information you gather is an opportunity to think critically about your teaching and to generate evidence that comes directly from your practice. We talk in detail about this process in the next chapter.

Teacher inquiry is a process of collecting and analyzing data to evaluate your instructional practices. The conclusions you reach through this process are practice-based evidence. Practice-based evidence is evidence that comes from real classrooms in real contexts. As we said earlier, not all evidence-based practices work in all settings and for all students. Practice-based evidence that *you* generate will give you contextualized information about which practices work for which students in which contexts, and what resources are needed for those practices to work. As a teacher, you produce practice-based evidence systematically. You consider what you want to know, collect data such as student assessments and other information, make sense of that data, and reflect on that information in order to determine whether the practice-based evidence you collected shows that the practice is "working" in a way that meets your goals.

Practice-based evidence gives you an opportunity to figure out which students might not succeed when you use a particular practice, to try and figure out why that may be, and then to adapt your teaching. This is the key difference between evidence-based practice and practice-based evidence. Evidence-based practice asks, "Does this practice mostly work better compared to another practice?" Practice-based evidence helps you to figure out "Does this work for all of my students, in this time, in this place, and does it work better for some students than others?" Both questions are important as you plan, teach, plan, and teach again.

As we stated earlier, there is less research about what works for rural students than in suburban and urban contexts. Practice-based evidence will provide you with important data to enable teaching and learning in your rural classroom. Not only that, but as you generate practice-based evidence, you can share what you learned, informally with your colleagues, and in more public forms to help build our knowledge about what works for rural students.

References

Brenner, D., Jayroe, T., & Boutwell, A. (2003). Building on the strengths of families: The Promising Readers program. *Language Arts, 80*(4), 275–283.

Coleman, D., & Pimentel, S. (2012). *Revised Publishers' criteria for the Common Core State Standards in English Language Arts and Literacy, grades 3–12.* Council of Chief State School Officers & National Association of State Boards of Education. www.corestandards.org/assets/Publishers_Criteria_for_3-12.pdf

Deci, E. L., Koestner, R., & Ryan, R. M. (2001). Extrinsic rewards and intrinsic motivation in education: Reconsidered once again. *Review of Educational Research, 71*(1), 1–27. doi: https://10.3102/00346543071001001

Eppley, K., Azano, A.P., Brenner, D., & Shannon, P. (2018). What counts as evidence in rural schools?: Evidence-Based Practice and Practice-Based Evidence for diverse settings. *The Rural Educator, 39*(2), 36–40. doi: https://10.35608/ruraled.v39i2.208

Foorman, B., Beyler, N., Borradaile, K., Coyne, M., Denton, C. A., Dimino, J., ... & Keating, B. (2016). *Foundational skills to support reading for understanding in Kindergarten through 3rd Grade: Educator's practice guide.* NCEE 2016–4008. What Works Clearinghouse. https://ies.ed.gov/ncee/wwc/PracticeGuide/21

Graham, S., & Hebert, M. A. (2010). *Writing to read: Evidence for how writing can improve reading: A Carnegie corporation time to act report.* Alliance for Excellent Education. https://production-carnegie.s3.amazonaws.com/filer_public/9d/e2/9de20604-a055-42da-bc00-77da949b29d7/ccny_report_2010_writing.pdf

Lehr, F., Osborn, J., & Hiebert, E. H. (2004). *A focus on vocabulary.* Pacific Resources for Education and Learning. http://textproject.org/assets/library/resources/Lehr-Osborn-Hiebert-2004-A-Focus-on-Vocabulary-Booklet.pdf

National Governors Association, Council of Chief State School Officers, et al., (2012). *K–8 publishers' criteria for the common core state standards for mathematics.* www.corestandards.org/assets/Math_Publishers_Criteria_K-8_Summer%202012_FINAL.pdf

Stanovich, P. J., & Stanovich, K. E. (2003). *Using research and reason in education: How teachers can use scientifically based research to make curricular & instructional decisions.* Partnership for Reading (Project), National Institute for Literacy, US Department of Education. https://lincs.ed.gov/publications/pdf/Stanovich_Color.pdf

18

Teaching as Inquiry: What Works in Rural Classrooms

As an Education Specialist, an integral part of my practice is helping my students make connections to what they are learning in our classroom while meeting their individual needs. Through my own experiences as a learner, I have determined that I retain more information when I make a personal connection to what I am learning. As I have been working on building relationships with our students over the past several months, I have observed that they, too, have greater academic success when they are able to make a personal connection to what we are teaching them. There is one critical incident that stands out in support of this direction for my question. My mentor teacher allowed me to design an English unit focused on a modified version of Mary Shelley's Frankenstein. An integral piece of the unit was the integration of journal prompts related to what we were reading in each chapter. The focus of these prompts was to encourage our students to personally connect to the text through creative writing. Another important component of this unit was anchor activities before reading and post-reading activities tied to the anchor activities. These focused on teaching students how to pull important details from the text as they read. Each chapter lesson concluded with a brief eight-question comprehension assessment.

Upon completing the anchor activity, reading, post-reading activity, and journal prompt for chapter two, I observed one of our students who struggles with assessments due to disorders in processing and memory as he worked through the chapter quiz. I realized that not only was he referring to the text to find answers to the quiz, he answered seven of the eight questions correctly. I later asked him why he thought he did so well on the quiz and he responded that he felt like he knew what was going on and was interested in the characters. For many, especially those in general education, this might be a given; however, for this student to express those ideas and achieve a high score on the assessment is uncommon. This moment of success prompted me to inquire more deeply into what I can do to promote more personal connections in fostering academic success for students with disabilities.

Tara West, Special Education Teacher, Oroville California

In Chapter 17, we talked about using evidence in your classroom and introduced the idea of practice-based evidence as a way to potentially consider what could work in your classroom. In this chapter, we introduce teacher inquiry as a way guide to the systematic study of your classroom to generate your own practice-based evidence.

Before we begin, we will talk just a bit more about evidence. In Chapter 17, we defined evidence-based practice as teaching practices that have been shown to work in studies that evaluate whether students learn more in classrooms using one practice compared to another. The practice being studied is considered evidence-based if students in the group that experienced the intervention score better on standardized assessments, even if only by a slim margin, than the group that received their regular classroom instruction.

One significant concern about these types of studies is that, even if a practice has been deemed evidence-based, there may be large numbers of students for whom a practice has not been effective. Also, most large-scale studies do not take place in rural schools and may not transfer well. While we think that this kind of research can provide important information to inform your teaching, large-scale studies are not the only kind of research you should consider and, often, you will not be able to find research that addresses your specific question. Additionally, we argue in this chapter that as a professional, you are well-equipped to answer your own questions and contribute to what we know about teaching. In fact, we see this as an essential component of what good teaching is.

How then can you find out what works in your rural classroom? How can you grow your professional voice? We suggest practice-based evidence. This chapter explains how to find out what works using teacher inquiry to generate practice-based evidence specific to your context.

Professional Decision Making in Rural Classrooms

Teachers make several instructional judgments per minute, which adds up to about 1,500 educational decisions per day. The decisions vary in importance and consequence. Everything from which book to read aloud and which student to call on during a class discussion to the topic of your next writing mini-lesson, to how to help Emelia, a new student, integrate into the group of children who have been together as a class since kindergarten. These decisions are made instantaneously but are based on your goals and your knowledge of your students and of effective practice.

The need to make all of these informed, thoughtful decisions is why teaching is an intellectual activity—a profession. Teacher inquiry, the intentional and systematic study of your practice, is a means through which you can grow your self-confidence, empathy, knowledge, and skills. Teachers must continually reflect on the decisions they make in order to improve their decision-making skills. This is particularly important in a time when policies are increasingly requiring teachers to use scripted curriculum and high-stakes tests in the classroom. Within this view of teaching, you are a technician whose job it is to implement decisions made by others. Teacher inquiry pushes back against this idea and elevates your voice and status as a professional. We believe that you are the authority on what should happen in your classroom, but the truth is that many people do not share this view. Teacher inquiry better positions you to be recognized as an authority about what is happening in your own classrooms. Your participation in decision-making processes is more likely if you have intentionally and systematically collected data that you use as the basis for your opinions and decisions.

Teaching as Inquiry

Teacher inquiry is not so much a method (though there is a method) as it is a habit of mind or a stance toward teaching and learning. Teacher inquiry is a practical pursuit. It can help you to maintain your professional authority and confidence in the face of a seemingly endless stream of pre-packaged curricular materials and programs, fads, and policies (see Chapter 10). You may suspect that some of these things, regardless of the slick advertising, the practiced presentations of well-paid representatives, and the popularity of a product, idea, or approach, are not good for your students. But how can you know for sure? Teachers must constantly make decisions about what works for students. Your need to know is immediate and ongoing. As you are teaching, you may have questions like:

- Would a particular student's behavior change if she ate breakfast at school?
- How could cooperative groups in math increase participation of emergent bilingual students who opt not to speak during whole-group time?
- How is homework experienced by students whose parents work in the evenings?
- What happens when students are given the option to choose their own topics for writing?
- How can parent involvement efforts be changed to involve parents who do not typically participate in school events?

Teachers work in highly stressful and politically charged environments and may not have time for extra projects, yet questions such as these are pressing. They are the ordinary problems of practice. Even as you are making day-to-day and moment-to-moment decisions, you also need to participate in curricular decisions, to nurture your curiosity about your practice, and for professional collaboration. We argue that these three characteristics are hallmarks of the excellent teaching that you strive to accomplish every day. This is where teacher inquiry comes in.

We intentionally use the term "teacher inquiry" here as opposed to similar terms such as teacher research, action research, and practitioner research. These terms all refer to teachers studying and committing to improve their practice. By teacher inquiry we mean the intentional, sys-tematic study of your own practice in order to investigate your professional curiosities about your work (Dana & Yendol-Hoppey, 2019). Teacher inquiry also has a distinct emphasis on professional collaboration. While it is likely that you regularly think about your practice and talk to others about your work, teacher inquiry differs in how these practices are done systematically and intentionally.

Inquiry is not separate from teaching. It is not something extra that takes your attention away from your "real" classroom responsibilities. It is not a project you do once and file away. Instead, teacher inquiry is a stance you adopt toward teaching, a way of doing your work. Teacher inquiry is the enactment of a particular vision about what teaching ought to look like and about what teachers ought to be doing in their classrooms.

If we have not yet convinced you to adopt the idea of teaching as inquiry, consider the role of teacher inquiry in addressing inequity and injustice, and the potential of teacher inquiry to think through contradictions between what "we" say and what we do. For example, we often say we value active learning, but we usually keep a tight rein on what we mean by "active" and when we allow it. We say that we value the knowledge that our students bring to the classroom, but we don't often change the curriculum to accommodate our students' lives outside of school. We want to believe that we value student voice, but often we do not provide meaningful time or space for students to examine how their voices are potentially silenced by oppressive language or practices at school. Teacher inquiry can help us work toward more just and equitable systems of schooling by its potential to illuminate how injustice and inequity are experienced in our classrooms and schools. This is not the kind of information that can be investigated, discovered, and set aside. Your ongoing engagement with difficult questions such as these illustrates another way in which teacher inquiry can only be understood as a frame of mind or as a stance.

For Discussion

Think about a time when you were trying to teach someone (of any age) something new. Your teaching could have happened anywhere: In a classroom, at home, or at a camp. Have you taught someone how to do something new with technology? Have you taught a younger sibling how to tie a shoe or swim? Did you tutor during high school? Have you helped coach a sport? Thinking back on that situation, what was difficult about it? What questions did you have about your teaching at the moment? These are the same types of questions that can be addressed by teacher inquiry.

What Do We Mean by Systematic Study?

As a thoughtful teacher, naturally you have questions about your work. These questions likely stay with you like a persistent "itch" (Chiseri-Strater & Sunstein, 2006). Your questions might creep into your mind when you are removed from the business of the school day, like while you are mowing the lawn or trying to fall asleep. Write them down! Teacher inquiry is the scratching of that itch. The itch is your question. To systematically answer your question (and scratch your itch), you will:

1. Find out what other people already know about your question.
2. systematically collect data to answer your question.

3 Make sense of that data so it can answer your question.
4 Make changes or plans for the future based on what you've learned.
5 Share what you learned.
6 Ask a new question.

We will elaborate on these six actions in the rest of this chapter, but first, what if a question does not immediately come to mind? Or as is common, you have so many questions, you don't know which one you want to focus on?

The National Writing Project (NWP) is a rich source of examples of inquiries on a variety of topics, only some of which are about writing. Your search for models of how inquiry can work in your classroom should begin at the NWP Teacher Inquiry web page at https://lead.nwp.org/kb/teacher-inquiry/.

How Do I Find My Inquiry Question?

You may experience the "itch" of a particular question. In this case, assuming you have access to the information (data) required to answer that question, the focus of your inquiry is clear. However, this is not always the case. You may need to cast a wide net to find your question.

Your professional curiosity prompts many questions throughout your day. The trick is to pay attention to the questions, and, importantly, your feelings and interest in the questions. The most pressing issue in your classroom right now, student absenteeism for example, is not necessarily the best potential topic of your inquiry. You want to focus on something that feels important, but doable. The topic should not feel overwhelming or fill you with dread. This is where having the opportunity to bounce ideas off a colleague can be critical. We suggest starting by writing down what piques your curiosity. These statements are sometimes called "wonderings." A list of wonderings is essentially a brainstorm. The simple act of writing your wonderings down is an important first step in embracing the habit of self-reflection. Here are some wonderings:

- The children in my kindergarten classroom seem to only want to play along strict gender lines. The girls play "girl things" with girls and the boys play "boy things" with boys. I wonder what might happen if I make some changes to their free time choices?

- One student in my tenth-grade geometry class consistently tries to engage me with confrontation. What might be causing him to respond that way? Is he more likely to be confrontational during some parts of class as compared to others?
- How might content-based picture books be a useful tool in my twelfth-grade American History class?
- There seems to be a distinct racial divide in my middle school biology class. How might racial tensions be affecting students' ability to engage with the content?

Some teachers have a structured journaling routine using a computer, an app, or a notebook, but others write down notes on scraps of paper, record voice memos, or take pictures as reminders of things they want to explore later. Most of what you write will remain unexplored, but some observations are significant (and repetitive) enough that you might choose to spend some time systematically studying them. A journal is a very good tool to help you notice patterns of interest and, ultimately, a topic you want to study.

If your inquiry involves studying a change in your teaching practice, at this point you should think about what you would like to see happen as a result of the change and, importantly, how you decide if your change was beneficial. For example, if you are focusing on student engagement, decide what you think that engagement should look like. Would you like to see more raised hands? More in-depth answers? Perhaps you will look for signs of engagement in completed work. What would that look like? If you are studying a specific change such as in these examples (as opposed to understanding something that is happening in your classroom), you must identify your desired outcome in advance and how you will determine the extent to which change happened.

How do I Find Out What Works?

Earlier, we listed six actions that teachers do when they engage in systematic study of their practice. Once you have your question, these six actions can help you investigate your inquiry question. Teacher inquiry is not a linear process, you might not march through these six actions in order every time or you might linger at one for a while as you inquire about your teaching or what is happening in your classroom. Each action can help you learn more about your wonderings.

Find Out What Other People Already Know About Your Question

Let's assume you have a question and you are ready to think and act systematically to learn about possible answers to that question. The first step is to find out what others know about your topic. It is here where you should decide, if you haven't already, whether you would like to work collaboratively or individually. We think your inquiry will be richer if you work with a colleague—someone in your building, district, or from elsewhere, if possible.

Finding out what others know about your topic is a logical first step. You may find an answer before you start. More likely, finding out what others know will help you refine your question and can potentially prompt you to think about your question in a way you had not yet considered. For example, perhaps you are interested in how your students experience the homework you give them. In this case, you may want to begin by talking to the other teachers in your building to learn about their homework programs and how yours compares. Other teachers are often your first source of information about what is happening in your classroom. Never, ever underestimate the expertise of your colleagues, even (or especially) those who don't often volunteer information or opinions.

As you are likely familiar, Google Scholar is an excellent source of scholarly articles (see Chapter 17). Although Google will return far fewer results than your college or university library, you likely will find that you can develop a good bit of background knowledge from this source. You should also consider articles in the media, blogs, and materials at school such as policies or curriculum guides. Cast a wide net to catch as much information about your topic as possible.

Your goal at this point is to learn as much as you can about your topic and to make sure that the answer to your question does not already exist. To return to the homework example, you would want to start reading broadly about homework, then focus on information that most closely connects to your own context. For example, research on homework suggests that there is very little benefit to assigning homework at the elementary level, and some benefit to homework in the higher grades (Bennett & Kalish, 2006). This information would be highly relevant as you think about homework for the grade level(s) you teach. Here, as always, you will need to keep your own students in mind as you determine if or to what extent what you are reading will apply to your own students. Teacher inquiry is how you fill the gap between what's known already and what you want to know.

You may find yourself aimlessly clicking from bit to bit online, but it is imperative that you keep track of what you are learning. You may find that free online citation organizers (Zotero, Mendeley, etc.) can help you keep track of your sources, but there is no need to use a different organizational method than what you used for your research in college, provided that worked well for you then. Advice in Chapter 17 focuses on being a critical consumer of research and other sources of information about education can be helpful to keep in mind as you search for information. While you want to collect information that relates as closely as possible to your topic, if you are organized, you may benefit from collecting more sources than you think you need. The information you need likely will change as you move further along into your inquiry. For this reason, you will likely continue to consult outside resources about your question in each stage of your inquiry.

Collect Data to Answer Your Question

You have a question. You have talked to others about your topic and potentially have found someone to work with. You have read a lot about your topic and, maybe, your question has become more focused as a result. If your inquiry involves studying the results of a change to your teaching, you have already thought that through (see above How Do I Find My Inquiry Question?). Implement that change and you are now ready to collect data.

"Data" are simply bits of information that can answer your question. If you are studying homework in your classroom, a key piece of data would be information about rates of completion. Data can take many, many forms: Interviews, surveys, tally sheets, video or audio recordings, observations, student work, self-reflections, logs, notes, test scores, documents, classroom materials, formal curriculum materials, photos, and objects. And this is just a start! In order to work more efficiently (after all you have a question that needs answering) focus on collecting data that answers your question. *Data that can answer your question is the only data you need to collect.* A "good" teacher inquiry is one that answers the question asked. You may need five different sources of data or one.

Inquiry Question	Data Source
What does emergent literacy look like for a high school student with developmental disabilities?	• student work • formal literacy assessment data • curriculum materials
What do second graders say about gender norms in their classroom?	• student interviews • observations
How does an online Spanish program motivate middle school students?	• student survey • curriculum materials • student work
What happens when I commit to a wellness routine for self-care?	• journal entries
How does the physical layout of my classroom influence student collaboration?	• photographs • student interviews • student surveys • audio recordings
What happens when I use music as a transition signal in my primary-age classroom?	• student interviews • video recordings
How do movement breaks support engagement in a high school Advanced Placement Literature class?	• student interviews • student surveys • audio recordings

It is important to note here that the data you collect should be as closely connected to your everyday work as possible. The reality is, teachers are incredibly busy. Teaching as inquiry is not an extra project on your to-do list. Instead, it is a systematic approach to understanding information *that you already have*, or have easy access to, such as using your phone to record yourself teaching. In your everyday life in the classroom, you reflect on your teaching. You talk to students. You analyze their work. You observe them. Doing these activities systematically, teaching as inquiry, is a process that allows you to capitalize on the work you're already doing.

For Discussion

Earlier, you thought about some questions you might ask about a time you taught something to someone else. If you could go back in time and ask those questions, what data might help you answer your questions? What information would you need to investigate your wonderings?

Data Analysis: Make Sense from What You Collected

In the same way that you will likely continue to try to find out what others know about your topic while you are completing your inquiry, you may also begin to make sense of your data even while collecting it. You may even opt to make changes in your teaching in response to early data analysis. Teaching as inquiry is not a linear process, it is a way of thinking and improving.

Data analysis simply means making sense of your data so it can answer your question. Your data collection and analysis are intended to answer your question. If the answer is clear early in the process, you should act accordingly. For example, say you wanted to study the potential need for your middle school students to have a mid-morning snack. You used information you learned from your early research on the topic to help you pitch your idea to the principal. You found funding from a local business, notified parents, and implemented the change. You intended to collect data (short daily student surveys) for two weeks, but after only four days, you analyzed the data you had collected at that point and found that it showed, conclusively, that the students not only liked the snack, but *needed* the snack because they had not eaten since the night before. Because teaching as inquiry is a way to think, not a project, you are now wondering how you can entice more students to eat breakfast at school. And so you begin again!

In other cases, you may not look at the data you've collected until you have finished. And, often, the data will be less clear than in our snack example. At this stage, it will be critically important that you stay focused on your inquiry question. This is the most important strategy to avoid becoming overwhelmed with the sheer amount of data you have and the many, many possibilities for its interpretation. To begin, read your inquiry question. Read it again.

What Does This Say? What Patterns Can I See?

A logical way to begin data analysis is to sort your data by type. For example, separate student work by assignment, then, perhaps, chronologically.

Your sorting decisions don't matter too much at this stage as they are only a mechanism to help you review what you have and set aside sources that you thought would be useful but that now seem likely to be irrelevant to your research question.

After you have imposed some sort of structure, read everything in your entire data set. Now find some sticky notes and highlighters and read again. This time, stopping to notice and note possible points of connection, questions, and surprises. For most questions you should be looking for connections within data types as well as across your whole sample. Because of this, you may want to focus at first on making sense of one type of data at a time. For example, once you feel like you understand what your twelve observation sheets say, *then* you can begin to think about how your observation sheets connect with what you heard in the student interviews. Some steps you can take during data analysis include:

- Organize your data by type.
- Read your complete data set.
- Make preliminary notes with stickies. Highlight especially relevant bits.
- Read your data set by type.
- Make more notes. Highlight especially relevant bits.
- Look for connections and repeating ideas between sources.
- Group like ideas across sources, paying attention to common ideas. Like ideas are themes or your "answers" to your question.

As you organize and analyze your data, you might refer back to the information you gathered about your question when you were framing your question. How does what you learned help you understand the data? What patterns are you finding that might be expected or are surprising based on what you read? How does your reading about homework, or hunger, or self-care, help you make sense of your data?

What Stories Are Here?

Only you will decide what your data says. While it is generally good practice to group like data together to create big ideas (or "themes"), you may find other possible answers to your question hiding among those hard-to-miss ideas that repeat over and over. Your data may have clear themes made up of ideas that stand out in each data type, but if you look closer, you may also notice quieter themes that are also worthy of investigation. Both types of data can answer your question. Ultimately, your goal is for your data tell a story about your question. Your story may have plot twists and messy spots, or it might be straightforward. In either event, it is very likely that your story will lead you to new insights about your teaching and, in turn, lead you to new questions.

Making sense of your data is another reason to work with a colleague. Having another perspective can be incredibly useful. You might both organize and read the data and compare the notes you are taking. You might share your initial patterns and hunches and see if your colleague sees the same patterns. Talking about the patterns you see might help you reflect and understand more about your teaching.

Make Changes or Plans Based on What You Learned

Your new insights will inspire change or plans. What you are learning should, and will, inform your teaching practice or your understanding of your students. If you tried something new, like a mid-morning snack or project-based learning, and you find it is working, you can plan to keep doing it. If your interviews with second graders reveal that many of the students have gender stereotypes, you might change some of the books you are reading or investigate possible strategies to engage your children in thinking about gender norms. Teaching as inquiry means that you are constantly observing, asking questions, collecting information, and analyzing that information to make adjustments to your teaching. This is what it means to be a professional.

Share What You Have Learned

When you engage in teaching as inquiry, you generate practice-based evidence (see Chapter 17). You are developing knowledge about what works, with which students, under which contexts, based on actual classroom practice and outcomes for students. The evidence you will be generating is valuable. You will be learning about practices that work for your students in your rural context. This information will be useful, not just to you but also to your colleagues. Sharing what you learned can take a variety of forms. From the most informal, talking with other teachers, to the most formal, submission of a paper to a research journal such as *Journal of Teacher Action Research* (www.practicalteacherresearch.com) or *Networks: An Online Journal for Teacher Research* (https://newprairiepress.org/networks/) or *The Rural Educator* (http://ruraleducator.info). Your insights are valuable and might be of interest to a larger audience, particularly other rural teachers. Sharing can also mean presenting at state and national conferences (see examples in Chapter 9) or writing about what you are learning in a blog, in a building newsletter, school district publication, or for your professional organization.

> See "Tips for Publishing: Bringing Classroom Practices, Reflections, and Research to Print," by the National Writing Project, for comprehensive guidance on writing for publication https://archive.nwp.org/cs/public/print/resource/1949.

Regardless of how you share your work, the data you have collected and the conclusions you have drawn will be an invaluable support for your professional voice. Data, systematically collected and analyzed, is far more powerful than your opinion or general impressions. Your data and conclusions will help you to explain what works in your rural classroom, demonstrate when something is not working, or to make requests for needed resources. You can also use what you learned in your communication with families, administrators, and your colleagues about your teaching and your students' learning.

Ask a New Question

Inquiry is never "done." Teacher inquiry is recursive in the sense that you will likely find some answers but will also find new questions you did not know you had. You investigate one idea, one question, one practice; you learn and reflect; and then you notice something else that makes you curious or concerned, and you begin the process over again. If you were studying a new strategy related to project-based learning, for example, you probably had some successes but found out that some things did not quite work the way you wanted them to. You have learned what you did right and what you did wrong. Now you will read a bit more, talk to your students and some colleagues, make a new plan, and try again.

A Word About Inquiry Communities

Although an individual teacher can effectively embrace a stance of teaching as inquiry, collaboration will enrich your efforts. We suspect you will find your inquiries, and, indeed, your teaching as a whole, far more rewarding and generative if you work with others. A trusted colleague to question your assumptions, look at your data with another perspective, and share in your successes (and failures) is invaluable for any teacher. However, you may find yourself in a school, large or small, in which teachers have not yet embraced collaboration. First, we would encourage you to take a leadership role by reaching out to your colleagues with a specific inquiry question in mind. Exhaust all of your in-building (or in-district) possibilities for collaboration. Have you invited the itinerant teachers?

If those efforts fail, however, you can find an active support network online. People you know, such as your peers from your student teaching days, your former mentor teachers, or teachers you know in other districts are good sources for potential collaborators. But even if you find no takers among people you know, there are active inquiry groups online on popular social media sites. As we discuss in Chapter 9, there are many ways to build your professional network, and your colleagues are potential collaborators as you engage in inquiry.

Even if your primary support network is not in your geographical location, it is important to share your learning with your on-site colleagues. Being vulnerable by sharing your learning with others can inspire a community of learning and is an important part of professional collaboration.

Why Is Teacher Inquiry Important for Rural Classrooms?

The inquiry process as described here can be used readily in any context. There is nothing specifically rural about teacher inquiry. There are, however, reasons why you may want to give special consideration to teacher inquiry in your rural classroom. If, for a variety of reasons, you find your school culture to be resistant to change, and/or lacking in a robust professional development program, teaching as inquiry can support your professional growth and professional voice. Systematic investigation of questions about your classroom will nurture your curiosity and lifelong learning habits. It is likewise important to challenge your own assumptions about teaching and learning as a way to make sure your instruction is equitable.

You already know that published research does not always speak accurately to rural classrooms. We see your role in the classroom not as a technician whose job it is to follow directions, but as an educated professional who is able to generate practice-based evidence about teaching and learning. When teaching is inquiry, you read what others have to say, but you also understand the limitations of large-scale research studies *and* have a powerful process to contribute to the evidence base about what works in your classroom. Being curious about your practice and disciplined enough to investigate your curiosities systematically can lead you to not only to uncover experiences that may be limiting the potential of some of your students but suggest ways that your classroom can be transformed.

References

Bennett, S., & Kalish, N. (2006). *The case against homework: How homework is hurting our children and what we can do about it*. Crown.

Chiseri-Strater, E., & Sunstein, B. (2006). *What works? A practical guide for teacher research*. Heinemann.

Dana, N., & Yendol-Hoppey, D. (2019). *The reflective guide to classroom research: Learning to teach through practitioner inquiry*. Corwin.

19

Thriving as a Rural Teacher

Upon receiving my student teaching placement, I recognized the significance of my assignment as an educator in the school and community that raised me. Having a local connection to, and personal insight into, Oroville, one issue above others stood out to me as it related to my students—the negative image of Oroville as a poor, drug-ridden, rural community that has been propagated for many years. The origins of this perceived negative image are unknown to me; however, growing up, it was impossible to avoid hearing comments, jokingly or not, about the town being the "meth capital of California."

This image problem is something that has both intrigued and perturbed me throughout my life, as I, too, have been one of the locals who has felt the need to defend my place of residence when others cast a downward eye towards it. Additionally, I found it very relevant to education because the youth of Oroville pick up on this stereotyped negative image of the town and are affected by it. From personal experience, I have seen individuals internalize and process the negative image of Oroville in both healthy and unhealthy ways. I identified one of my roles as an educator to help students move past Oroville's negative label and instead develop a more positive sense of place. In doing so, it may just lower any mental barriers students may have as a result of internalizing the community's tarnished image and promote a healthier mindset.

Austin Roughton, Science Teacher and Outdoor Educator
Read more about Austin at http://iamaruralteacher.org

What are your motivations for becoming a teacher? For many, becoming a teacher was always in the cards. As we have noted elsewhere, maybe you come from a family of teachers and the career choice was something you always imagined doing. You read to your toys. You led every group project in middle school. You embrace leadership roles any chance you get. Or maybe you want to become a teacher because you had positive learning experiences. You were good at school, formed lasting relationships with peers and teachers, and engaged in school activities. Maybe you had a favorite teacher or coach who inspired, encouraged, and cheered you on through some of your toughest years, and you dream of playing a similar role in the lives of young people. But for others, you might find yourself wanting to teach because of a *motivating discontent.* Some of us come to our calling as an educator because we were discontented with an aspect of education—maybe our own schooling—and we believe something "better" can be done. We see ourselves as a change agent and advocate, and we are motivated by a deep desire to *make it right.* In the vignette above, Austin was annoyed that throughout his life he had to defend a place he valued and that others so quickly dismantled and devalued. As a teacher, he wants to promote a healthier mindset by helping students develop more promising views of their place and themselves in it.

For Discussion

Can you name three motivating factors for wanting to become a teacher? How have they influenced you in wanting to become a teacher? Do you have a motivating discontent as well? If so, can you name it and share how it has influenced your career goals?

"Personal history—the formative, contextualized experiences of our lives that influence how we think about and practice our teaching—provides a powerful mechanism for teachers wanting to discern how their lived lives impact their ability to teach or learn" (Samaras, Hicks, & Berger, 2004, p. 905).

Like Austin, and as the quote suggests, your life experiences will also shape the ways you come to think of your purpose as a rural teacher. This book has covered many topics—the theories, ideas, and practical takeaways—that we imagine will continue to influence how you think of yourself as a rural teacher. In this final chapter, we want you to *do the work* of examining how these topics intersect with your values and beliefs. Through the rural lenses introduced in this text, you will articulate your purpose, intention, and vision for thriving as a rural teacher.

Defining Your Purpose: What Do You Believe?

As you read this chapter, you will be asked to complete a series of exercises and respond to questions about your beliefs. By doing so, you will be building a philosophy statement that allows you to articulate your vision and purpose as a teacher. We rely on five components about beliefs that present big ideas for thinking about and structuring your statement, including:

1   Beliefs about being a rural educator: Who are you?
2   Beliefs about rural schools and communities: Where will you teach?
3   Beliefs about rural students: Whom will you teach?
4   Beliefs about instruction in rural classrooms: How will you teach?
5   Beliefs about relationships with rural partners: How will you make connections?

As you move through this chapter, you will complete a series of activities that will allow you to explore the ideas above. Then, at the end of the chapter, we will ask you to consider your notes and craft a statement that does three important things:

- Describes what you believe are the one or two most essential qualities needed for rural learners
- Describes how you will foster those qualities as a rural teacher
- Discusses how your purpose is particularly important for rural classrooms

We will circle back to these questions later, but first, we invite you to work thoughtfully through the activities outlined below.

Beliefs about Being a Rural Educator

For this initial component, you will think about where you have come from and where you are going as a rural teacher. Your experiences of rurality will impact not only how you understand the students in your rural school but also your role as a teacher. If you believe your students only need certain kinds of knowledge to live in rural places, you may limit your curriculum to the skills and current circumstances of the community. But if you believe that students possess the abilities to create change and think crea-tively about the future of their communities, then your teaching strategies will engage students in innovative approaches to helping their community thrive. The following activity can help you reflect on your purpose as a teacher as it relates to the place where you will teach.

For Discussion

Reflect on your experience of place as a young student. Do you identify as having grown up rural, not rural, or somewhere in between? Consider the following table as you talk about these differences with a peer.

If you	Discuss . . .
Grew up rural	What are the characteristics you would use to describe your rural upbringing? Were you conscious of this identity as a child or did you become aware of this identity at a later point in your life? Did you believe other rural people lived as you did? How did your rural identity make you feel? (proud, lucky, ashamed) In what ways do you now identify with a rural identity?
Grew up not rural	Were you aware of rural places that were different from where you lived? Do you recall thinking about rural places? How did you learn about rural places? (TV, books, visiting) What did those sources teach you about rural places? Describe any experiences throughout your life that compli-cated your perspectives of rural places. In what ways do you relate to rural places or people now?
Grew up somewhere in between	Describe how your upbringing has shaped your under-standing of rurality and rural people and places. Use the questions for rural and not rural to help shape your response.

As you share your responses to the questions above, observe to what extent you share life experiences and perspectives, or not, with your col-leagues and classmates. Although shared life experiences often lead to shared views of the world, this is never *always* the case. As you read in Chapter 3, even the characteristics of rural towns differ from place to place.

However, a good starting point is to acknowledge that we identify with places in particular ways.

Our identities as individuals are integrally connected to who we are as teachers. Sometimes we share personal characteristics with our students that help us to relate to them and generally understand their perspectives, whether we agree with them or not. Other times, we may have vastly different views based in different life circumstances and understanding students' perspectives may be more challenging. Regardless of what we have in common, or how we are different, it is of great importance that as teachers we intentionally reflect on how *who we are* impacts *what we do* in the classroom and how we develop relationships with our students. These relationships are important in all school communities but are particularly important for beginning teachers in small and rural communities.

Beliefs about Rural Schools and Communities

You may be from a rural place yourself, or you may have grown up somewhere more urban or suburban. Whatever your background, it shapes how you see yourself, others, and the world. For example, if you belong to a particular religion, your values and beliefs are likely shaped in some ways that stem from that religion's doctrine. These ideas will be reflected in your behaviors as you enact your belief system. Your gender and how you express it, your racial identity, the language you speak at home, the culture or cultures you belong to, will all play some part in shaping the ways you understand others, and knowing this is particularly important as you develop your purpose as a teacher. One of the reasons why it is so important for rural teachers to deeply reflect on their beliefs about rural places is to challenge any narrow assumptions or stereotypes one might have internalized over the years. If your rural community taught you that your best future is some place other than where you were from, or if you grew up in a suburb and have relied on television sitcoms and media stereotypes to shape your view of rurality, then your views of rural may be significantly incomplete and/or biased. As discussed in Chapter 2, negative constructions of rurality go as far back as the seventeenth century in Europe and have only gotten more widespread with globalization and mass media (Theobald & Wood, 2010).

In the opening section of this book, you read about the histories of rural places, the notion that rural places are socially constructed (rather than geographic constructions), and that teaching is always a political act. What do those ideas mean to you and how do they influence your beliefs about teaching in a rural community?

For Discussion

Axiology is the study of ethics and aesthetics, asking: What is good, true, and beautiful? How do you value rural places? How will you situate your own instruction in a rural place in ways that you will defend as "good" teaching? What do you know and believe and value about rural schools and communities? Complete the sentence starters below.

1. I want to teach in a rural school because…
2. My favorite things about a rural community are…
3. Some of the challenges in my rural community include…
4. There are stereotypes about rural places because…
5. I am from (away/here) and expect that to help me because…
6. I am from (away/here) and expect that to be a challenge because…
7. My actions as a teacher are political because…

As you discuss these questions, are you able to articulate why exactly you want to teach in a rural school? Are you honest about what makes you most excited and most worried? Are you able to consider the complicated histories of rural places to think through rural stereotypes? Importantly, can your group discuss what it means to "teach for social justice" in rural communities?

Beliefs about Rural Students

Throughout the book we have covered topics related to rural students and ways of thinking about their learning. Ontology is the study of existence by asking the question: What makes a human *human*? What do you believe about your students and their existence? What do you believe students should be able to do now, when they leave your classroom, and when they leave school? Think about Chapter 4, Why Place Matters, Chapter 5, Rural Literacies, and Chapter 15, Diversity in the Rural Classroom. How do critical understandings of place or the ways students might come to think of their membership in rural places matter?

For Discussion

For this exercise, write a defense of, or a dissent from, the following statements:

1. Place matters to rural students and should be an integral way of thinking about teaching in rural places.
2. Rural literacies are part and parcel of rural community membership.
3. Rural students are diverse in myriad ways.
4. Rural students deserve equal opportunities to achieve.
5. Rural students should learn about their local community and how it relates to power and privilege on a global stage.

As you discuss your defense of or dissent from these statements, consider—Which statements did you agree and disagree with and why? What have you read in other sections of this book that support your point of view? How might your views of these statements impact your work as a teacher?

Beliefs about Instruction in Rural Classrooms

Having a sense of your community and your students allows you to articulate your beliefs about instruction. Epistemology is the study of knowledge, asking: What counts as knowledge and who decides? Even when you are teaching a standardized curriculum, you will have to make decisions about prioritizing and modifying content. As we argue in Chapter 10, Policy and the Rural Teacher, nearly every decision in the classroom is influenced by an outside policy decision. Reflect on Chapter 17, about evaluating and using evidence and Chapter 18, about teaching as inquiry. How will you learn from your experiences and apply them to build practice-based work with your rural students?

How will you leverage opportunities and negotiate constraints? How will you put your beliefs about rural communities and rural students into *practice*? Your beliefs about instruction and what counts for knowledge will influence what students learn and how they will learn it—both in explicit and implicit ways. What contribution do you want to make in what students learn? Will that contribution transform students in ways that influence their thinking about local and global power?

For Discussion

For this activity, use either "will" or "will not" to complete the statements that articulate beliefs about instruction in rural classrooms.

1. I will/will not use trauma-informed practices because ...
2. I will/will not implement a critical pedagogy of place because ...
3. I will/will not integrate technology in my instruction because ...
4. I will/will not seek out evidence to help me decide what and how to teach because ...
5. I will/will not practice teaching as inquiry to examine the impact of my instructional practices because ...

Share your responses to these questions. What do they reveal about what you already plan to do as a teacher, and what you still need to learn before you can feel effective and accomplished as a rural educator?

Beliefs about Relationships with Rural Partners

In Chapter 8, From Here or Away, we spend time considering the pros, cons, and pitfalls of teaching in the place where you grew up (or similar rural community) as opposed to teaching in a relatively unfamiliar rural setting. How you view yourself in that continuum can influence the ways you think about relationship building. Here, we want you to consider: What do you most value about relationships with students, families, and communities? What is your vision for being a student ally? A family advocate? A reliable colleague? An engaged community member?

Across several chapters (e.g., Chapter 6, Community Assets, Chapter 7, Families and Communities as Partners, Chapter 9, Find Your People), we discuss the importance of learning about the community where you'll be working and finding professional networks that will support and sustain your efforts in and out of the classroom. Think back to Chapter 9. Do you anticipate being a "lone wolf" (the only math teacher at your school) or an itinerant teacher (the gifted resource teacher serving multiple schools) as described in Chapter 12? How might that experience create a need to foster relationships with others in your school district and beyond?

For Discussion

For this exercise, we want you to make a grocery list of what you hope to obtain and gain from your efforts in building meaningful relationships. We have organized your list in five parts:

1. Relationships with students
2. Relationships with colleagues
3. Relationships with families
4. Relationships with community members
5. Relationships with professional networks

Hopefully, your list shows that in your role as teacher, you have a network. As a teacher you are part of an interconnected web of allies and advocates who can support you in your work and help you achieve your goals. As you share your list with colleagues or classmates, what new ideas and supports come to mind?

Parameters That May Impact Your Purpose

Determining your purpose as a teacher is not without its parameters or complexity. For example, if you are teaching in a public school, you are a public employee—your salary is paid by taxpayers and you are responsible to your community (the local and state government) for your work. As an employee of the government, you are required to uphold the Constitution of the United States. By upholding the First Amendment, you will need to ensure that you neither promote nor deny the practice of any religion. In some small communities, where most of the teachers share the same religion as most of the students, this constitutional protection may be harder to notice, but the Constitution guarantees that all students are free to practice, or not to practice, the religion of their choice and the teacher is responsible to defend this freedom. Refer back to Chapter 10 about several other policies and implications for your teaching.

As government employees, public school teachers are expected to avoid partisan politics. However, your position is inherently political because knowledge is power. That is, any time knowledge is used to empower, it has a political impact (Apple, 2013). Providing students with particular knowledge, and denying or omitting access to certain other knowledge impacts your students' abilities to act on that knowledge or not. For example, how a science teacher addresses creationism in a biology class influences the students' understanding of both of those concepts. Teaching about environmental impacts of the local mining industry may result in your students devising ideas to make a difference in those impacts. Even the way you respond to a student using a racial slur on the playground demonstrates what knowledge is allowable, what people are valued at school, and what kinds of behavior are tolerated. Your actions in all of these examples reflect your purpose as a teacher.

Finally, it is important to consider your school's stated mission and vision statements as guidelines once you are working in a rural school. These can be supportive to you when providing a rationale for the decisions you make in the classroom. For example, a school's mission statement may state something like this: "We are dedicated to ensuring a *quality education* in an environment that produces *responsible, compassionate* individuals by providing a *relevant curriculum* enabling all students to become *productive citizens.*"

As a teacher, the italicized terms in the mission statement above may provide important reinforcement for choosing to do certain things as a teacher. For example, if you want to incorporate place-based projects, you can argue that they are a successful way to bring relevancy into your curriculum. Or, if you want students to read about racial and economic inequality, you can defend that by explaining how this helps to make them compassionate individuals. In the event that your school's mission statement is in significant contrast to your purpose as a teacher, you will need to examine how to navigate your role in that district or perhaps contemplate other contexts that are more philosophically aligned with your purpose.

It is ultimately your professional responsibility to consider what and how to best teach your students in your classroom, while using the laws, regulations, and professional teaching standards to guide you. Knowing what factors will support you in your purpose, and which may prove to be barriers, will assist you in enacting your goals and responsibilities as a teacher.

Drafting Your Statement

To begin, what is the title of your statement? We like to think it would be about *thriving* in rural classrooms, schools, and communities. Look over the ways you have moved through this chapter and the ways you articulated your beliefs about being a rural educator, about rural schools and communities, about rural students, about instruction, and about relationships. Are you prepared to write an essay that elaborates on who you are, where you will teach, who you will teach, how you will teach, and how you will make connections?

As you articulate the kind of teacher you want to be, and what you believe education is for, you can focus on those aspects of teaching and learning that matter most to you. You can evaluate what you see in classrooms and what you learn in your classes against your philosophy. Refer back to those questions asked at the start of this chapter. As a rubric of sorts, be sure your statement does the following:

1   Describes what you believe to be one or two of the most essential qualities of an educated person in a democracy.
2   Describes what should happen in your classroom in order for your students to achieve those qualities.
3   Discusses why this purpose is particularly important for rural classrooms and what makes this your rural teaching purpose statement.

Questions 1 and 2 ask you to think about what education is for and how to get there. If your purpose is to make sure students have a deep understanding of biology, how do you help your students use that information as a citizen of your community and the world? If you believe your purpose is to create competent and efficient workers, then what do you teach to prepare them for that? If you believe the youth are the future leaders of our society, what does that mean for how you teach them leadership? If you believe that students should have voice and choice in the classroom, think about how you would provide opportunities to amplify their voice and act on their ideas. You will eventually have to consider how schools encourage those ways of learning and how you would navigate schools where those practices are not typical.

Alyssa Detloff, a rural student teacher, responds to questions 1 and 2, below:

The purpose of schooling is to set students up to participate in a diverse and inclusive democratic society by putting a large focus on collaboration and cooperation over competition to create a sense of community where students can practice the skills necessary to become active members of our democracy. If we expect our youth to become adults who use reflective judgment, take responsibility for themselves and their community, and take part in shaping their country, then the environment in which they are taught must teach them how to do this by giving them real practice in responsibility and personal authority.

Question 3, above, asks you to specifically address rurality in your purpose statement. As you recall from Chapter 2, this book utilizes Fraser's (2009) framework for understanding justice. Distributive justice works to dismantle barriers to economic equity. It asks whether resources are distributed fairly. Cultural justice asks whether all groups of people are recognized and equally valued, including people from rural places. Political justice works to ensure that all voices are represented in decision making processes. In what ways do you feel it is your role as a teacher to enact curriculum and instruction that contributes to justice in rural communities? How do you see your role as an ally to students and families that are historically marginalized in your community or in our country? To what extent is it your goal to prepare students to participate in making changes that will result in more equity for more people in our society?

Dillon Johnson, also a rural student teacher, wrote explicitly about rurality in his statement:

> *Upon reading into how educational philosophers and practitioners view rural America, it bothers me that they don't seem to mention any of its strengths. I want to teach in a rural community. I grew up in one and have always valued that. It is part of my identity and I believe many people underestimate the advantages of the strong sense of community a rural area has the ability to develop. My positive outlook on rural communities mainly is founded upon the potential to make a meaningful difference. It may be selfish of me, but in urban areas I feel an overwhelming sense of insignificance and lack of purpose. In a rural community, there is often a shared sense of struggle, as well as common goals, and with that more meaningful relationships are created. I look forward to taking on the challenges of rural education faces and bring to light some of the benefits that I think are overlooked all too often.*

The teachers we have quoted in this chapter—Austin, Dillon, Alyssa—have all thought about their *why*, their purpose for being a teacher in a rural community. They understand that, as Gruenewald (2003) wrote "Places make us: as occupants of particular places with particular attributes, our identity and our possibilities are shaped" (p. 621). They feel a connection to rural places and a responsibility to help their students develop a positive sense of place that will contribute to their sense of themselves as learners and as members of a community.

We invite you to think about what it means to be a rural teacher as you draft a purpose statement for yourself and consider how being in a rural place impacts the ways in which you view your roles as a teacher. Having clearly articulated your purpose and goals as a teacher will serve as a compass as you make daily and monthly decisions in service to your students. Your personal ideas about who you think you should be as a teacher will shape what it means to teach, and to thrive, in a rural community. Periodically you can reflect on that purpose and assess the extent to which you are able to be that which you believe. This is a measure of the integrity of a teacher (Schulte, 2009).

Conclusion

As a teacher, you will be a community leader and this is even more true in a rural place. In that role, we hope that you will adopt the asset-based views of rural schools and communities and advocate for policies and actions that serve your students and improve the vitality of your communities. For communities that have experienced significant traumas, we hope you will engage in practices that support recovery and resiliency not only for your students and their families, but also for yourself.

Because everyone wears several hats, smaller communities have more opportunity for leadership. Over the life of your career we hope that these principles and strategies will give you a foundation for taking a leadership role in your community, school, district, and state. We imagine you may become involved on a national level, bringing attention to practice-based evidence, strategies that work, and the unique needs of schools and children in rural places. As you gain experience as a teacher, you might consider earning an administrative credential and leading your school district as a principal or superintendent. There are many platforms for critiquing inequities and for sharing positive stories about success that serve to change the narrative—social media, popular press, policy, and every day in your rural classroom.

We invited you at the beginning of this book to think about rural teaching as an act of social justice. Rural places, and the people who live there, have to varying degrees, been subject to injustice in terms of economic, social, and political capital. Rural students of color have had the additional burden of institutional and individual racism. Rural places historically may not have been seen as a priority, but rural students deserve fully prepared teachers, and we hope this book provides you with a greater understanding of the reasons why teaching in a rural place is an amazing opportunity. We also hope that you have learned tools and strategies to help you thrive no matter where that rural place is.

References

Apple, M. W. (2013). *Knowledge, power, and education: The selected works of Michael W. Apple*. Routledge.

Fraser, N. (2009). *Scales of justice: Reimagining political space in a globalizing world*. Columbia University Press.

Gruenewald, D. A. (2003). Foundations of place: A multidisciplinary framework for place-conscious education. *American Educational Research Journal, 40*(3), 619–654. doi: https://10.3102/00028312040003619

Samaras, A. P., Hicks, M. A., & Berger, J. G. (2004). Self-study through personal history. In J. J. Loughran, M. L. Hamilton, V. K. LaBoskey, & T. L. Russell (Eds.), *The international handbook of self-study of teaching and teacher education practices* (*Vols. 1 & 2*, pp. 905–942). Kluwer Academic.

Schulte, A. K. (2009). *Seeking integrity in teacher education: Transforming my student teachers, transforming my self*. Springer.

Theobald, P., & Wood, K. (2010). Learning to be rural: Identity lessons from history, schooling, and the U.S. Corporate Media. In K. Schafft & A. Y. Jackson (Eds.), *Rural education for the twenty-first century: Identity, place, and community in a globalizing world* (pp. 17–33). Pennsylvania State University Press.

Index

Page numbers in italics refer to figures.